Senegal

NATIONS OF THE MODERN WORLD: AFRICA
Larry W. Bowman, *Series Editor*

SECOND EDITION

SENEGAL

An African Nation Between Islam and the West

SHELDON GELLAR

Westview Press

A Division of HarperCollins*Publishers*

Nations of the Modern World: Africa

Copyright ©1995 by Westview Press, Inc., A Division of HarperCollins Publishers, Inc.

Published in 1995 in the United States of America by Westview Press, Inc., 5500 Central Avenue,
Boulder, Colorado 80301-2877, and in the United Kingdom by Westview Press, 12 Hid's Copse Road,
Cumnor Hill, Oxford OX2 9JJ

Library of Congress Cataloging-in-Publication Data
Gellar, Sheldon.
    Senegal : an African nation between Islam and the West / Sheldon
Gellar.—2nd ed.
        p.   cm.—(Nations of the modern world. Africa)
    Includes bibliographical references and index.
    ISBN 0-8133-1020-2
    1. Senegal.   I. Series.
DT549.22.G44   1995
966.3—dc20   95-16606
                                                                                CIP

The paper used in this publication meets the requirements of the American National Standard for
Permanence of Paper for Printed Library Materials Z39.48-1984.

10   9   8   7   6   5   4   3   2   1

In memory of Pat,
who shared my love
of Senegal

Contents

1 THE HISTORICAL BACKGROUND   1

2 GOVERNMENT AND POLITICS   21

3 THE ECONOMY   55

4 SENEGAL AND THE WORLD   83

5 CULTURE AND SOCIETY   109

6 TOWARD THE YEAR 2000:
WHITHER SENEGAL?   133

Figures and Tables

Preface to the Second Edition

I MET ISMAILA DIA, my Senegalese "big brother," in 1962 on board the French liner *Ancerville* sailing from Marseilles to Dakar. Ismaila was returning to Senegal after nearly a decade of studies in France, where he had obtained advanced degrees in biology and pharmacology. I was on my way to conduct fieldwork for my doctoral dissertation.

Ismaila wore impeccably tailored French woolen suits and read *Le Monde* and *L'Humanité*, the French Communist daily, regularly. Despite outward appearances, Ismaila was no Black Frenchman. He came from a noble Tukulor family on the Senegal River. His father, who died when Ismaila was a young boy, had been a respected Muslim religious leader. Ismaila himself had studied at Koranic schools in Mauritania before attending and excelling in French colonial public schools in Saint Louis.

Over the years, as the memories of French colonial rule receded into the past, Ismaila, like Senegal, became both more cosmopolitan and more traditional. Although he still read French newspapers, France was no longer the only focal point of Western culture for him. He had sent a younger brother to Germany to study engineering. Like many Western-educated Senegalese, he developed an interest in learning English. At the same time, Islam became a more important part of his life. He went on pilgrimage to Mecca and came to prefer the traditional African *boubou* to Western clothes.

Ismaila Dia took me under his protection and brought me into his family circle. Through him and his family, I was able to develop more than just an academic interest in Senegal. We shared personal and family triumphs and tragedies. He lost a younger brother; I a wife to cancer. Ismaila is now struggling to put his three oldest children through college and dreaming of doing a *doctorat d'état* on Senegalese traditional medicine.

It is now more than thirty years since I first came to Senegal and more than a decade since the first edition of this book came out. In 1962, Dakar had but one traffic light and the great mosque of Touba had not yet been completed. The legacy of French colonial rule was very evident. French officials still occupied most of the upper echelons of the Senegalese civil service; Renaults, Peugeots, and Citröens monopolized traffic; and the peanut dominated the economic life of the country. Today, Dakar is no longer an ex–colonial capital but a cosmopolitan city where world-class international conferences and daily traffic jams are routine events. The Senegalese bureaucracy and universities have been Africanized, and French cars must now share the roads with Hondas, Toyotas, and Mercedes. Islam no longer coexists with French culture; it has become ascendant. Touba, the capital of the Mourides, has become a prosperous religious and commercial center and soon will become Senegal's second-largest city.

In the countryside, the peasantry, though dwindling steadily, has become less docile and more organized in its struggle to survive. Women have become more vocal and represent perhaps the most dynamic social force in the country. Senegal is moving through a difficult transition as it attempts to build a modern and competitive economy to replace the old colonial peanut-based economy. The 1994 devaluation of the CFA franc set the stage for economic recovery but required even more belt tightening for Senegal's urban populations.

Senegal remains a multiparty democracy but one under siege because of chronic political, social, and economic crises. The current political class seems to be tired; it is running out of steam and losing the confidence of the people. It is possible that a new generation of political leaders with fresh ideas and energy is waiting in the wings to bring Senegal into the twenty-first century.

This book provides a general introduction to Senegal and its people. It is based on more than thirty years of research, frequent trips to Senegal, and friendships with many of Senegal's people. This revised and updated edition incorporates much of the material presented in the 1982 edition but adds new perspectives and information.

I would like to thank the following Senegalese for their help and friendship over the years: Ismaila Dia and his family, the late Abdoulaye Malick Fall, Ibrahima Famara Sagna, Michel Dembelé, Carrie Dailey Sembène, Papa Kane, Tidjiane Dia, Pathé Diagne, and Fatou Sow. I also have learned much from Senegalese development practitioners such as Pape Sène, Benjamin Diouf, Cissé Ben Mahdi, and Jacques Bugnicourt and Senegalese scholars such as Babacar Kanté, Tafsir Malick Ndiaye, Mamadou Diouf, Momar Coumba Diouf, Boubacar Barry, Benois Ngom, Cheikh Tidjiane Sy, Abdoulaye Bara Diop, and Mamadou Niang.

This book also owes a tremendous intellectual debt to North American scholars who have worked on Senegal and have shared their ideas, research, and writing with me: Jonathan Barker, Robert Charlick, Lucie Colvin Philips, Clem Cottingham, Lucie Creevey, William Foltz, Wesley Johnson, Martin Klein, Robert Meagher, Diane Painter, David Robinson, John Waterbury, and Richard Vengroff. My appreciation also goes to scholars such as Jean Copans, Christian Coulon, Robert Fatton, Gerti Hesseling, Donal Cruise O'Brien, René Pélissier, François Zuccarelli, and Régine Van-Chi-Bonnardel for their work in enriching the literature on Senegal. I would also like to thank Arthur Fell, Don Brown, John Van Dusen Lewis, and David Shear from the United States Agency for International Development (USAID) for their help and collaboration while I worked with them on consulting assignments in Senegal.

Series editor Larry Bowman carefully read several versions of the manuscript, and Barbara Ellington of Westview Press gently prodded me to finish it. I thank Connie Oehring and Katherine Streckfus for their meticulous editing of the manuscript. I would also like to thank Professor Naomi Chazan and the Truman Institute for giving me moral and logistical support and head librarian Cecile Panzar and her staff at the Harry S Truman Institute for providing me with updated materials on Senegal.

Sheldon Gellar
Jerusalem, Israel

Acronyms and Abbreviations

ADS   Alliance Démocratique Sénégalaise
AJ-PADS AND JEF   Parti Africain pour le Démocratie et la Socialisme
BCEAO   Banque Centrale des Etats de l'Afrique de l'Ouest
BDS   Bloc Démocratique Sénégalais
BMS   Bloc des Masses Sénégalaises
BNDS   Banque Nationale du Développement Sénégalais
BPS   Bloc Populaire Sénégalais
BSD   Banque Sénégalaise de Développement
BSS   Bokk Sopi Senegaal
CDP/Garab-gi   Convention des Démocrates et Patriotes/Garab-gi
CEAO   Communauté Economique de l'Afrique de l'Ouest
CFD   Coordination des Forces Démocratiques
CILSS   Comité Inter-Etats de Lutte contre la Sécheresse dans le Sahel
CNTS   Conféderation Nationale des Travailleurs Sénégalais
COSAPAD   Comité de Soutien à l'Action du President Abdou Diouf
CUD   Communauté Urbaine de Dakar
ECOWAS   Economic Community of West African States
EDF   European Development Fund
EEC   European Economic Community
FAIS   Féderation des Associations Islamiques au Sénégal
FIDES   Fonds d'Investissement et de Développement Economique et Social
FLAM   Forces de Libération des Africains de Mauritanie
FNS   Front National Sénégalais
FONGS   Féderation des Organisations Non Gouvernmentales du Sénégal
GES   Groupements Economiques du Sénégal
GIE   Groupement d'Intérêt Economique
GRESEN   Groupe de Rencontres et d'Echanges pour un Sénégal Nouveau
IFAN   Institut Fondamental d'Afrique Noire
IFZ   Industrial Free Zone
IMF   International Monetary Fund
IOM   Indépendants d'Outre-Mer
LD/MPT   Ligue Démocratique/Mouvement pour le Parti du Travail
MFDC   Mouvement des Forces Démocratiques de la Casamance
MPS   Mouvement des Paysans Sénégalais

MRP Mouvement Républicain Populaire
MRS Mouvement Républicain Sénégalais
NGO Nongovernmental Organization
NIEO New International Economic Order
NPA Nouvelle Politique Agricole
NPI Nouvelle Politique Industrielle
OAU Organization of African Unity
OCA Office de Commercialisation Agricole
OCAM Organisation Commune Africaine et Malgache
OIC Organization of the Islamic Conference
OMVG Organisation de Mise en Valeur du Fleuve Gambie
OMVS Organisation de Mise en Valeur du Fleuve Sénégal
ONCAD Office National de Coopération et d'Assistance au Développement
OPEC Organization of Petroleum Exporting Countries
PAI Parti Africain de l'Indépendance
PAIGC Partido Africano da Independência da Guiné e Cabo Verde
PDS Parti Démocratique Sénégalais
PDS/R Parti Démocratique Sénégalais/Rénovation
PE Parti des Ecologistes
PIT Parti de l'Indépendance et du Travail
PLO Palestine Liberation Organization
PLP Parti pour la Libération du Peuple
PRA-Sénégal Parti du Rassemblement–Sénégal
PS Parti Socialiste
PSS Parti de la Solidarité Sénégalais
PSS Parti Socialiste Sénégalais
PT Parti des Travailleurs
RDA Rassemblement Démocratique Africain
RDAs Regional Development Agencies
RND Rassemblement National Démocratique
SAED Société d'Aménagement et d'Exploitation des Terres du Delta
SAL Structural Adjustment Loan
SFIO Section Française de l'International Ouvrière
SMIG Salaire Minimum Interprofessionnel Garanti
SONOCOS Société Nationale de Commercialisation des Oléagineux au Sénégal
SUDES Syndicat Unique et Démocratique des Enseignants du Sénégal
UDF Union pour la Démocratie et le Féderalisme
UDS/R Union Démocratique Sénégalaise/Rénovation
UGTAN Union Générale des Travailleurs d'Afrique Noire
UNACOIS Union Nationale des Commerçants et Industriels Sénégalais
UNCTAD United Nations Conference on Trade and Development
UNESCO United Nations Educational, Scientific and Cultural Organization
UNIGES Union des Groupements Economiques du Sénégal

UNSAS   Union Nationale des Syndicats Autonomes du Sénégal
UNTS   Union Nationale des Travailleurs Sénégalais
UPIS   Union pour le Progrés Islamique au Sénégal
UPS   Union Progressiste Sénégalais
UTLS   Union des Travailleurs Libres du Sénégal

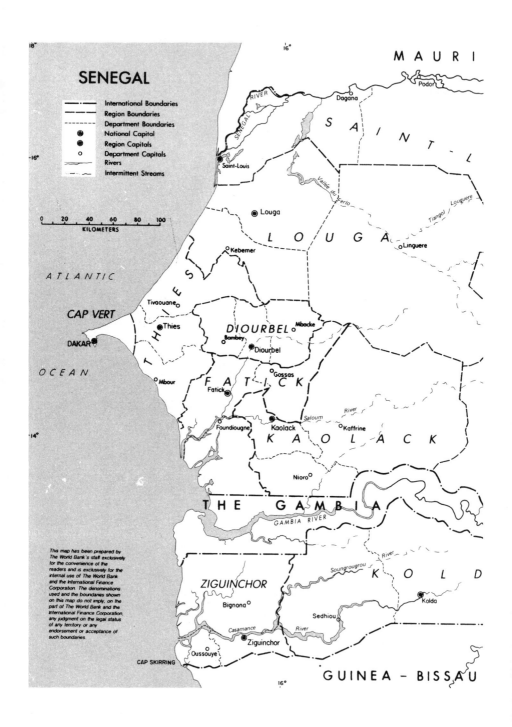

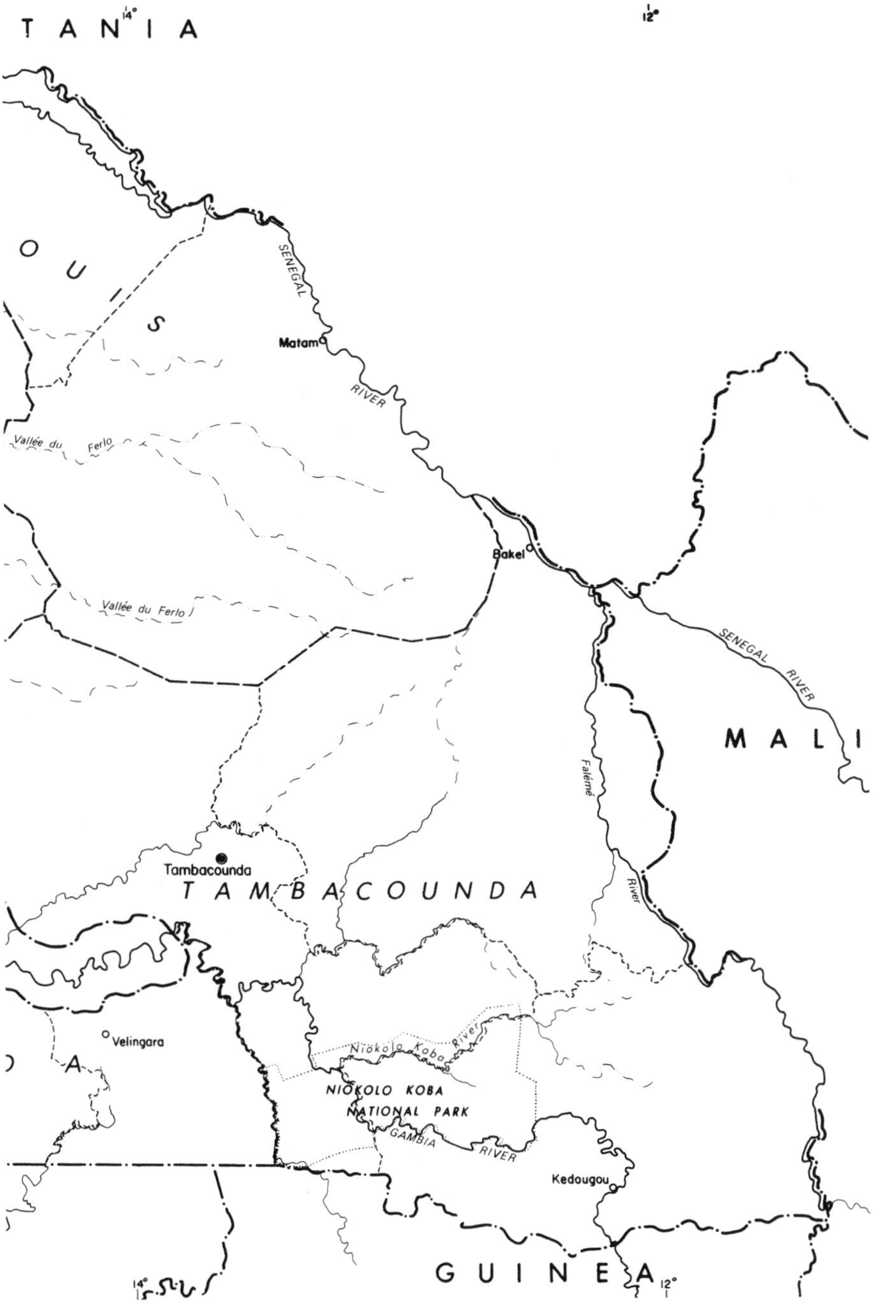

TANIA
14°
12°
OUIS
SENEGAL
RIVER
Matam
Vallée du Ferlo
Vallée du Ferlo
Bakel
SENEGAL RIVER
MALI
Falémé River
Tambacounda
TAMBACOUNDA
Velingara
Niokolo Koba River
NIOKOLO KOBA NATIONAL PARK
GAMBIA RIVER
Kedougou
GUINEA
14°
12°

1

THE HISTORICAL BACKGROUND

M ODERN SENEGAL'S NATIONAL DEVELOPMENT has been profoundly affected
by its strategic location and dual vocation as both a Sahelian and an Atlantic
country. Sahelian Senegal's long involvement in trans-Saharan trade exposed it to
Islamic currents from North Africa. Thus, more than a millennium ago the peoples inhabiting the banks of the Senegal River were among the first in West Africa
to embrace Islam. And because of its proximity to Western Europe and the New
World, Atlantic Senegal became one of the first areas to develop direct commercial ties with Europe, more than five centuries ago, and to send large numbers of
slaves to the Americas. Senegal's geography has brought its people into close contact with North Africa and the West and has made Senegal a crossroads where
Black African, Islamic, and European civilizations have met, clashed, and blended.
Today, Senegal plays an active role on the world scene as a bridge between Africa
and the West and an Islamic nation with strong ties to the Muslim world—two
roles that Senegalese have been playing for many centuries. Although Islamic and
Western influences have done much to shape modern Senegal, the Senegalese
people remain deeply attached to traditional Black African values and world
views.

Precolonial Senegal

Little is known about the origins of the peoples who now inhabit modern
Senegal—the Wolof, Serer, Lebu, Tukulor, Fulbe, Sarakollé, Mandinka, and
Diola—or how and when they first arrived in the region. The late Senegalese his-
torian and cultural nationalist Cheikh Anta Diop has argued that most of
Senegal's peoples originated in the Nile River Valley and then emigrated to West

1

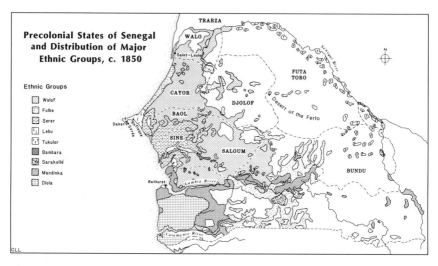

Figure 1.1

Africa.[1] Diop based his theory on similarities between the language and culture of ancient Egypt and those found in Senegal and other parts of West Africa.

While Europe was passing through the Middle Ages, precolonial Senegal had already been organized into chiefdoms and larger political units patterned on the Sudanic state model, which flourished in West Africa during the ascendancy of the mighty Ghana and Mali empires. In the Sudanic state system, a dominant ruling lineage usually established its hegemony over other peoples through conquest.[2] Power derived from control over people rather than territory. Because land was plentiful then, the ruler was more concerned with exacting tribute from as many villages and social groups as possible than with exercising direct political sovereignty over a given territory. At the local level, villages, towns, and social groups that were incorporated into the dominant political unit enjoyed a considerable measure of autonomy as long as they acknowledged the authority of the ruling lineage, paid their taxes, provided men for public works and military service, and extended hospitality to visiting officials. However, revolts were frequent, and territorial boundaries expanded and contracted with the rise and decline of the military prowess of the ruling lineage. The capitals of Sudanic states usually were not fixed but were located wherever the ruler decided to establish his court.

Tekrur, a densely populated kingdom situated in the Middle Senegal River Valley and founded more than a thousand years ago, was one of the oldest and most prominent of Senegal's precolonial African states.[3] Thanks to its strategic location reaching to the edge of the desert, Tekrur prospered from the trans-Saharan trade between North and West Africa, which involved gold and slaves moving north and cowries, salt, and weapons coming south. During the eleventh century, Tekrur's Tukulor ruler, War Jabi, came under the influence of Muslim traders and missionaries from North Africa and converted to Islam. The great majority of the Tukulor people soon followed War Jabi's example, and the Tukulor became the first major Senegalese ethnic group to embrace Islam en masse. From Tekrur arose the Almoravid movement, which swept through Morocco and Spain during the last third of the eleventh century. Over the years, Tekrur became a training ground for Muslim clerics and missionaries operating throughout modern Senegal and West Africa.

During the thirteenth century, Tekrur became a vassal state of the powerful Mandinka Mali Empire to the east. At the same time, the Wolof were being unified under the leadership of the legendary Ndiadiane N'Diaye. After the Wolof of Djolof chose N'Diaye as their ruler (*bourba*), he conquered the Wolof states of Walo, Cayor, and Baol and united them to form the Djolof Empire toward the end of the thirteenth century. Eventually the Djolof Empire extended its dominion to include the predominantly Serer kingdoms of Sine and Saloum.

Although exposed to Islamic influences through Muslim clerics, traders, and court advisers, the Djolof Empire, unlike Tekrur, resisted Islamization and most of its leaders and people remained firmly attached to their traditional religious practices. The Djolof Empire reached its peak during the fifteenth century, when it controlled much of modern Senegal's heartland north of the Gambia River. The empire disintegrated during the second half of the sixteenth century when Baol, Cayor, Walo, Sine, and Saloum broke away to establish their own independent kingdoms. Although the original core state of Djolof survived, it never recaptured its former glory.

Senegal's state structures and social patterns were comparatively stable by the end of the sixteenth century. Most of Senegal's peoples lived in highly stratified societies based primarily on blood relationships. Precolonial Senegalese society was divided into three main social categories: freemen, servile artisan castes, and slaves. Some scholars estimate that as much as one-half to two-thirds of the population were slaves.[4] Less than 10 percent were artisans.

The main characteristic shared by freemen, including royalty and the poorest commoner, was their agricultural vocation and strong attachment to the land. Members of the royal lineages were at the top of the social hierarchy of freemen. Only men with royal blood could aspire to the succession. Bloodlines tended to be traced from the mother's side. The nobility consisted of those families related to the royal lineage by birth, marriage, and tradition; to local chiefs; and to prominent military commanders. The commoners were freemen who had no royal or noble blood, and most were peasants.

Sharp differences in social status differentiated the freemen and the servile castes. Artisans constituted the majority of precolonial Senegal's casted population and supplied most of the goods and services required by a preindustrial agrarian society. The most prominent caste occupations in descending order of status were jewelers, blacksmiths, weavers, leather-workers, and *griots,* who were the musicians, praise-singers, and guardians of oral tradition. Occupations were inherited, and intermarriage rarely took place outside of the caste. Casted women shared the status of their spouses and often practiced similar occupations. Despite their inferior social status, casted Africans frequently enjoyed higher living standards than the average free peasant eking out a hard existence from the soil.

Slaves occupied the bottom rung of society. There were considerable differences in status and treatment among the various categories of slaves. Domestic slaves (i.e., those born into slavery in the household of the master) generally could not be sold. Unlike chattel slaves in the New World, domestic slaves in Senegal, although obliged to work for their masters, were usually given some land of their own to farm and were permitted to marry and raise families. Trade slaves, however, usually captured in war and sold before they could form any permanent ties with the local community, had no rights. Crown slaves constituted a third category. The less fortunate ones performed the most grueling and dangerous forms of manual labor; others served in the ruler's household or were recruited into the ruler's army.

The warrior crown slaves (*ceddo*) were a special class. Despite their lowly slave status, many *ceddo* who displayed exceptional military prowess held high-ranking positions. A warrior slave could become a general, lead the ruler's armies, acquire great wealth, and own other slaves. As a group, the *ceddo*, like the Roman Praetorian Guard, often played a decisive role in determining who would rule by supporting or opposing rival claimants for the crown.

The power and prestige of rulers depended largely upon the number of warriors and clients they could maintain in their personal entourages. Rulers were expected to be generous and even extravagant in rewarding their followers. In return, they could count upon their entourages' loyalty and devotion. A ruler's entourage cut across class, caste, and kinship lines and included members drawn from all segments of society. Rulers needed warriors to fight their battles, *griots* to sing their praises and mock their enemies, courtiers to provide good counsel and service, skilled artisans to fabricate weapons and luxuries, and slaves to work their fields and mines and serve in their households.

Precolonial Senegal was by no means homogeneous in social organization. Caste lines and slavery, for example, were less developed among the Serer and the Diola than among the Tukulor, Wolof, and Mandinka. The Diola and other ethnic groups in the Casamance region usually had less complex and relatively more egalitarian political units than those found in the north. The status of women also was usually higher in the Casamance, where men and women shared agricultural duties.

The peoples of Senegal began to trade with Europe with the arrival of the Portuguese in the mid-fifteenth century. Until the end of the sixteenth century, the Senegambian region was the largest supplier of slaves to Europe.[5] During the seventeenth century, Europeans began to turn their attention to the more densely populated areas of West and Central Africa in their quest for slaves to work the sugar plantations of the New World. However, Senegambia remained an important source of slaves, exporting an average of 2,000 to 3,500 slaves a year until the end of the eighteenth century.

The rise of the Atlantic slave trade and the heightened competition for slaves to export spurred warfare within the Senegambian region, disrupted food production, and often brought misery and famine to the masses. The constant warfare was accompanied by a marked increase in the size and power of the warrior class and a widening gulf between nobles and warriors, on the one hand, and the peasants, who were the main victims of slave raids and *ceddo* plundering of the countryside, on the other. The intensification of the slave trade in the Senegal River region during the latter half of the seventeenth century gave rise to a popular but unsuccessful movement (1673–1677) led by Muslim clerics, or marabouts, in revolt against the tyranny of the slave-trading traditional aristocracy. The aristocracy, however, crushed the revolt with the help of firearms supplied by the French from Saint Louis.[6]

The French had originally come to Senegal to reap the benefits of the Atlantic slave trade and to assert France's position as a major European naval power. They gained a solid foothold in Senegal after establishing a fort and trading post at Saint Louis in 1659 and driving the Dutch from the isle of Gorée in 1677.

European Imperialism and Islam

British and French rivalry for empire and control over West African trade during the eighteenth century often pitted these two powers against each other in the Senegambian region. France controlled Saint Louis and Gorée; the British had established themselves further south near the mouth of the Gambia River. Neither power was strong enough to drive the other out of the region or to penetrate the interior, which remained under African rule. Their presence, however, laid the groundwork for the eventual partition of the Senegambian region into the British colony of Gambia and the French colony of Senegal in the late nineteenth century.

The growing imperialist rivalry between France and Britain also coincided with a militant Islamic revival in Senegal.[7] In 1776 a group of Tukulor marabouts led a successful revolution that overthrew the Denianké dynasty, rulers of Futa Toro since the sixteenth century. After establishing a theocratic oligarchy, the leaders of the clerical party began to send missionaries throughout Senegal and to develop close ties with other resurgent Islamic movements in Guinea and elsewhere in West Africa.

During the mid-nineteenth century, Tukulor clerics from Futa Toro led many of the jihads, or holy wars, that sought to overthrow pagan rulers and create Muslim theocratic states in the region. The most eminent of the Muslim clerical warriors was Al Haj Umar Tall. While on pilgrimage to Mecca in the 1820s, Tall was initiated into the Tijaniyya brotherhood, an organization that had been founded in Fez (Morocco) by Ahmad al-Tijani in the late eighteenth century. As the appointed Tijani Khalife (caliph) for the western Sudan, Tall acquired a large following after visiting the major West African Muslim courts at Kanem, Sokoto, Macina, and Futa Djallon. In 1852 he organized an army and made preparations for a jihad to build a Tijani Islamic empire. After conquering vast stretches of pagan and Muslim territory from Medina to the Niger Bend, Tall moved to extend his power to Senegal. There he came into conflict with the French, who were themselves embarking on a campaign to extend their power.

France's program for expansion began shortly after Major Louis Faidherbe was named governor of French Senegal in 1854. Faidherbe first launched a successful military campaign to subjugate the Moors of Trarza, who controlled the lucrative gum trade on both sides of the Senegal River, and then in 1855 he annexed Walo, which became the first indigenous African state to come directly under French rule. Next Faidherbe built forts at Matam, Bakel, and other points along the Senegal River to ensure French control and to stop Tall's westward advance. By the end of 1859, several of Tall's efforts to dislodge the French had failed, and the Tukulor leader once again turned to the east, where he consolidated his hold over a vast empire before dying in battle in 1864. Tall's Islamic reform movement was the first to come into open conflict with European imperialist ambitions in West Africa, and Tall himself became a rallying point for African resistance to the French.

Other Islamic reformers followed Tall's example and clashed with the French as well as with pagan states and peoples resisting conversion to Islam. One of the most prominent of these warrior reformers was Ma Ba, a Tukulor cleric and disciple of Al Haj Umar Tall's who in 1861 launched a holy war and religious revolution against the pagan Mandinka chiefdoms and states along the Gambia River. Ma Ba's religious wars pitted the party of the marabouts against the traditional rulers and *ceddo*. By the mid-1860s, Ma Ba's forces also controlled much of Saloum and Djolof and he had converted several prominent Wolof leaders to Islam, including Lat Dior of Cayor and Alboury N'Diaye of Djolof, who both played major roles in the Islamization of their home states and led the resistance against the French. Ma Ba died in 1867 during a decisive battle in which the pagan Serer state of Sine dealt a devastating defeat to his forces, temporarily halting the rapid advance of Islam in the region.

Meanwhile, the French were busy extending their control over the Senegal River from Saint Louis to Bakel and gaining a foothold over the mainland further south. In 1857, the French established a military post in the Lebu village of Dakar and gradually acquired control over the rest of the Cap Vert Peninsula. They then built several forts along the coast and sent troops and gunboats to the interior to protect French commerce and affirm France's hegemony over the inland states. Resistance to the French conquest and occupation of African soil was widespread in Senegal. In many areas, particularly in the Wolof states, Islam became a catalyst for armed resistance. After the final defeat of the Wolof armies and the death of Lat Dior in 1886, the French were able to exercise direct control over most of Senegal with the exception of the Casamance, where the Diola and other ethnic groups continued to fight the French into the twentieth century.

The French conquest of Senegal had the greatest impact on the Wolof, whose military defeat was accompanied by the dismemberment of their states and tremendous social upheavals. The defeat of the Wolof nobility and the disbanding of the *ceddo* class destroyed the power and the prestige of the "pagan party" that had earlier resisted Islamization. At this point, the Wolof masses turned for guidance to holy men like Amadou Bamba, who founded the Mouride brotherhood, and Malick Sy, founder of Senegal's most prominent Tijaniyya religious dynasty. The Islamization of the Wolof toward the end of the nineteenth century, and their integration into Muslim brotherhoods led by venerated marabouts, created new authority structures that initially aroused the suspicion of the French, who were attempting to impose the authority of the colonial state.

Social structures underwent fewer dramatic changes in Futa Toro, Sine, and the Casamance. In Futa Toro, the French named members of the *grandes familles* who had collaborated with the French to be the canton chiefs (*chefs de canton*) in the colonial system; in Sine, the pagan Serer were allowed to retain their traditional political structures for a while. However, in all instances the French eventually dismantled the conquered African states, divided them into smaller units, and superimposed French administrative structures on them.

Just as precolonial Senegal had been one of the first areas in West Africa to develop commercial ties with Europe and participate in the Atlantic slave trade, in the nineteenth century, after the demise of the slave trade, it quickly became integrated into the modern industrial capitalist system. Senegal entered this system in 1840 when it sent a shipload of peanuts to France, where the cargo was used to produce cooking oil and soap for European consumers. Within a few decades, the peanut trade, or *traite*, had become the cornerstone of the economy for many Africans and peanuts had become Senegal's main export, supplanting gum and slaves.

Until the mid-nineteenth century, trading relationships between Europe and the African states of precolonial Senegal were based on more or less mutual reciprocity. African rulers and chiefs were able to improve their terms of trade by taking advantage of the national and commercial rivalries among the European powers trading in the Senegambian regions. Moreover, the Africans were able to levy customs duties on imports and exports passing through their territory. Faidherbe's military campaigns were initially instigated primarily for economic reasons. They were intended to establish a French presence on the mainland that could protect French commerce and end African control over inland trading routes and trading posts. The military campaigns that followed the Berlin

Congress of 1884–1885 had a far more ambitious aim—the establishment of French sovereignty over Senegal and other African territories destined to become part of republican France's vast West African empire.

The Colonial Era, 1885–1945

Senegal's colonial experience has profoundly affected its modern national development. Colonial rule in Senegal, as elsewhere in Africa, was essentially a system of political, economic, and cultural domination forcibly imposed by a technologically advanced foreign minority on an indigenous majority. As a system, colonialism justified itself largely through ideologies that asserted the superiority of the colonizer and the inferiority of the colonized. France defended its acquisition of colonies on the grounds of a "civilizing mission" that would bring peace, prosperity, and the benefits of French civilization to the "backward and primitive" peoples fortunate enough to come under French rule. The colonial situation permitted France to deny its colonial subjects the political and civil rights that its own people enjoyed at home and to make policy largely on the basis of what was good for France or for French nationals living in the colonies.

Senegal was the only colony in Black Africa in which France attempted to apply assimilationist ideals.[8] Thus, Senegal had its own territorial assembly (Conseil Général), municipal councils patterned on those found in metropolitan France, and a representative who sat in the French Chamber of Deputies in Paris. Since the seventeenth century, France had considered its coastal settlements in Senegal as an overseas extension of the *métropole*. With the advent of the Third Republic and political democracy in France, Africans born in the urban communes of Dakar, Gorée, Rufisque, and Saint Louis were granted full French citizenship rights in Senegal. This meant that male African "citizens" from the "Four Communes" could participate in modern electoral politics, hold political office (if they met certain educational qualifications), and escape the servitude imposed on the less fortunate inhabitants of the interior, who were regarded as "subjects" by the French colonial authorities. The Senegalese citizens were a tiny privileged minority, constituting less than 5 percent of the colony's total population. In addition to enjoying the benefits of French citizenship, this elite group also had greater access to Western education and employment in modern economic activities.

The location of the federal capital of French West Africa in Senegal was another sign of that colony's privileged status. Created in 1895, the French West African Federation was headed by a French governor-general. From 1895 to 1902, when the federal capital moved to Dakar from Saint Louis, Senegal's governor served in this post. However, in 1902, the two positions were separated and the powers of the governor-general increased. Housed in the luxurious colonial palace, the governor-general soon became the main symbol of France's imperial presence. Dakar itself was transformed into an imperial city containing the most advanced administrative and social services in French Black Africa. And Senegal enjoyed preeminence over the federation's other colonies—French Soudan, Mauritania, Guinea, Ivory Coast, Upper Volta, Niger, and Dahomey.

Colonial Senegal was divided into two distinct political and administrative entities that reflected the sharp differences in status between the citizens of the Four Communes and the subjects of rural Senegal. Although economically dominated by the French, the Four Communes had a vibrant political life based on competitive electoral politics and was one of the rare areas in colonial Africa where Europeans and Western-educated Afro-Europeans and Africans could engage in politics on an equal basis. Rural Senegal, in contrast, was governed along more autocratic lines by colonial administrators.[9]

Outside the Four Communes, the country was divided into fifteen administrative districts (*cercles*) each headed by a French *commandant*, whose military title accurately reflected the authoritarian character of his role. The colonial system of "native justice" (*indigénat*) gave the commandant the right to arrest and jail without trial African subjects for such offenses as not paying taxes, resisting servitude on forced-labor crews, and not showing the proper respect for French authority. *Commandants* could also impose collective fines on entire villages and expropriate village land by administrative fiat. As representatives of the colonial state, they were responsible only to the French colonial governor of Senegal, whose policies they carried out.

The main administrative unit below the *cercle* was the canton. Each *cercle* was divided into several cantons headed by African canton chiefs named by the colonial administration and directly incorporated into the colonial bureaucracy. Although the French often chose as canton chiefs local leaders with high traditional status, in some areas they chose outsiders or people of low social status who knew how to read and write in French and who enjoyed the confidence of the colonial authorities. Canton chiefs had the unpopular tasks of collecting taxes and recruiting men for labor gangs. Some abused their authority by extorting money from the people in their districts. Their dependence upon the French colonial administration for their position and their subordinate rank in the colonial bureaucracy undermined their legitimacy with the rural masses, who regarded them primarily as agents of the French.

The great disparity in status between citizens and subjects gave rise to two markedly different styles of political leadership. In the communes, the prototype of the political leader was the urbane, Western-educated Senegalese intellectual; in the countryside, it was the marabout.

Mastery of the French language and familiarity with French culture and institutions were prerequisites for political leadership in the Four Communes. The Western-educated Senegalese citizens who were actively involved in colonial elec-

Figure 1.2 Election time in colonial Dakar (from a colonial postcard collection). (Photo by Michel Renaudeau)

toral politics clearly identified with the egalitarian ideals embodied in the French Revolution and the Declaration of the Rights of Man. Members of an "auxiliary" elite playing a subordinate role within the colonial system, they were more concerned with ending racial discrimination than with winning political independence. They wanted equality with the French and worked hard to make French assimilationist ideals a reality in Senegal.Senegalese intellectuals followed international events and political developments in France and Europe very closely, a trait that remains characteristic of the Senegalese political elite today.

In 1914, Blaise Diagne, a colonial customs official, became Senegal's first Black African deputy in the French parliament. Diagne held the seat until his death in 1934. His election marked the ascendancy of Black African leadership in Senegalese politics, which previously had been dominated by French and Afro-French (*métis*) politicians.[10] By 1920, the majority of local elective offices was also in African hands.

Blaise Diagne's long and brilliant career was marked by several major political developments that became integral features of Senegalese colonial politics: (1) the active involvement of the Senegalese deputy in metropolitan politics; (2) the polarization and personalization of party politics around the figure of the deputy; and (3) the growing involvement of Muslim religious authorities in electoral politics.

In 1915 and 1916, Diagne recruited Black African troops throughout French West Africa to fight for France in World War I in exchange for legislation that permanently guaranteed the rights of French citizenship to his African constituents in the Four Communes in the face of efforts by colonial administrators and French residents to disenfranchise them. During the early 1920s, Diagne became a leading spokesman for the Bordeaux trading companies then controlling Senegal's colonial export economy and allied himself with the so-called Colonial party, a group of French deputies and senators promoting metropolitan colonial economic interests. Regarded as a dangerous radical by the French in 1914, Diagne by the end of his career had become a pillar of the colonial establishment, enjoying the confidence of French colonial officials and the French business community.

While Diagne was championing assimilationist policies and defending the rights of the citizens, the subjects in the interior were attempting to adjust to colonial rule. Unlike the westernized citizens in the communes where mastery of the French language and culture was an instrument for political, social, and economic advancement, the subjects had little reason to embrace French culture or French political institutions, which they saw expressed primarily in the form of an autocratic colonial bureaucracy. The decline of chiefly authority and the peaceful spread of Islam throughout much of Senegal was accompanied by the rise of Muslim brotherhoods, which provided a new form of political leadership for the rural masses. At first, the French sought to stifle the growing influence of the marabouts by deporting popular leaders like Amadou Bamba, who underwent exile twice, first to Gabon (1895–1902) and then to Mauritania (1903–1907). However, Bamba's exile made him even more of a hero to the rural Wolof masses, and his return from exile was marked with great celebration.

Toward the end of the first decade of the twentieth century, the French colonial authorities in Senegal reversed their anti-Islamic policies and moved to reach a modus vivendi with Muslim religious leaders willing to preach acceptance of the authority of the colonial state. Prominent Muslim leaders like Amadou Bamba, Malick Sy, and Seydou Nourou Tall realized that they could not drive the French out by military force and thus decided to make their peace with the colonial regime in exchange for a free hand in preaching and organizing their followers within the framework of the Muslim brotherhoods. During World War I, many prominent marabouts demonstrated their loyalty to France by recruiting African troops for the war effort.

Although the marabouts made their peace with the colonial state, they kept their distance from westernizing influences. Thus, they discouraged their followers from attending French schools and created their own network of Koranic schools and pioneer youth colonies. For their part, the French kept Catholic missionaries out of Muslim areas. As a result, Catholic missions in the interior were restricted primarily to territories occupied by the then predominantly pagan

Serer and Diola populations. Even there, Islam advanced more rapidly than Christianity.

Although the marabouts resisted cultural assimilation, they were very much involved in Senegalese colonial politics, offering their support and that of their following to Senegalese citizen politicians in exchange for certain favors such as government subsidies for building mosques, jobs and trading licenses for their faithful followers, and redress against abuses perpetuated by the colonial administration. The Mourides, for example, financed much of Blaise Diagne's successful 1914 campaign for deputy in the hope that Diagne would defend them against administrative persecution.

In addition to preaching obedience to the colonial authorities, the marabouts urged their *talibés* (disciples) to grow peanuts in the new areas where they were settling. The French were delighted with this practice, as it promoted the expansion of peanut production, the foundation of the colonial economy. Because of its interest in extending peanut production, the colonial administration granted many prominent Mouride and Tijani marabouts large tracts of land that became peanut estates and often supported the marabouts in their disputes with Fulbe herders fighting to retain control over their traditional grazing lands that were being taken over by the peanut farmers. It would be difficult to exaggerate the significance of the rise of the peanut export economy in shaping the contours of Senegal's economic life.[11] Peanut exports began before the advent of colonial rule, but French colonial investments in ports, roads, and railroads facilitated the rapid expansion of peanut production by making it easier to transport peanuts from the interior. The first railroad in West Africa—the Dakar–Saint Louis line—was opened in 1885. Between 1885 and 1914, peanut production increased from 45,000 to 300,000 tons[12] and followed the eastward expansion of the Dakar-Niger railroad toward Tambacounda. The heart of the peanut zones lay within the boundaries of what formerly had been the states of Cayor, Baol, Walo, Sine, and Saloum. The railroads set the geographical boundaries of commercial agriculture, as 93 percent of Senegalese peanuts were produced in regions serviced by the Dakar–Saint Louis and Dakar-Niger railroads.[13] Conversely, regions like Futa Toro, Eastern Senegal, and much of the Casamance, which had no railroads to link them to the coast, remained largely outside the cash-crop economy.

The pattern of commercialization during this period of rapid economic growth was accompanied by the development of three distinct but interdependent economic and geographic sectors in Senegal: (1) a modern sector concentrated in the federal capital of Dakar, where the major import-export houses and colonial banks had their headquarters, and to a lesser extent in Saint Louis, Rufisque, and the larger towns in the interior; (2) a cash-crop sector that corresponded with the main peanut-producing regions; and (3) a predominantly subsistence sector devoid of cash crops, which encompassed the so-called peripheral regions and exported labor to the towns and peanut zones.

Figure 1.3 A typical colonial peanut trading post in Louga (from a colonial postcard collection). (Photo by Michel Renaudeau)

By World War I, the foundations of Senegal's export economy had been solidly established and the colony's prosperity was inextricably linked to the peanut. Growing peanuts for the market became the main source of cash income for most of Senegal's rural population. Peanuts sparked the growth of trade and generated more revenues for the colonial state. By the end of the 1930s, nearly two-thirds of Senegal's rural population was engaged in peanut farming; more than 60,000 tons of peanuts were produced in a good year.

Although its peanut production and exports made Senegal the wealthiest colony in French West Africa, the peanut economy was, at best, a mixed blessing for Senegal's African population.[14] In the first place, the expatriate import-export companies and colonial banks, which dominated the peanut trade, derived most of the benefits. Second, during the inter-war years (1919–1939), Senegalese peanut farmers suffered from a sharp deterioration in their terms of trade as peanut prices dropped relative to the prices of the goods they bought. Third, many farmers went heavily into debt when crops failed or when peanut prices fell, and they found it increasingly difficult to get out of debt. Fourth, the expansion of peanut production often took place at the expense of traditional food crops. Fifth, French colonial policy, with its heavy emphasis on peanut production, neglected the development of the agricultural potential of the regions lying outside the main peanut zones and locked Senegal into an increasingly unremunerative single-crop economy. Finally, the French did little to improve the productivity of Senegalese farmers.

Dakar's special status as the administrative and commercial capital of French West Africa was another major factor shaping colonial Senegal's economic development. The French built up Dakar as an imperial city from which France would govern and develop its West African empire. Following the transfer of the federal capital from Saint Louis to Dakar in 1902, Dakar soon became the center for French West Africa's most advanced government services, providing secondary schools, hospitals, and research facilities to serve the entire federation. At the same time, the French spent heavily to modernize Dakar and make it the hub of economic life in the French West African Federation. Improvements in port facilities quickly transformed Dakar into French West Africa's most important port. The construction of the Dakar-Niger railroad connecting Senegal to French Soudan (now Mali) spurred peanut production and made Dakar a major entrepôt for French trade with the region. Attracted by Dakar's modern infrastructure and urban amenities, most major French and other European trading companies doing business in French West Africa set up their overseas headquarters in the federal capital. Soon afterward, Dakar replaced Saint Louis, the once proud territorial capital, as Senegal's largest city. By the end of the 1930s, its population had soared to more than 100,000, including a French population of nearly 10,000, the largest European community in all West Africa.

The Lebanese were another important non-African group active in Senegal's colonial development. First coming to Senegal toward the end of the nineteenth century, they helped extend the boundaries of the peanut economy by offering cash for peanuts and operating in areas previously neglected by the French. Because of their willingness to accept lower standards of living, Lebanese traders had a competitive edge over French and Senegalese middlemen.

The 1930s were a difficult and turbulent period in Senegal's colonial history. Drought and the Great Depression brought drastic declines in the living standards of Senegal's rural population when world peanut prices and domestic production plummeted. Although French protectionist policies contributed to the recovery of peanut production by guaranteeing markets for Senegalese peanuts in the metropole, rural living standards remained depressed as local peanut prices stayed well below predepression levels. During this period, French colonial banks and import-export houses reinforced their hold over the Senegalese economy while the Lebanese became the main intermediaries in the peanut trade.

In the political arena, Galandou Diouf, Blaise Diagne's successor as deputy (1934–1940), also aligned himself with the Dakar-based colonial establishment. His main opponent was Lamine Guèye, Senegal's first Black African lawyer and founder of the Parti Socialiste Sénégalais (Senegalese Socialist Party—PSS), which established formal links with the French Socialist party. Guèye's star rose with the coming to power of the Socialist-led Popular Front government (1936–1938), which restricted the use of forced labor in the colonies, gave Africans the right to form their own trade unions, and simplified naturalization procedures for Africans seeking to become French citizens.[15] Taking advantage of the more liberal political climate, Guèye began to organize Socialist party units in the interior and to encourage Western-educated subjects to play a greater role in Senegalese politics, which had previously been limited almost exclusively to the Four Communes. The demise of the Popular Front in 1938 brought an abrupt halt to colonial reform and a reversal of Guèye's political fortunes.

The outbreak of World War II led to a marked deterioration in the political and economic status of Senegal's African population.[16] As in 1914, France called upon Senegal and its other African colonies to provide troops and materials for the war effort. After the fall of France in 1940, the reactionary Vichy regime abolished Senegal's representative assemblies, outlawed all trade unions, and denied Senegal's African citizens the prerogatives and rights of French citizenship. Most Senegalese suffered under the Vichy regime as the colonial administration stepped up its use of forced labor and confiscation of African stocks of rice, millet, and other raw materials. After taking its tribute for the war effort, the colonial administration left little for the Senegalese.

In November 1942, French colonial officials in Senegal rallied to General Charles de Gaulle, leader of the Free French forces. Despite the elimination of Vichy rule, economic conditions remained harsh for Africans and the French did not restore Senegalese political institutions until the end of the war.

The Road to Independence, 1945–1960

With the victory of the Allies in sight, General de Gaulle organized a conference to discuss the future of France's Black African colonies. The Brazzaville Conference (November-December 1944), held in the capital of French Equatorial Africa, formally committed the metropole to postwar colonial reform and marked the end of the old autocratic colonial era. General de Gaulle and the colonial officials who dominated the conference defined reform largely in terms of the metropole's making a greater effort to promote the social and economic well-being of its overseas populations and granting them a larger voice in the administration of their territories. The Brazzaville Conference had little to say about political reform, however, and pointedly excluded independence as a possible option for France's Black African colonies.

In 1946, overseas African deputies worked closely with metropolitan deputies from the French left to push through reforms that drastically altered the relationships between France and her colonies. These reforms included: (1) the abolition of forced labor and the *indigénat;* (2) the elimination of distinctions in status between citizens and subjects; (3) the extension of the suffrage and greater African representation in metropolitan assemblies; and (4) the creation of the Fonds d'Investissement et de

Développement Economique et Social (Economic and Social Development Investment Fund—FIDES) to subsidize overseas development programs.

A distinctive feature of postwar Senegal's political development was the great involvement of Senegal's political leaders in metropolitan and inter-African politics.[17] While he was a deputy (1945–1951), Lamine Guèye was one of the most influential Africans in the French parliament. As leader of the group of African deputies and member of the executive bureau of the French Socialist party, Guèye gave his name to the 1946 law that obliterated the distinction between citizen and subject. He also championed legislation to provide equal pay for equal work for African civil servants, who had been subjected to lower pay scales than their French counterparts throughout the colonial era. His influence began to wane both at home and in Paris after the French Socialists with whom he was allied lost control of the Overseas Ministry.

In 1948, Léopold Sédar Senghor, Senegal's second deputy and a *protégé* of Lamine Guèye, broke away from the Socialists and formed a new political party, the Bloc Démocratique Sénégalais (Senegalese Democratic Bloc—BDS). At the same time, Senghor aligned himself with the Catholic-based Mouvement Républicain Populaire (People's Republic Movement—MRP) in France and assumed the leadership of a loose coalition of African parliamentarians called the Indépendants d'Outre-Mer (Overseas Independents—IOM). During the late 1940s and early 1950s, Senghor and the IOM were primarily concerned with economic issues; Senghor himself became one of the most forceful advocates for increasing the volume of FIDES credits and constantly reminded the metropole of its obligation to provide better educational and health facilities for its overseas African populations.

In 1953, Senghor attempted to transform the IOM from a loose parliamentary alliance to a disciplined interterritorial African movement similar to the Rassemblement Démocratique Africain (African Democratic Assembly—RDA), then headed by Félix Houphouêt Boigny of the Ivory Coast. The IOM did not become a powerful interterritorial party as Senghor had hoped, but it did provide him with a platform during the mid-1950s to call for new political arrangements between France and French West Africa in which each African territory would have its own parliament and executive and would become integrated into a French federal republic with a federal parliament and executive in Paris. In October 1954, Senghor proposed that the West African territories join a French federal republic as two separate entities, one with its capital in Dakar (which would include Senegal, Mauritania, French Soudan, and Guinea) and the other with its capital in Abidjan (which would include the Ivory Coast and the rest of the French West African territories).

At home, the 1946 colonial reforms led to major changes in Senegal's political life.[18] In the first place, the extension of the suffrage to the rural population ended the citizens' monopoly of Senegalese politics and greatly enhanced the power and influence of the marabouts. The emergence of the BDS as Senegal's majority party in 1951–1952 was largely due to its capitalizing on the subjects' resentment of the citizens' past privileges and condescending attitudes and its success in winning the support of most of Senegal's prominent Muslim leaders. Although it remained strong in the Four Communes, Lamine Guèye's once dominant Socialist party never regained power again because of its lack of electoral support in the countryside. A second major development was the appearance of trade unionists, Marxist intellectuals, and university students as important actors in Senegalese politics. Espousing a more nationalistic and radical brand of politics, they tended to regard both the BDS and the Senegalese Socialists as establishment parties too closely wedded to the French. Lacking a mass base, they remained outside the mainstream of Senegalese electoral politics. Third, despite a sharp increase in the size of the French community in Senegal—from 16,500 in 1945 to 38,000 during the 1950s—European participation in Senegalese politics became virtually nonexistent as few Europeans sought political office. Fourth, French colonial administrators were no longer a law unto themselves and became increasingly subjected to pressures exerted by Senegal's political leaders.

Although the postwar colonial reforms accelerated the pace of political decolonization, they did little to alter the structures of Senegal's peanut-based export economy or to transfer economic power from the French to the Senegalese. French firms and businessmen still controlled the peanut trade, and the more advanced sectors of the economy continued to import skilled workers and middle-level managers from the metropole rather than upgrade the skills of the African work force. As in the past, Dakar received a disproportionate share of French investments in Senegal, which were aimed at modernizing its administrative infrastructure and transportation networks and transforming the Cap Vert Peninsula into a major industrial region serving French West Africa and the metropole. The priority given to Cap Vert widened still further the economic gap between Dakar and the countryside. And despite some modest improvements in wages and peanut prices due to vigorous trade union activities and metropolitan subsidies, living standards remained low for most African farmers and workers during the postwar era.

As nationalist demands for independence grew, the French attempted to dampen them by initiating the Loi-Cadre of 1956, which set the stage for self-government by broadening the powers of the territorial assemblies and providing for an African-controlled government in each territory. At this time, the BDS, led by Senghor and Mamadou Dia, his trusted political lieutenant, was moving to the left. When several prominent Marxist intellectuals joined the BDS, the party changed its name to the Bloc Populaire Sénégalais (Senegalese People's Bloc—BPS) to reflect the ideological shift. After the BPS defeated Lamine Guèye's Socialists in the March 1957 territorial elections, Mamadou Dia assumed the reins of Senegal's first territorial government. In April 1958 the Socialists merged with the BPS to form the Union Progressiste Sénégalaise (Senegalese Progressive Union—UPS).

General de Gaulle's return to power following the May 13, 1958, uprising in Algeria created a new political situation. De Gaulle held out three options for France's

Black African territories: (1) total integration with France, an option that no one took seriously; (2) political autonomy as self-governing republics within the framework of a French community dominated by France, which would continue to be responsible for foreign affairs, defense, financial and monetary matters, and higher education—the option preferred by de Gaulle; and (3) immediate independence.

The latter two options were intensely debated in Senegal and throughout the French West African Federation. Militant trade unionists, students, and the left wing of the UPS wanted immediate independence. Senegal's marabouts, however, opposed independence on the grounds that the radicals could take power and launch a campaign to undermine the marabouts' authority. Fearing the defection of the marabouts and economic reprisals by France, Senghor decided to ask the UPS to opt for self-government within the framework of the French community. After a stormy debate, the radical wing of the UPS walked out and formed a new party to campaign for immediate independence in the September 28, 1958, referendum, in which the territories were asked to maintain or sever their formal ties with France. A yes vote meant opting for self-government within a French community dominated by France; a no vote meant opting for immediate independence and the possibility of seeing all French aid terminated abruptly. Despite a vigorous campaign for a no vote by Senegalese nationalists in Dakar, Saint Louis, and parts of the Casamance, the final results showed more than 97 percent following the UPS appeal to vote yes.

The UPS consolidated its power in 1959 by firmly crushing a general strike launched in January by radical trade unionists and by sweeping the March 22, 1959, national elections with nearly 83 percent of the vote and taking all eighty seats in the National Assembly. The main opposition to the UPS in the 1959 elections was the conservative Parti de la Solidarité Sénégalais (Party for Senegalese Solidarity—PSS), headed by Ibrahim Seydou N'Dao, who had led the conservative wing of the UPS before losing control over his political base in the Sine-Saloum region and resigning from the UPS. The PSS also had the backing of dissident marabouts like Cheikh Tidjiane Sy and anti-federalist elements. The Parti Africain de l'Indépendance (African Independence Party—PAI) boycotted the elections, and the Parti du Rassemblement Africain–Sénégal (African Assembly Party of Senegal—PRA-Sénégal), the UPS's main opposition on the left, fared poorly.

As the only Black African territory to choose immediate independence despite reprisals by France, Guinea set a precedent that encouraged Senegal and other francophone African states to seek full independence. In 1959, Senegal began negotiations with France to obtain its independence as a constituent unit of the Mali Federation,[19] which comprised Senegal and the former French Soudan. By the end of 1959, de Gaulle had become resigned to accepting independence as a legitimate option, provided that the former colonies agreed to maintain close political, economic, and cultural ties with France. The Mali Federation formally became independent on April 4, 1960, a date that is still celebrated in Senegal as Independence Day. However, the federation did not last long, primarily because of personal rivalries between Senegalese and Soudanese political leaders and conflicting ideas about the form and future direction that the federation should take. Senegal feared being dominated by its larger neighbor and wanted a loose federation that would permit Senegal to retain its political autonomy and party structures. Senghor also worried about political intrigues between Senegalese and Soudanese politicians to replace him as Senegal's leader and thwart his ambitions to become president of the Mali Federation. The federation broke up on August 22, 1960, when the Senegalese arrested the Soudanese leader, Modibo Keita, in Dakar and shipped him back to Bamako in a sealed railroad car. Immediately afterward, the Senegalese National Assembly met in emergency session to declare Senegal's secession from the Mali Federation. By the end of September 1960, Senegal had its own constitution and a seat in the United Nations.

Notes

1. See, for example, Cheikh Anta Diop, *L'Afrique noire pré-coloniale* [Precolonial Black Africa] (Paris: Présence Africaine, 1960).

2. For an analysis of the Sudanic state system, see J. Spencer Trimingham, *A History of Islam in West Africa* (London: Oxford University Press, 1962), pp. 34–37.

3. For a comprehensive history of the Senegambia's precolonial history, see Boubacar Barry, *La Sénégambie du XVè au XIXè siècle: Traite négrière, Islam, et conquête coloniale* [The Senegambia from the Fifteenth to the Nineteenth century: The African Slave Trade, Islam, and the Colonial Conquest] (Paris: Editions L'Harmattan, 1988). For a succinct discussion of the development of Senegal's precolonial African states, see G. Wesley Johnson, Jr., *The Emergence of Black Politics in Senegal: The Struggle for Power in the Four Communes, 1900–1920* (Stanford: Stanford University Press, 1971), pp. 7–17.

4. For example, see Philip D. Curtin, *Economic Change in Precolonial Africa: Senegambia in the Era of the Slave Trade* (Madison: University of Wisconsin Press, 1975), p. 36; and Majhemout Diop, *Histoire des classes sociales dans l'Afrique de l'Ouest: Le Sénégal* [History of Social Classes in West Africa: Senegal] (Paris: François Maspero, 1972), pp. 27–31.

5. For a detailed discussion of the Senegambian slave trade, see Curtin, *Economic Change in Precolonial Africa,* pp. 153–196; and Barry, *La Sénégambie du XVè au XIXè siècle,* pp. 99–184.

6. See Boubacar Barry, *Le Royaume du Waalo: Le Sénégal avant la conquête* [The Kingdom of Waalo: Senegal Before the Conquest] (Paris: François Maspero, 1972).

7. For some of the best works on the Islamic revival and the advance of French imperialism, see Martin A. Klein, *Islam and Imperialism in Senegal: Sine-Saloum, 1847–1914* (Stanford: Stanford University Press, 1968); Martin A. Klein, "Social and Economic Factors in the Muslim Revolution in Senegambia," *Journal of African History* 13 (1972): 419–441; David W. Robinson, *Clerics and Chiefs: The History of Abdul Bokar Kane and the Futa Toro* (New York: Oxford University Press, 1976); and David W. Robinson, *The Holy War of Umar Tal: The Western Sudan in the Mid-nineteenth Century* (Oxford: Clarendon Press, 1985).

8. For a full discussion of this point, see Michael Crowder, *Senegal: A Study of French Assimilation Policy* (London: Oxford University Press, 1962).

9. For two major studies of the French colonial administration in Africa, see Robert Delavignette, *Freedom and Authority in French West Africa* (London: Oxford University

Press, 1950); and William B. Cohen, *Rulers of Empire: The French Colonial Service in Africa* (Stanford: Stanford University Press, 1971).

10. For a detailed analysis of this important phase in Senegalese colonial politics, see Johnson, *Emergence of Black Politics in Senegal,* pp. 121–219. For a description of early political life in Senegal, see François Zuccarelli, *La vie politique sénégalaise (1789–1940)* [Senegalese Political Life (1789–1940)] (Paris: CHEAM, 1987), pp. 9–98.

11. The most extensive quantitative study of the development of peanut production in Senegal is André Vanhaeverbeke, *Rémuneration du travail et commerce extérieur: Essor d'une économie exportatrice et termes de l'échange des producteurs d'arachides au Sénégal* [Remuneration of Labor and Foreign Trade: Progress of an Export Economy and the Terms of Trade of Peanut Producers in Senegal] (Louvain: Centre de Recherches des Pays en Développement, 1970).

12. All tons are metric.

13. Vanhaeverbeke, *Rémuneration du travail et commerce extérieur,* p. 16.

14. For more on this point, see Sheldon Gellar, *Structural Changes and Colonial Dependency: Senegal, 1885–1945* (Beverly Hills, Calif.: Sage Publications, 1976), pp. 49–66.

15. For more details on Senegalese politics during this period, see Ruth Schachter-Morgenthau, *Political Parties in French-Speaking West Africa* (London: Oxford University Press, 1964), pp. 127–134. For a full description of the Popular Front years in Senegal, see Nicole Bernard Duquenot, *Le Sénégal et le Front Populaire* [Senegal and the Popular Front] (Paris: Editions L'Harmattan, 1986).

16. See Jean Suret-Canale, *Afrique noire, occidentale et centrale: L'Ere coloniale, 1900–1945* [West and Central Black Africa: The Colonial Era, 1900–1945] (Paris: Editions Sociales, 1964), pp. 567–600 for a detailed discussion of the war years (1939–1945).

17. For more details, see Schachter-Morgenthau, *Political Parties in French-Speaking West Africa,* pp. 32–124; and Edward Mortimer, *France and the Africans, 1944–1960: A Political History* (New York: Walker and Company, 1969).

18. For extensive analysis of postwar Senegalese politics, see Schachter-Morgenthau, *Political Parties in French-Speaking West Africa,* pp. 134–165; Kenneth Robinson, "Senegal," in W.J.K. Mackenzie and Kenneth Robinson, eds., *Five Elections in Africa* (London: Oxford University Press, 1960), pp. 281–390; and Sheldon Gellar, "The Politics of Development in Senegal," Ph.D. dissertation, Columbia University, 1967, pp. 148–228.

19. For the story of the rise and fall of the Mali Federation, see William F. Foltz, *From French West Africa to the Mali Federation* (New Haven, Conn.: Yale University Press, 1965).

2

GOVERNMENT AND POLITICS

Despite severe strains on the political system, aggravated by the chronic economic crises of the 1980s and 1990s, Senegal remains one of the most democratic and least repressive regimes on the African continent.[1] Skillful political leadership, the support of Senegal's Muslim leaders for the regime, the commitment to democratic values and traditions on the part of most of the Senegalese elite, the professionalism of the military, and a political culture that prefers to resolve conflicts through dialogue are all factors contributing to Senegal's long-standing political stability.

Senegalese Politics:
The Senghor Era, 1960–1980

In January 1981 Léopold Sédar Senghor became the first African head of state to voluntarily step down before the end of his term and transfer power to his successor in a peaceful and orderly manner. Senegal, to a large extent, owes its legacy of political stability to the political skills of Senghor, who led the country during its first two decades of independence.

Senegalese politics during the postcolonial Senghor era went through three distinct periods: (1) 1960–1963; (2) 1964–1975; and (3) 1976–1980. The first (1960–1963) was characterized by fiercely competitive electoral politics, the consolidation of the UPS's hold over the country, and the emergence of Senghor as Senegal's undisputed national leader.[2] During this period, the UPS experienced its gravest internal crisis as a result of a power struggle between President Senghor and Prime Minister Mamadou Dia. The crisis, which divided the party into two camps, reached its peak in mid-December 1962 when a majority of UPS deputies introduced a motion of censure against the prime minister. Dia responded by arresting four of the UPS deputies who had led the effort to oust him, and Senghor intervened on the side of the deputies in the name of constitutional legality. The army resolved the crisis by supporting Senghor and arresting Dia. The prime minister was tried for attempting a coup d'état, found guilty, and sentenced to life imprisonment.

With Dia out of the way, Senghor moved to change the 1960 constitution to eliminate the office of prime minister and to concentrate greater power in the hands of the president. In a national referendum held on March 3, 1963, the country approved a new constitution that established a strong presidential regime. Senghor and the UPS then prepared for the December 1, 1963, national elections. The unified opposition list included leaders of the PRA-Sénégal, the party that had led the campaign for a no vote in 1958; elements of the PAI, which had been banned in 1960; partisans of Mamadou Dia; and followers of Cheikh Anta Diop, the leader of a faction of the short-lived Dakar-based Bloc des Masses Sénégalaises (Bloc of the Senegalese Masses—BMS). The elections themselves were marred by rioting in Dakar and outbreaks of violence in several rural districts. The official election results gave 94.2 percent of the votes to the UPS, a figure that surely exaggerated the party's margin of victory.

The second period (1964–1975) saw Senegal transformed into a one-party state.[3] Throughout this period, the UPS held all seats in the National Assembly and faced no formal political opposition in national or local elections. In October 1964, the government outlawed the Front National Sénégalais (Senegalese National Front—FNS), a coalition of the supporters of Mamadou Dia (called *Diaistes*) and of Cheikh Anta Diop. The legal opposition disappeared completely when PRA-Sénégal rallied to the UPS and its leaders—Abdoulaye Ly, Assane Seck, and Moktar M'Bow—were rewarded with ministerial posts and places in the UPS Political Bureau. In the February 28, 1968, national elections, the UPS did not have to face any rival political parties.

Despite the absence of opposition parties, the late 1960s were stormy years for Senghor and the UPS. They were marked by an attempt to assassinate President Senghor in 1967, student and trade union unrest in the spring of 1968, and general rural discontent popularly known as the "*malaise paysanne.*" During this period, Senghor managed to survive by making timely concessions to Senegalese students, workers, and businessmen; co-opting their leaders; and using force when necessary to preserve the regime, as was the case when the army was called upon to crush student and trade union strikes and restore order in May and June 1968.

In response to pressure from the postindependence generation of technocrats in the party, Senghor revised the constitution in 1970 to restore the office of prime minister and named Abdou Diouf, a young technocrat and *protégé* of Senghor's, to fill it. Senghor and the UPS again ran unopposed in the national elections of January 28, 1973. With the political opposition reduced to impotence, Senghor began to move cautiously to liberalize the regime and to restore the semblance of multiparty democracy.[4] In April 1974, he authorized the release of an unrepentant Mamadou Dia and other prominent political prisoners to demonstrate the regime's desire for national reconciliation. A few months later, the government formally recognized the Parti Démocratique Sénégalais (Senegalese Democratic Party—PDS), led by Abdoulaye Wade, as the country's first legal opposition party since PRA-Sénégal's merger with the UPS in 1966. In 1975 a presidential pardon permitted Majhemout Diop, the leader of the outlawed PAI, to return to Senegal after fifteen years in exile.

The third period (1976–1980) of the Senghor era was marked by further liberalization, movement toward a competitive multiparty system, and preparations for Senghor's departure from the political scene. Revision of the constitution in April 1976 permitted a three-party system in which each of the three competing parties would be identified with one of the "ideological currents" designated in the constitution: social democratic, liberal democratic, and Marxist-Leninist/Communist. The UPS declared that it incarnated the social democratic position, changed its name to Parti Socialiste (Socialist Party—PS), and joined the Second Socialist International to demonstrate its commitment to this ideological position. Since the government determined which party was to operate under which label, the PDS was obliged to be the liberal democratic party, despite protests by its leaders that it was really closer to Great Britain's Labour party in ideological orientation. Majhemout Diop's resurrected PAI became the officially sanctioned Marxist-Leninist party.

In allowing only three official parties, the 1976 constitutional reforms left opponents of the PS who did not wish to affiliate with either the PDS or the PAI outside the system. Thus, Cheikh Anta Diop's Rassemblement National Démocratique (National Democratic Assembly—RND) was denied official recognition, and Mamadou Dia was refused permission to form his own political party. However, the government permitted Diop, Dia, and other political opponents to publish newspapers that often contained scathing attacks on the Senghor regime.

All three legal political parties competed in the national presidential and legislative elections of February 26, 1978, the first to be contested since 1963. The electoral campaign featured mass meetings and televised debates between spokesmen of the contending parties. The PDS and PAI claimed that the state-controlled radio and television stations favored the UPS and that local administrative officials were far from neutral in supervising the elections. The official results gave the PS approximately 82 percent of the vote; Abdoulaye Wade and the PDS received nearly 18 percent. The PAI ran a poor third, garnering fewer than 3,800 of the nearly 1 million votes cast. The percentage of abstentions—slightly more than 37 percent—was the highest since independence, a fact that the opposition attributed to growing popular dissatisfaction with the regime and the "illegal" opposition's call for a boycott of the election. After the election, Mamadou Dia and other opposition leaders claimed that the PS was, in fact, a minority party because a majority of the voters had either abstained or voted against Senghor and the PS.

The Senegalese constitution was again revised in 1979 to make room for a fourth political party to carry the banner of the right. The government formally recognized the Mouvement Républicain Sénégalais (Senegalese Republican Movement—MRS) as the country's fourth legal party in February 1979. The conservative MRS championed private property, free enterprise, and traditional Islamic and African family values and was headed by Boubacar Guèye, a prominent Dakar lawyer and nephew of Lamine Guèye.

In liberalizing Senegalese politics, Senghor was setting the stage for his eventual withdrawal from the political scene. Since reestablishing the office of prime minister in 1970, Senghor had been grooming Abdou Diouf to be his successor. The constitution was revised in April 1976 to permit the prime minister to automatically take over the duties of the president in the case of the president's death or resignation from office and to continue as president until the next presidential election. Senghor also built up Diouf's stature as a national leader by sending him to represent Senegal on important diplomatic missions. By resigning at the end of 1980, Senghor ensured that his successor could remain in office without having to face the electorate until February 1983, when the president's term was scheduled to end. Abdou Diouf took office on New Year's Day, 1981, marking the beginning of the post-Senghor era in Senegalese politics.

Senghor's political legacy was a mixed one. On the one hand, he had provided Senegal with a degree of peace, political stability, tolerance, and freedom of expression that was rare in Africa. Unlike most African leaders, he knew when and how to give up power gracefully. On the other hand, though committed to democratic principles, he tended to govern in the style of a presidential monarch. By concentrating so much power in his own hands and the presidency, Senghor had reduced the National Assembly to a rubber stamp for his policies and discouraged lively debate and initiative within the government. By establishing a de facto one-party system built on his control of state resources and mastery of clientelist politics, Senghor had contributed to the decline of his own party's dynamism and thwarted the development of a vigorous and loyal opposition that could openly challenge national policies that had failed to stem Senegal's economic decline.

The Struggle for Democracy: The Diouf Era, 1981–1994

Although groomed to succeed Senghor for more than a decade, the new president did not have a reputation as a strong political personality. Instead, Diouf was widely regarded as a modest, if not timid, technocrat who had faithfully served Senghor and the state. Some questioned whether the mild-mannered president would have the necessary authority, strength, and political skills to lead the country in such difficult times or to control the various factions contending for power within his own party.[5]

Figure 2.1 Léopold Sédar Senghor offering advice to Abdou Diouf, his successor. (Photo by Michel Renaudeau)

Diouf moved quickly to assert his authority and style of political leadership. To underscore continuity with the Senghor regime, he retained most of the ministers who had served in the previous government and named Habib Thiam as his prime minister. Shortly after taking office, Diouf also became secretary-general of the PS, taking over the reins of the party from Senghor, and wisely named several leaders of the "old guard" as deputy secretaries-general. This display of respect for the graybeards of the party, who had seen their power wane with the rise of the younger technocrats, won Diouf their support and warm pledges of loyalty. At the same time, Diouf placed his closest political collaborators in key organizational posts within the PS, thereby insuring his control over the party apparatus.

The new president then took several bold measures in his first 100 days in office to enhance his personal prestige and status as a national leader in his own right.[6] These included: (1) a triumphal visit to Saudi Arabia, which established his credentials as a prominent Muslim leader and spokesperson for Africa within the Islamic world; (2) the organization of an Etats-Généraux de l'Enseignement (Estates-General of Education), a conference that brought together representatives of the government, teachers' unions, parent associations, and other groups to discuss the future of Senegal's educational system; and (3) the establishment of an unlimited multiparty system. With these steps, Diouf addressed some of the sore spots that had developed under Senghor.

Although a predominantly Muslim country, Senegal had been led by the Catholic Senghor for its first twenty years of independence. Senegalese television coverage of the 1981 Islamic conference held at Taif in Saudi Arabia showed Diouf praying in the holy city of Mecca and graciously being received by Saudi leaders as the official spokesman for the Muslim Sahelian countries. When Diouf returned home, he received a hero's welcome from Senegal's Muslims, who were proud to see Senegal recognized as a Muslim nation led by a Muslim leader, something that had not been possible under the Catholic Senghor.

By addressing the dissatisfaction of a large segment of the Senegalese intelligentsia toward Senegal's educational policies policies at the Etats-Généraux de l'Enseignement on January 28–31, 1981, Diouf managed to defuse a potentially explosive situation and open up a dialogue between the government and growing numbers of alienated students, teachers, and urban youth.[7] The 1979–1980 school year had been marked by student strikes and violence, an unsuccessful attempt to strike by the Syndicat Unique et Démocratique des Enseignants du Sénégal (Democratic Teachers Union of Senegal—SUDES), the radical antigovernment teachers' union, and the firing of most of SUDES's leaders from their teaching posts.

The Etats-Généraux de l'Enseignement was an enormous success for the Diouf regime. Both the government and SUDES dropped their confrontational stances and sat down together to discuss their respective points of view in a spirit of reconciliation. At the end of the conference, the government committed itself to a major reform of the educational system and co-opted many of the educational policies advocated by SUDES and Senegalese nationalists on the left. The government thus promised to institute universal primary school education by 1990, accelerate the use of national languages as a medium of instruction, and sharply reduce the number of foreign teachers serving in the school system with the objective of phasing out all technical assistance personnel within ten years. Diouf's conciliatory stance and willingness to repudiate some of Senghor's most cherished educational policies disarmed SUDES and the opposition and were widely acclaimed by the general public.

In late March 1981, Diouf announced that he would ask the National Assembly to authorize recognition of all political parties. In April the National Assembly voted to eliminate the constitutional provisions limiting the number of legal parties to four.[8] This move demonstrated that Diouf knew how to effectively deal with the political opposition, which had challenged Diouf's right to assume the presidency without going before the people in national elections.

Instead of cracking down on the opposition and reestablishing a one-party state, as some elements within the right-wing of the PS were demanding, Diouf opted to liberalize the regime by bringing the "illegal" opposition back into the system. In June 1981, the government formally recognized Cheikh Anta Diop's

RND, which had been fighting for legal status since 1976, and several smaller parties on Senegal's fragmented left.

The liberalization measures took some of the steam out of the opposition, weakened the position of Abdoulaye Wade, leader of the PDS, and split the left into a multitude of small parties. By 1982, the number of illegal opposition parties had jumped to eleven. The opposition remained fragmented as Abdoulaye Wade failed in his efforts to unify these groups under his banner. Opposition elements on the left did not see Wade as a viable alternative. As it became evident that Diouf was gaining popularity in the country, Wade began to have problems within his own party as several PDS deputies quit to rally to the PS. By the middle of 1982, the number of PS deputies in the National Assembly had fallen to ten.

The February 27, 1983, national presidential and legislative elections were the most free-wheeling and open elections since the 1959 national elections, the last to be held before Senegalese independence.[9] Colorful political rallies were held by the opposition throughout the country. Marxist-Leninist parties campaigned in towns as far away from the capital as Kédougou, where the red flag with hammer and sickle was displayed at rallies. Opposition parties were granted 50 percent of the time allocated for political debate during the electoral campaign in the national media and used the opportunity to present their positions and platforms to a wide audience. Eight of the fourteen officially recognized political parties participated in the legislative elections, but only four candidates ran against Diouf for president. Cheikh Anta Diop, the popular nationalist leader and head of the RND, declined to run.

The official election results gave Diouf 83.45 percent of the vote. His closest rival, Abdoulaye Wade, garnered 14.79 percent, and Mamadou Dia received 1.39 percent. In the legislative elections, the PS won nearly 80 percent of the vote and took 111 of the 120 seats in the National Assembly. The PDS won close to 14 percent of the vote and saw its representation reduced to 8 seats in the National Assembly, and the RND, with 2.7 percent of the vote, took the last remaining seat.

Although the opposition complained that the elections were rigged and presented many examples of corrupt electoral practices, particularly in Dakar, the evidence indicated that Diouf and the PS had clearly won the elections. Diouf retained the support of Abdoul Lahat Mbacké, the Grand Khalife (spiritual leader) of the Mourides and most of Senegal's Muslim establishment; he also had the backing of many Senegalese independents, who had organized into support groups such as the Comité de Soutien à l'Action du President Abdou Diouf (Support Committee for President Abdou Diouf—COSAPAD) and the Groupe de Rencontres et d'Echanges pour un Sénégal Nouveau (Encounter and Exchange Group for a New Senegal—GRESEN). Moreover, Diouf and the PS had the advantage of being the party in power, with its control over patronage, the state-run media, and territorial administration.

Although the elections firmly established Diouf's legitimacy as Senegal's president, his personal victory and image were tarnished by his inability to control and later to acknowledge widespread fraudulent practices by PS stalwarts. The opposition protested the failure of election officials to require voters to show their identity cards and asked the Supreme Court, without success, to nullify the election results. The PDS and the RND responded by having their deputies boycott the sessions of the new National Assembly. President Diouf's political honeymoon was over, and the remaining years of the 1980s were marked by a deterioration of the dialogue between the regime and the political opposition.

In April 1983, Diouf surprised the country by announcing the elimination of the office of prime minister and the restoration of a strong presidential regime. The PS Party Congress held in January 1984 saw the departure of most of the old party "barons" who had flourished under Senghor, such as Amadou Cissé, Magatte Lo, and Alioune Badara Mbengue; the takeover of the party by close Diouf associates; and the emergence of Jean Collin as the éminence grise of the regime.

In consolidating his own personal power, Diouf became increasingly isolated within the country and within his own party. Although the departure of the old barons had opened important party posts to young technocrats, the fact remained that the barons all had solid electoral followings in their constituencies. In 1984 Habib Thiam resigned from the party in protest against a move to reduce his mandate as president of the National Assembly to one year, and Foreign Minister Moustapha Niasse, another prominent PS leader, was forced to resign following an incident in which he slapped Djibo Ka, a younger minister and close associate of Diouf's, during a cabinet meeting.

In 1984 Diouf faced growing hostility to the regime from several sectors. Student protests began in March 1984 and were to periodically plague the regime throughout the rest of the decade and into the 1990s. Lack of jobs for university graduates and the government's failure to implement promised educational reforms undermined support for Diouf among the students. All but one of the opposition parties boycotted the November 25, 1984, municipal and rural council elections, and the opposition refused to heed Diouf's appeal to them to put aside their grievances and work with his government to overcome the severe economic and social crises the country was experiencing. Finally, the armed insurrection in the Casamance, which had begun in 1982, became more serious as separatist bands stepped up their attacks against government targets.[10]

In the face of growing street demonstrations initiated by the opposition, the regime became more repressive. Abdoulaye Wade and Abdoulaye Bathily, leader of the Ligue Démocratique/Mouvement pour le Parti du Travail (Democratic League/Labor Party Movement—LD/MPT), were arrested following an unauthorized demonstration against apartheid in August 1985. Shortly afterward, the government banned the Alliance Démocratique Sénégalaise (Senegalese Democratic Alliance—ADS), a loose coalition of opposition parties. Diouf's efforts to reach an understanding with Wade and other opposition leaders in 1986 and 1987 foundered when Diouf refused to reform the electoral code and provide greater safeguards against fraud. Without such safeguards, the opposition feared that the regime in power would always rig the elections and prevent the opposition from ever taking power. Diouf's failure to support electoral reform dissipated much of the support and good will he had acquired in the early 1980s by opening up the electoral process to all parties. The political and social climate deteriorated steadily with more student and street demonstrations and more government repression. The April 1987 police strike touched off by prison sentences given to several Senegalese policemen accused of beating a prisoner to death also severely shook the regime's authority.[11] Diouf responded by firing the entire police force, using gendarmes as replacements, and naming Collin as interior minister to restore order in the ministry.

During the February 28, 1988, national elections, the Diouf regime benefited from divisions in the opposition. Part of the opposition decided to boycott the elections; the rest failed to choose a single candidate to run against Diouf. After a hotly contested electoral campaign that put the PS on the defensive in the midst of charges of corruption, incompetence, and capitulation to the *diktat* of the International Monetary Fund (IMF) and the World Bank, the final results gave Diouf 73.2 percent of the vote and Wade, his principal adversary, 25.8 percent.[12] In the legislative elections, the PS took 71.34 percent of the vote and 103 seats in the National Assembly and the PDS received 24.7 percent of the vote, taking 17 seats. Voter turnout was again low as an estimated 42 percent of registered voters abstained.

Election day itself was relatively calm following violent confrontations between PS and PDS supporters in Thiès a few days before. The next day, however, rioting broke out in Dakar amid opposition claims, widely believed among urban youth, that the PS had stolen the election from Wade. Diouf responded firmly to the violence by arresting Wade and other opposition leaders, declaring a state of emergency, and putting Wade on trial for inciting rioting and threatening the security of the state. Wade was found guilty in May and given a one-year suspended sentence. The regime closed the university following a stormy student strike and the students lost credit for the entire 1987–1988 academic year.

Following the elections, Senegal's international image as a stable democratic African state became tarnished as articles appearing in the French press and elsewhere pointed to the limits of Senegalese democracy. Within Senegal, the legitimacy of the regime was seriously questioned. Wade claimed that he had won the elections[13] and insisted that he was the country's duly elected president. The opposition stepped up its attacks on Diouf and Collin and called for their resignations and new elections. Wade increased his appeals to disenchanted urban youth to demonstrate, and Diouf criticized the "unhealthy pseudo-youth" who responded to Wade's appeals, hinting that he was willing to take even stronger measures to save Senegalese democracy.

The July 1988 Round Table Forum, which brought together the PS and eleven opposition parties, failed to defuse the political crisis. Diouf and the PS refused to accept the opposition's demands for major revisions of the electoral code and greater access to the media.[14] In 1989, the political crisis deepened further with a strike by university professors and the outbreak of the Senegalese-Mauritanian conflict in the Senegal River Valley. The government had difficulty controlling anti-Moor rioting that broke out in Dakar and other urban centers in April 1989. Diouf appealed to the patriotism of the opposition and sought their views; however, the attacks on the regime continued. The opposition was especially critical of Jean Collin, the former French colonial administrator and Senegalese citizen who had faithfully served both Senghor and Diouf and who had managed to systematically eliminate most of Diouf's real and imagined potential rivals within the PS while leaving himself as the indispensable person in the president's entourage.[15]

In 1990 Diouf took several important measures to reverse his declining political fortunes and end his political isolation. First, Jean Collin had to go. Collin left his government post as the powerful secretary-general of the presidency and, in April, resigned from all his party offices. This change set the stage for Diouf's reconciliation with old party barons and other prominent PS leaders who had opposed Collin's dominant position within the party and government. Second, at the July 28–30 Party Congress, Diouf reached out to the old barons, giving them a role in arbitrating internal factional disputes, democratized party procedures, and provided greater opportunities for women, youth, and popular local leaders to rise in the PS. Third, Diouf renewed his efforts to bring about a reconciliation with the political opposition and create a broader-based government.

In April 1991, Diouf announced that he was restoring the office of prime minister and named Habib Thiam to the post. For the first time since independence, the government included leaders of opposition parties. Abdoulaye Wade, Diouf's arch-rival, agreed to join the government as minister of state, a position second only to that of prime minister. Amath Dansonko, leader of the Parti de l'Indépendance et du Travail (Independence and Labor Party—PIT), also joined the government, as did three other PDS leaders.

Ten years earlier, Diouf had disarmed the political opposition by permitting an unlimited multiparty system. In 1991 he did it again by co-opting his main opponent, reforming the electoral system with the participation of nearly all of Senegal's political parties (fourteen out of seventeen), and providing the opposition with greater access to the state-controlled media.

Unlike the old electoral code, the new one created the conditions for minimizing fraud and making the elections more transparent. Henceforth, each voter would have to present a national identity card bearing his or her photo. All political parties would participate in drawing up electoral registration lists, and voting registration cards would be distributed in the presence of representatives of the political parties, who would also be permitted to witness the conduct of the election at each polling station. Voters would cast their ballots in secret, thus escaping the direct pressure of local notables and administrative officials. In the past, the administration had controlled the entire voting registration process, had not required proper identity cards, had discouraged the secret ballot, and had often excluded representatives of opposition parties from verifying the vote tally.[16]

By mid-1992, Senegal's political parties were already gearing up for the February 21, 1993, presidential elections and the May 9, 1993, national legislative elections. The big question in Senegal was whether Wade would run against Diouf in 1993. Wade's participation in the government presented him and the PDS with a dilemma. Having castigated the Diouf regime in the past, how could Wade and the PDS do the same again after serving in the Diouf government? Wade's "cohabitation" with Diouf made him a less credible candidate and dampened some of the ardor of PDS militants. On October 18, Wade and the other PDS ministers resigned from the government, thus setting the stage for another Diouf-Wade duel in 1993.

After leaving the government, Wade expressed more skepticism concerning the will of the Diouf government to implement the electoral reform and warned that there would be serious disturbances if the elections were not clean. For his part, Diouf insisted that the elections would be honest and invited foreigners to come to Senegal as observers.

Several new parties entered the political arena—the Parti des Travailleurs (Workers' Party—PT); the Parti des Ecologistes (Ecologists Party—PE); the Union pour la Démocratie et le Féderalisme–Mbooloo Mi (Union for Democracy and Federalism—UDF–Mbooloo Mi), a party committed to the panafricanist principles of the late Cheikh Anta Diop; and the Convention des Démocrates et Patriotes–Garab-gi (Convention of Democrats and Patriots—CDP/Garab-gi). Led by Iba Der Thiam, an historian and former education minister, CDT/Garab-gi had strong support among students and teachers and close ties with Senegalese Islamic reformers and was clearly the most popular of the new political parties.

As usual, Wade constituted the main threat to Diouf in the race for president. And, as usual, the political opposition remained fragmented and unable to rally around a single candidate. A few small leftist parties joined forces to back Landing Savané, who had run before and now had the support of Mamadou Dia. Abdoulaye Bathily, Babacar Niang, Iba Der Thiam, and Mamadou Lo, Senegal's first independent candidate for president who claimed to be the spokesperson for Senegal's civil society, also threw their hats into the ring. Wade predicted that he would win the elections if the government played by the rules of the game. Unlike the PDS, the PIT remained in the government and pledged its support to Diouf.

The 1993 Presidential and Legislative Elections

To head his reelection campaign, Diouf named Ousemane Tanor Dieng, his trusted *directeur de cabinet*.[17] At the same time, he made up with Daouda Sow, Moustapha Niasse, and the old barons he had displaced in the 1980s. In unifying the party behind him, Diouf also brought in new blood. As in 1988, the Diouf campaign set up various "nonpartisan" support groups representing different elements of Senegal's civil society to work for his reelection. Although Diouf wooed the heads of the Muslim brotherhoods, he was not able to get the same degree of

Figure 2.2 Abdou Diouf seeking votes in February 1993 presidential campaign. (Photo courtesy of Le Soleil)

overt support as in the past. The Grand Khalife of the Mourides, for example, refrained from giving his *ndigel,* or orders, to vote for Diouf.

The reelection campaign portrayed Diouf as a world-renowned figure whose leadership had enhanced Senegal's international prestige. Thus, under Diouf, Senegal had become a model for democracy in Africa, a fact duly acknowledged by Western nations. Senegal had also become a prominent player in the Islamic world, being the first Black African country to host the Islamic Conference in 1991. Senegal's prestige in the international arena was reflected in the large amounts of foreign aid it received from both the West and the Islamic world. At home, Diouf promised to lead Senegal to economic prosperity and to create 20,000 new jobs a year for Senegalese youth.

For his part, Wade presented himself as the candidate of change (*sopi*) and the only opposition candidate capable of winning the elections. Although he was critical of Senegal's economic performance under Diouf, his own economic platform did not differ much from that of his opponent. Instead, Wade offered new ideas to further democratize the political system and reinforce civil society.[18] Thus, he called for granting more power to the National Assembly, establishing a more independent judiciary, giving the opposition a greater formal role in governance, and creating private radio stations and a second independent TV channel. If elected, Wade promised to set up a broad coalition that would

TABLE 2.1 Results of February 21, 1993, Presidential Elections

Candidate	Votes	Percent of Votes
Abdou Diouf (PS)	757,311	58.40
Abdoulaye Wade (PDS)	415,295	32.03
Landing Savané (AND JEF)	37,787	2.91
Abdoulaye Bathily (LD/MPT)	31,279	2.41
Iba Der Thiam (CDP)	20,840	1.61
Madior Diouf (RND)	12,635	0.97
Mamadou Lo (Independent)	11,058	0.85
Babacar Niang (PLP)	10,450	0.81
Total	1,296,655	100.00

SOURCE: *Africa South of the Sahara, 1994* (London: Europa Publications Limited, 1993), p. 740.

bring peace to the Casamance and deal more effectively with Senegal's economic crisis.

The parties on the left focused on Senegal's poor economic performance, the negative social consequences caused by the Diouf government's adherence to the IMF/World Bank–imposed structural adjustment programs, government corruption, and the lack of commitment to democratic reforms in the PS.

Despite a long and costly registration campaign, fewer than 2.6 million Senegalese out of 4 million eligible voters were officially enrolled. On February 21, only 51.46 percent of the registered electorate voted. Official election results gave Diouf 58.4 percent of the vote, and Wade received 32.03 percent.[19] The rest of the opposition polled 9.45 percent, with Savané (2.91 percent), Bathily, (2.41 percent), and Thiam (1.61 percent) leading the pack of opposition candidates (Table 2.1).

Diouf's margin of victory was the lowest of any presidential incumbent since independence and down nearly 15 percent from 1988 when he had garnered 73 percent of the vote. He owed his victory primarily to his strong performance in the rural areas, particularly in the Fleuve (Senegal River Valley) and the old peanut basin, where the rural populations were reluctant to change leaders, the PS patronage machine was solidly entrenched, and the administrative apparatus was less subject to surveillance by the opposition parties. His margin of victory was much lower in the Casamance, where election day violence initiated by the insurgents had cost the lives of twenty-seven persons.

Wade did best in the highly urbanized Dakar-Thiès metropolitan area, carrying Dakar, Pikine, and Thiès. He also did relatively well in the Casamance. Wade's voting strength in the capital led him and his followers to claim victory. Landing Savané, who came in third, also did well in the Casamance region, winning more than 8 percent of the vote there. Although Senegalese youth came out in droves to attend opposition candidates' campaign rallies, relatively few actually voted.

Representatives of the seven opposition parties sitting on the National Vote Counting Commission (Commission Nationale de Recensement des Votes) refused to validate the preliminary results and kept the country in suspense for three weeks. Ironically, many voters who had supported Wade and other opposition candidates believed that the government was delaying the release of the results because Diouf had lost, when it was, in fact, the opposition parties who were not respecting the rules of the game and accepting the raw results that had been validated by their own representatives at the polling stations. Kéba Mbaye, the distinguished Senegalese jurist who had been the "father" of the 1991 electoral code establishing the National Vote Counting Commission, resigned as president of the Constitutional Council because the credibility of Senegal's electoral reform institutions had been undermined. The council's proclamation of the official results on March 13 declared Diouf to be the victor, but, in contrast to the events of 1988, this outcome did not touch off widespread protests and street violence.

Six lists contested the 120 seats up for grabs in the May 9, 1993, legislative elections. The electoral system provided for 70 seats to be distributed among the national party lists on the basis of proportional representation. Thus, a party winning 50 percent of the vote would theoretically get 35 seats. The remaining 50 seats were to be apportioned on a winner-take-all basis from 30 departmental lists. This system favored the PS because of the fragmentation of the opposition and the lack of provision for a second round of voting in areas where one party did not get the majority of the vote. Nevertheless, the new electoral system provided small opposition parties with greater opportunities for representation in the National Assembly than the old system had offered, especially if they decided to form a common list with other parties.

Wade's PDS decided to run alone, as did Bathily's LD/MPT. Four presidential candidates—Landing Savané, Iba Der Thiam, Madior Diouf, and Mamadou Lo—joined forces to form a new list called JAPPOO to contest the elections. Amath Dansonko's PIT, which had backed Diouf in the presidential elections, presented its own list. Mamadou Fall, an old-time politician and union leader headed the Union Démocratique Sénégalaise/Rénovation (Senegalese Democratic Union/Renewal—UDS/R), the sixth list to run in the May 9 elections.

Slightly less than 41 percent of those registered voted in the May 9, 1993, legislative elections.[20] The abstention rate of nearly 60 percent was the highest since Senegal had become independent. The PS maintained a comfortable majority in the National Assembly, winning 56.56 percent of the vote and 84 seats, while the PDS, with 30.21 percent of the vote, obtained 27 seats. JAPPOO and the LD/MPT won 3 seats each; PIT took 2 seats; and Mamadou Fall's USD/R earned 1 seat. The PS did worse in Dakar, where it took only a third of the vote. The PDS again carried Dakar and Pikine and did well in the urban areas, and the PS won the most votes in the remaining 28 electoral districts, carrying the rural areas by large majorities (see Table 2.2).

TABLE 2.2 Results of May 9, 1993, Legislative Elections

Party	Votes	Percent of Votes	Seats
PS	602,171	56.56	84
PDS	321,585	30.21	27
JAPPOO[a]	52,189	4.90	3
LD/MPT	43,950	4.13	3
PIT	32,348	3.04	2
UDS/R	12,339	1.15	1
Total	1,064,582	100.00	120

[a]An electoral alliance of AND JEF, the CDP, RND, and independent candidates.

SOURCE: *Africa South of the Sahara, 1994* (London: Europa Publications Limited, 1993), p. 741.

Shortly after the legislative elections, the assassination of Babacar Sèye, the vice president of the Constitutional Council, on May 15 rocked the country.[21] One of the alleged killers implicated Wade and the PDS in the murder. Wade and two of his lieutenants were arrested and released, and the affair torpedoed secret negotiations to bring Wade back into the ruling government coalition and cast a shadow over his political future.

Though excluding Wade and the PDS, the new government formed by Diouf in June 1993 included Amath Dansonko, leader of the PIT; Abdoulaye Bathily, head of the LD/MPT; and Serigne Diop of the Parti Démocratique Sénégalais/Rénovation (Senegalese Democratic Party/Renewal—PDS/R).[22] Landing Savané, Iba Der Thiam, and other JAPPOO leaders rejected Diouf's overtures inviting them to join his government, preferring to stay in the opposition.

Despite the entry of a large number of young PS ministers, close associates of Diouf again held the key ministries. Diouf's old friend Habib Thiam remained as prime minister, and the rehabilitated Moustapha Niasse became minister of foreign affairs, a post he had been forced to resign in 1984. Ibrahima Famara Sagna, who did not get along well with Thiam, left his post as finance minister to become the president of the Economic and Social Council. Diouf replaced him with Pape Ousemane Sakho, a technocrat, who along with Mamadou Lamine Loum, a junior minister responsible for the national budget, elaborated the Sakho-Loum emergency recovery plan, which called for a 15 percent cut in public-sector salaries in August 1993.

The brightest spot on the Senegalese political scene during the second half of 1993 was the signing of a cease-fire agreement between Casamance separatists and the government on July 8. By the end of 1993, the prospects were good that peace would return to the Casamance.

In his 1994 New Year's address to the nation, Diouf admitted that the state was bankrupt and called for a "National Pact" among all Senegalese, including those still in the opposition, to work out a solution to the crisis.[23] The January 11, 1994, devaluation heightened political and social tensions, which were further aggravated by rioting following an unauthorized march on February 16 that led to the deaths of five policemen and one demonstrator.[24] The authorities claimed that the violence had been planned and blamed the political opposition, which had recently formed a coalition called the Coordination des Forces Démocratiques (Coordination of Democratic Forces—CFD), for instigating the riots. The government responded by outlawing the Moustarchidines, a radical Islamic movement headed by Moustapha Sy, who had been jailed in November 1993 on charges of disturbing the peace, and arresting Abdoulaye Wade and Landing Savané and other opposition leaders. Notwithstanding protests by the opposition and Senegalese intellectuals that the government had violated the principle of parliamentary immunity in arresting and jailing Wade and Savané, there was remarkably little public reaction to these arrests. Wade himself denounced the violence and refrained from aggravating the tense situation by not inciting his followers to take to the streets.

In May 1994, the Senegalese Appeals Court dismissed the charges that Wade, his wife, Viviane, and two PDS deputies had been involved in the May 1993 assassination of Babacar Sèye on the grounds of insufficient evidence. However, Wade, Savané, and other opposition leaders were held on charges of instigating the February 16 riots. They were released in late June following a hunger strike. On August 30, a Dakar court dismissed the charges against Wade and Savané, and by early September, rumors were circulating that the government was negotiating to bring Wade back into the government.

Meanwhile, Wade and other opposition parties joined forces to create Bokk Sopi Senegaal (Bloc for Change in Senegal—BSS), a loose coalition headed by Wade calling for a pact to maintain social peace and the elaboration of a national consensus program to resolve Senegal's political, economic, and social crisis. Wade presided over the coalition, which consulted with various employer associations and trade unions.

In January 1995, Diouf invited Wade to the presidential palace, thus touching off speculation that Wade's return to the government was imminent. Diouf also consulted other opposition party and trade union leaders who had contested his economic policies during the early months of 1995 as he reached out to seek a broader government coalition.

The Political Process:
Clan Politics and Party Structures

It would be impossible to comprehend the flavor and essence of Senegalese politics without some understanding of the important role played by "clan politics" in the country's political life.[25] During the postwar era, Senegal's two major political parties were built around coalitions of different groups of leaders and their followers. At the local level, clan politics incorporated large numbers of people into the game of electoral politics and linked the mass of the population to regional and national leaders. When interparty electoral competition declined after independence, clan politics persisted, primarily in the form of intraparty factionalism among rival politicians jockeying for control over local and regional party organizations. With the rebirth of an unlimited multiparty system in the 1980s, clan politics and factionalism became part of the dynamics of opposition parties.

Senegalese clan politics is highly personalized and revolves around the prestige of the clan leader and his ability to reward followers with favors, material resources, and reflected glory. In the context of Senegalese politics, clan leaders are not necessarily professional politicians. They can also be religious leaders, rural notables, heads of ethnic communities, businessmen, or trade unionists vying for power within their own communities or organizations.

Clan politics were clearly a major ingredient in the 1962 power struggle between Senghor and Mamadou Dia that led to the latter's downfall. As prime minister, Dia took advantage of his control over government jobs and resources to build a large following of local and regional clan leaders. The showdown between Senghor and Dia was instigated by growing polarization between pro-Dia and pro-Senghor clans. After ousting Dia, Senghor proceeded to purge the government and his party of clan leaders who had sided with the prime minister.

Although he often denounced the evils of clan politics—"*la politique politicienne*"—Senghor himself was a master of this style of politics. He knew how to keep on the good side of the dominant factions controlling the Muslim brotherhoods and how to play off rival clan leaders against each other to weaken or win control of trade unions or business organizations. He was particularly adept at squashing potential challengers before they could establish independent power bases within the party.

The formal party structures that Diouf inherited after taking Senghor's place as secretary-general of the PS in January 1981 did not differ very much from those in place at independence.[26] As a mass party, the PS was organized at all levels of society, from village and urban neighborhood committees at the base to the Political Bureau at the national level. Party units coincided with administrative districts at the rural community, department, and regional levels. The party also had its women's, youth, and student organizations and close ties with trade union leaders in the Conféderation Nationale des Travailleurs Sénégalais (National Confederation of Senegalese Workers—CNTS). Party councils and national conferences served to place the official party stamp of approval on the government's domestic and foreign policies and to reaffirm the party's confidence in the national leader. Within the party, clientelist politics prevailed as Diouf and other party leaders responded to appeals from the rank and file by providing government jobs, loans, social services, and development projects for their supporters and constituencies.

By the early 1980s, the PS, after more than twenty years in power, had lost much of its dynamism. The extreme centralization of power in the presidency, the diminished role of the National Assembly, and the absence of a real threat from opposition parties in national and local elections had contributed to widespread party apathy. The decade was a period of decline for the PS. Despite his frequent calls to revitalize the party by bringing in new blood and promoting democracy at the base, Diouf, in fact, contributed to party demobilization by alienating the old clan leaders—the so-called barons who had strongly supported Senghor and had large followings; eliminating popular leaders of his own generation like Habib Thiam, Moustapha Niasse, and Daouda Sow; and placing Jean Collin and technocrats with little popular support in high party posts. Party militants also did not appreciate Diouf's flirtation with independents and opposition elements or his efforts to place himself above the party in national elections.

Although Diouf lacked the personal touch and campaigning skills of a Senghor, he partially compensated for this weakness by fostering the creation of autonomous political support groups like COSAPAD and GRESEN, which incorporated different groups within Senegalese society to rally around his candidacy for the presidency.[27] Despite their endorsement of Diouf, these groups maintained their autonomy from the PS and their leaders often refused to join the party, even when offered high positions in the national administration. This situation created friction between the support groups and the party during the election campaigns and between Diouf and PS leaders who resented sharing the spoils of victory with people who had not been loyal party members. In contrast with Senghor, who had tried to integrate various groups in Senegalese society under the party banner, Diouf sought to appeal to those who were disillusioned with the PS and to put himself above crass party politics. In the 1993 presidential elections, Diouf's campaign again organized a wide range of nonpartisan support groups to work for his reelection.

In his attempts to reform and revitalize the PS, Diouf ran against the conservative wing of the party, which resisted opening up the party and the system to newcomers and opposition elements. After the special March 1989 PS Congress, Diouf named a twelve-person executive bureau, composed mostly of reformers,[28] to take over the party and oversee the democratization of the party in preparation for the 12th Party Congress. This congress, which took place in July 1990 after Jean Collin left the political scene, established tighter control over the sale of party cards; introduced proportional representation in local party elections; strengthened the role of regional party units; expanded the PS Political Bureau and Central Committee to make them more representative; and created the post of *controleur*, a largely honorary position as troubleshooter and adviser designed for old-guard party stalwarts who had been pushed out by Diouf during the 1980s.[29] That the congress did, in fact, succeed in injecting some new blood and life into the party became evident when a larger number of young men and women candidates ran on the PS list in the November 1990 municipal and rural council elections. The December 1992 Party Congress reinforced this trend and set the stage for large numbers of new PS candidates to run for deputy in the May 9, 1993, legislative elections. At a special PS Party Congress held in July 1994, Diouf promised to remain head of the PS as long as he had the confidence of party militants and dismissed rumors that he was grooming a "dauphin." Diouf also insisted that women and youth should be given a greater role in party affairs and that the PS should implement its pledge to give women 25 percent of the party offices.

The PDS was the only other Senegalese party to have a mass base of support outside the capital.[30] During the 1980s and early 1990s, the PDS relied heavily upon its women militants, and in 1993 it presented more women as candidates for the National Assembly than the PS.

Most of the smaller opposition parties had similar party structures but little party organization outside of Dakar. The 1993 elections gave the smaller opposition parties more opportunities to campaign and organize in the countryside than they had managed in the past. For the first time, the leftist opposition parties did as well outside the capital as they did in Dakar.

The Political Process: Ideological and Interest-Group Politics

Unlike clan politics, which is based on patron-client relationships and a share of the spoils of office, ideological politics in Senegal are largely concerned with winning the hearts and minds of the Western-educated intellectual elite. During the 1960s and 1970s, most of Senegal's intellectuals and political parties affirmed their allegiance to some variant of socialist ideology. Since then, ideology has been increasingly less important in Senegalese politics. While still claiming to be a socialist party, the PS has placed more emphasis on democratic rather than socialist ideals in recent years. The decline of the French Communist party in France, the demise of communism in the Soviet Union and Eastern Europe, and the end of the Mao era in China have all contributed to a decline in the ideological fervor of Senegal's small Marxist-based parties.

It is difficult to understand Senegalese ideological politics without some appreciation of the influence of the French left on Senegalese intellectuals, particularly during the postwar era (1945–1960) when most Senegalese university students attended school in France and many adopted Marxism or Marxism-Leninism as their guiding philosophy.[31] At that time many French university professors were themselves Marxists, and the French left, particularly the French Communist party, supported anticolonial independence movements throughout Africa and the Third World. After finishing their studies, former militant student leaders like Majhemout Diop, founder of the PAI, returned to Senegal in the late 1950s to agitate for independence and organize the radical Senegalese left.

Meanwhile, Senghor and Dia were in the process of formulating a non-Marxist, socialist ideology that had much in common with the communitarian socialism espoused by Emmanuel Mounier, the editor of *Esprit* and one of the leading lights of the French Catholic left. Senghor formulated the philosophical and political bases of African Socialism, and Dia developed its economic components.[32]

African Socialism became the official ideology of the regime and remained so until the mid-1970s when the UPS changed its name and joined the Socialist International, which was dedicated to democratic socialism. Throughout the 1960s, ideological opposition from the Marxist left continued to be strong. Senegalese intellectuals in this faction argued that African Socialism was not a valid socialist ideology but simply a rationale for defending the status quo and the preservation of neocolonial relationships with France. The disappearance of legal opposition political parties and contested national elections deprived the Marxist left of a public forum to express its views and forced ideological politics underground.

The freer political atmosphere of the late 1970s and early 1980s led to a resurgence of Marxist and nationalist critiques of the moderate socialist ideology of the regime. Different Marxist currents—pro-Soviet, pro-Chinese, Trotskyite, and so on—set up their own political parties and newspapers when Diouf liberalized the multiparty regime in 1981.[33] The Senegalese left focused its attack on the government's economic policies as reflected in the IMF/World Bank–sponsored structural adjustment program, corruption, and the failure of the regime to implement fully democratic practices. Fortunately, for the regime, Marxist ideologies did not have the same hold on Senegalese students and intellectuals that it had during the 1960s. Marxism no longer dominated the thinking of Senegalese university students as a return to Islam attracted more and more of the Western-educated Senegalese elite. Moreover, the PDS, the major opposition party, was not a Marxist party. Instead, the regime during the 1980s faced ideological attacks by radical Muslim fundamentalists who contended that secular Western values were polluting Senegalese society and demanded the establishment of an Islamic state. The PS, however, managed to counter these attacks by co-opting and supporting more moderate Islamic ideological currents.

Under Diouf, socialism became a less important ideological theme for the regime than it had been under Senghor, who had to justify his socialist credentials. Instead, Diouf spoke about the need for less government, a stronger private sector, and an "historical compromise" that would bring together the PS and the opposition to revitalize the nation at a time of severe social and economic crisis.[34] During the late 1980s and early 1990s, Diouf placed more and more emphasis on Senegal as a democratic model. For its part, the opposition also talked more about democracy than socialism in criticizing the regime in light of the developments taking place throughout the Communist world.

Interest-group politics make up another major dimension of the Senegalese political system and take place at two levels. At one level, different political actors and parties strive to win the support of key groups within Senegalese society. At the second level, interest groups attempt to wrest concessions from the government while the government pressures the interest groups to go along with its policies.

Four key groups tend to dominate Senegalese interest-group politics: students, trade unionists, African businessmen, and Muslim leaders. Despite their numerical predominance, rural producers have not been able to organize themselves to become a major pressure group.

During the postwar era, university and high school students were the most radical elements in Senegalese society and led the nationalist opposition to French colonial rule. Since independence, students have also been the most persistent source of opposition to the regime despite the fact that they constitute one of the most privileged groups in Senegalese society, receiving monthly stipends and other benefits that exceed those of many Senegalese industrial workers. During the 1960s, radical student organizations became the main centers of legal opposition to the regime following the establishment of a de facto one-party system. In May 1968, university students launched a strike that set off a wave of social unrest and shook the foundations of the regime.

During the Senghor era, the regime sought to neutralize student opposition by establishing UPS/PS-affiliated youth and student groups, co-opting radical leaders with offers of good positions in the government, giving priority in government spending to secondary and university education over primary education, and accelerating the pace of Africanization of the public sector to provide more employment opportunities for university and secondary school graduates.

Diouf's conciliatory stance during his first years in office won some respite from student agitation. By the end of the 1980s, however, student strikes and protests had again become commonplace. The rapid expansion of the number of Senegalese university and secondary school students, coupled with the decline in employment opportunities in the public sector, increased student anxiety about their future. By the beginning of the 1990s, Cheikh Anta Diop University in Dakar, which had been built to accommodate 3,000 students, was overflowing with more than 13,000 students. During the late 1980s and early 1990s, university strikes had become annual events, disrupting studies and forcing the government to come up with funds to meet student demands for better living conditions. The 1991–1992 school year was a difficult one for student-government relations despite the drop in political tension due to Wade's joining the government. Strikes at Cheikh Anta Diop University and the University of Saint Louis, which had opened in 1990, were accompanied by widespread secondary school strikes in major population centers throughout the country. Secondary school and university strikes continued to be frequent events during the early and mid-1990s. In 1994, a combination of student and faculty strikes resulted in a decision to cancel the 1993–1994 academic year for both Cheikh Anta Diop and Saint Louis Universities.

The collaboration of Senegal's trade unions for workers in both the public and private sectors is essential for maintaining political and social stability. After the 1959 national elections, the Dia government moved quickly to domesticate the trade union movement by crushing the radical Union Générale des Travailleurs d'Afrique Noire (General Union of Workers of Black Africa—UGTAN) and promoting a UPS-dominated trade union movement, the Union Nationale des Travailleurs Sénégalais (National Union of Senegalese Workers—UNTS). By the end of 1962, all of Senegal's trade unions were unified under the banner of the UNTS, which had to maintain a delicate balance between defending the interests of its members and supporting the economic programs of the government. In May 1968, the UNTS called for a general strike to protest government policies that had frozen wages since 1961. The Senghor government retaliated by arresting union strike leaders, dissolving the UNTS, and setting up the CNTS.

After crushing the strike, Senghor met some of labor's demands by raising the minimum wage, stepping up the Africanization of the modern sector, and offering trade union leaders official representation in the party and the government. In 1976 the government again permitted the creation of new trade unions not affiliated with the CNTS.

Diouf continued Senghor's policy of "responsible participation," which offered CNTS leaders important party and government posts.[35] During the ascendancy of the UNTS, all trade union members had to belong to the UPS. However, when the CNTS was formed, all PS members had to join the union but union members did not have to join the PS, thus leaving room for opposition elements within the union and the potential for union autonomy. Despite its alliance with the PS, the CNTS under the leadership of Madia Diop, its secretary-general since 1983, has not automatically supported government policies or stopped workers from striking. For example, the CNTS fiercely opposed government efforts to revise the Labor Code to make it easier for employers to fire personnel for economic reasons. During the late 1980s and early 1990s, labor agitation increased considerably, as evidenced by strikes by university professors, bank employees, and electricity and public transport workers.

On September 2, 1993, Senegal's trade union movement organized a successful one-day general strike to protest the government's decision to cut state employees' salaries by 15 percent to comply with donor demands for greater cutbacks in government spending. The Intersyndicale, a broad trade union coalition headed by the CNTS but also including independent unions, and those close to the PDS and other opposition parties joined forces to fight the government's austerity program.[36] Pressure from the rank and file forced the CNTS, despite its affiliation with the PS, to strongly oppose the government's emergency program. After the Intersyndicale agreed to negotiate with the government, the Union Nationale des Syndicats Autonomes du Sénégal (National Union of Autonomous Senegalese Trade Unions—UNSAS), the second most important union in the coalition, broke away from the Intersyndicale and organized unsuccessful strikes in October and December 1993. Under the leadership of Mademba Sock, UNSAS continued its militant activities in 1994 as part of its bid to woo workers away from the progovernment CNTS. In January 1995, UNSAS backed off from its threats to conduct a general strike and shut down Senegal's power supply during a state visit by the Ivoirian president when the government made it clear that such a strike would be unacceptable.

The PS and the government can no longer take Senegalese trade union support for granted. However, at the PS Extraordinary Party Congress held in Dakar in July 1994, the PS and the CNTS renewed their partnership and agreed to continue the system of "responsible participation" to give CNTS trade union leaders a direct voice in the party's governing circles.

Senegalese businessmen constitute a third major interest group in Senegalese politics. Before 1968 the government did little to promote the development of a modern Senegalese private sector, thus frustrating the aspirations of Senegalese businessmen to replace the French and Lebanese who dominated the leading sectors of the economy. In mid-1968, an important group in the private sector created the Union des Groupements Economiques du Sénégal (Union of Senegalese Economic Groups—UNIGES) to protest the lack of Africanization. Although the regime set up a rival group of progovernment businessmen, it took steps to meet some of UNIGES's demands. In 1969, the Dakar Chamber of Commerce, which had been directly controlled by the French, was Africanized, and the following year UNIGES merged with its rival to form the Groupements Economiques du Sénégal (Economic Groups of Senegal—GES), a highly politicized organization with close links to the government. Government support for the Senegalese private sector generally followed political lines with loans, licenses, and state contracts going to progovernment businessmen. In the 1980s, changes in regime ideology and economic policies calling for less state intervention and regulation of the economy improved the relative status of the Senegalese business class, which included many former state officials and their relatives who had profited from government ties.[37] During the mid and late 1980s, measures to reduce tariffs on imported industrial products hurt Senegalese industrialists, and the restoration of higher customs taxes in the late 1980s aroused the opposition of Senegalese importers. In both instances, the government had not consulted the Senegalese private sector but had instead followed the advice of the IMF and the World bank.

During the early 1990s, however, Senegalese businessmen, though still dependent on the government, were beginning to emerge as a more autonomous and influential interest group. Following the announcement of the government's economic program in August 1993, various business groups joined forces to support the trade unions in their protest against government economic policy. The most militant of the business groups was the predominantly Mouride Union Nationale des Commerçants et Industriels Sénégalais (National Union of Senegalese Merchants and Industrialists—UNACOIS), which left the coalition, with the progovernmental GES, to ally itself with the UNSAS, which organized strikes in October 1993. Senegalese business interests were also consulted when the government sponsored a meeting in the summer of 1994 to forge a common economic strategy to deal with the consequences of devaluation.

The heads of Senegal's major Islamic brotherhoods constitute the most influential interest group in the country, largely because of their hold over their mass following.[38] In exchange for their support, the marabouts extract various concessions from the government—subsidies for mosque construction, easy access to state loans, jobs for their followers, preferential treatment from state development agencies, and higher prices for their peanut crops. Unlike the urban-based student, labor, and business interest groups, which are heavily dependent upon the government financially, the marabouts, thanks to their large landholdings and the contributions of their followers, have an autonomous economic base that gives them greater freedom vis-à-vis the ruling party. During the 1970s and 1980s, many Islamic leaders expanded their business activities in the urban areas. The Mourides set up extensive trading networks throughout West Africa, Europe, and the United States.

Toward the end of the Senghor era, Muslim leaders began to put more distance between themselves and the government. Since coming to power, Diouf has succeeded in retaining the support of the heads of Senegal's major brotherhoods. Diouf's ability to defeat the opposition in the 1983 and 1988 national elections was in no small measure due to the strong backing he received from Abdoul Lahat Mbacké, the Grand Khalife of the Mourides. With Abdoul Lahat's death in June 1989, Diouf lost a powerful ally. In the 1993 national elections, the new Grand Khalife, Saliou Mbacké, did not order the Mourides to vote for Diouf and the PS. Direct, overt maraboutic support for the regime is no longer automatic. Nevertheless, Diouf and the PS still rely on the marabouts to serve as a crucial counterbalance to urban-based opposition from students, intellectuals, and workers and other Islamic forces that are more radical and not directly connected with the brotherhoods (see Chapter 5).

The proliferation of rural-based nongovernmental organizations (NGOs) and peasant associations during the 1980s and 1990s has created the basis for a peasant movement to defend rural interests. In January 1993 the Féderation des Organisations Non Gouvernmentales du Sénégal (Federation of Senegalese Nongovernmental Organizations—FONGS) organized a national forum that brought together diverse peasant groups and rural cooperative movements to discuss ways of defending and promoting rural interests. In March 1993, the Mouvement des Paysans Sénégalais (Senegalese Peasant Movement—MPS) became the first peasant-based Senegalese political party to run in a national election. However, the MPS decided to withdraw before the May 9 legislative elections.

Government Institutions

As in most African countries, the presidency in Senegal is the main locus of political power.[39] The 1960 Senegalese constitution provided for a so-called bicephalous, or two-headed, regime giving broad powers to both the president and the prime minister. The president was the head of state and conducted foreign policy; the prime minister was chief executive and ran the day-to-day affairs of government. This arrangement satisfied neither Senghor nor Dia and was one of the major underlying causes of the breakup of the Senghor-Dia tandem in 1962 and the establishment of a strong presidential regime in 1963.

The 1963 constitution transferred the functions previously carried out by the prime minister to the president, placed few checks on presidential power, and stifled ministerial initiative. In 1969 several Senegalese intellectuals and civil servants close to President Senghor called for constitutional reforms to increase the responsibility of cabinet ministers. The subsequent revisions of February 1970 reestablished the office of prime minister.

Although once again giving the prime minister control over administration, the 1970 constitutional reforms still left the president clearly in command. In effect, the prime minister had to be the "president's man" because it was the president who appointed him in the first place and who had the power to dismiss him. Moreover, the president exercised direct control over foreign policy, defense, the army, and the appointment of magistrates and high-ranking government officials and had the authority to initiate constitutional changes.

In 1983 the constitution was again revised to eliminate the office of prime minister and concentrate more power in the hands of the presidency. The General Secretariat to the Presidency, which had drafted much of Senegal's legislation during the Senghor era, became even more powerful under the direction of Jean Collin—to the detriment of the cabinet ministers. Collin's departure in 1990, the restoration of the office of prime minister in April 1991, and the establishment of a new government with fewer but stronger ministries marked a new phase in presidential rule that gave the prime minister and the cabinet greater responsibility and initiative in ruling the country and also left Diouf more free to concentrate on foreign policy.

The National Assembly's role as a major decision-making body reached its peak shortly after independence. Ironically, the power of the National Assembly was greatest during the Dia years (1959–1962), when it asserted significant influence over budgetary matters, despite the deputies' complaints about executive dominance and inadequate participation of deputies in the planning process. With the installation of the presidential regime in 1963, the National Assembly saw its influence reduced still further as the ratification of government-initiated legislation became more or less automatic, given strict party discipline within UPS/PS ranks and the absence of a parliamentary opposition until 1978.

After 1978 the National Assembly again became a lively forum for debating the major political and economic issues confronting the country despite the PDS's occasional boycotts. Although the executive branch continues to introduce nearly all of Senegal's legislation, there seemed to be some movement in the early 1990s toward giving Senegalese deputies and the National Assembly a more active role in governing the country following the April 1991 revisions in the Senegalese constitution, which gave the National Assembly greater powers to challenge government policy and to bring down the government. The presence of thirty-four deputies from several different opposition parties elected in May 1993 will no doubt liven debate and make the National Assembly less of a rubber stamp for ratifying government policy.

Until May 1992 Senegal's judicial branch was headed by a Supreme Court that, as the last court of appeals, ruled on the constitutionality of government laws, regulations, and actions and served as the guardian of the rights and freedoms inscribed in the constitution.[40] In principle, the independence of the judiciary is guaranteed by the constitution. Magistrates cannot be removed from office without their consent, and in carrying out their duties they are not to be pressured by the executive or legislative branches. In practice, however, the courts have rarely ruled against the government in important constitutional cases or political trials, a fact that should not be surprising, as the magistrates are named by the president.

Since the liberalization of Senegalese politics in the mid-1970s, the courts have become a major political battleground. During the late 1970s, Cheikh Anta Diop, the leader of the RND who challenged the section of the 1974 constitution defining the number and types of parties that could be recognized, lost his appeal on a technicality. The Supreme Court threw out the case on the grounds that the RND had filed too late in attempting to register as a legal party. A 1982 revision in the electoral code that gave the Supreme Court responsibility for resolving election disputes and declaring the official results led to repeated opposition appeals to the Supreme Court to declare the 1983 and 1988 elections illegal because of alleged widespread electoral fraud and violations of the law. When their appeals were rejected, the opposition claimed that the Supreme Court was not neutral and used the results to delegitimize the Diouf regime.

During the 1980s and 1990s, the Diouf regime placed more emphasis on strengthening the legal system and establishing Senegal as an *état de droit* (country ruled by law) that respected human rights and civil liberties. Senegal was one of the first to sign the Banjul African Charter of Human Rights in 1981. For their part, the opposition accepted this premise but insisted that the government did not always practice what it preached when it selectively banned political demonstrations and rallies and arrested opposition politicians and journalists.

A constitutional revision in May 1992 abolished the Supreme Court, created different appeals courts, and established the Conseil Constitutionnel (Constitutional Council), which assumed most of the functions previously handled by the Supreme Court in ruling on national election disputes and litigations and the constitutionality of Senegalese laws. The Constitutional Council became an important focus of Senegalese politics during the 1993 national elections when it was forced to intervene to settle the results of the February 21 presidential elections and to examine complaints by the PS and opposition parties concerning electoral fraud following the May 9 legislative elections.

The 1963 constitution set up the Economic and Social Council as an advisory body to the government. Made up of representatives of diverse sectors of the

Senegalese economy—for example, government employees, workers, farmers, artisans, industrialists, and experts designated by the government—the council gave citizens a voice in formulating national economic policy. Under Senghor, the Economic and Social Council tended to reflect the views of the Senegalese and French business communities. It served primarily as an organ of the presidency and was often used as a conduit for dispensing honorific titles for party leaders not serving in the government or the National Assembly. During the 1980s, the council declined in importance as an institution. In 1992, President Diouf attended its opening session for the first time since 1987. It is unlikely that the Economic and Social Council will regain the status and influence it had under Senghor, when it served as a useful forum for behind-the-scenes debates of Senegalese economic policies in a period when most business and trade union organizations were more or less appendages of the state. Nevertheless, it could become more active with the naming of former Finance Minister Ibrahima Famara Sagna as its new president in June 1993.

Although not a formal government institution like the National Assembly or the Economic and Social Council, the Senegalese army stands out as one of the nation's major institutions. Since intervening on Senghor's behalf, the army has been one of the main pillars of the regime and is often singled out for special recognition and praise during Senegal's annual Independence Day celebrations. Over the years, the Senegalese army has demonstrated its firm commitment to civilian rule and loyalty to the regime in power. During the early 1980s, it turned a deaf ear to appeals by various opposition groups to overthrow the government or intervene more directly to ensure fair elections. The postelection disturbances following the 1988 national elections, however, tempted some military officers to think about intervening if the situation got out of hand. Army Chief of Staff General Taverez Da Souza's decision to meet secretly with several high-ranking officers to discuss measures to be taken in case order would break down created considerable discomfort within the regime.[41] Diouf named Mansour Seck to replace Da Souza as chief of staff in June 1988, and in 1989 Diouf recalled the former general from his post as Senegalese ambassador to Germany to face charges that he had acted improperly in planning for a military takeover. Da Souza denied that he had acted improperly, and the affair was settled quietly. Da Souza lost certain privileges and minor punishment was handed out to his associates. The integrity of the army's commitment to civilian rule was reaffirmed once again.

Diouf continued Senghor's policy of building up the army and using it as an instrument of Senegalese foreign policy. During the late 1970s, Senghor had sent the Senegalese troops to Lebanon as part of the UN peacekeeping mission and to Zaire to shore up the Mobutu regime in Shaba Province. Under Diouf, Senegalese troops were sent to Gambia to save the Jawara regime in 1981 and to Saudi Arabia in 1990 during the Gulf War following Iraq's invasion of Kuwait. In 1994 Senegal also sent more than a thousand troops to Rwanda.

The army was also used to put down the insurgency in the Casamance and to ensure peace and order on Senegal's borders with Mauritania and Guinea-Bissau in the late 1980s and early 1990s when Senegal had border disputes with those two countries. Senegal's military forces number about 15,000 and are among the best trained in Africa.

In June 1993 Diouf made major personnel changes in Senegal's armed forces and named General Mouhamadou Keita, who had led Senegal's troops in the Gulf War, as chief of staff, replacing Mansour Seck who had held that post since 1988.

Postcolonial Administrative Reforms and Local Government

Those who took power at independence gained control of the administrative structures, legal system, and police powers of the French colonial state. Reformers rather than revolutionaries, Senegal's national leaders did not wish to dismantle the state structures they had inherited. Instead, they sought to Africanize them and to make the postcolonial state an instrument for promoting national rather than metropolitan goals and priorities. This task required some modification of the inherited colonial administrative structures and the creation of new ones.

The first major reform took place in January 1960 when the Dia government redrew administrative districts and divided the country into 7 *régions,* 28 *cercles,* and 85 *arrondissements* to replace the 13 *cercles,* 27 *subdivisions,* and 135 *cantons* established under colonial rule. The government abolished the unpopular *chef-feries (canton* chiefs) and Africanized the territorial administration by replacing the remaining French officials with Senegalese. Subsequent changes in official nomenclature sought to eliminate all vestiges of colonial rule and reaffirm the national identity of the Senegalese administration. Thus, in 1964 the *cercle* became the *département* and the old colonial titles of *commandant* and *chef* were replaced by *préfêt* and *sous-préfêt.* Louga was established as an eighth region in 1976 and the number of Senegalese regions was expanded to ten in 1984 when the Sine-Saloum was subdivided into the regions of Fatick and Kaolack and the Casamance into the regions of Ziguinchor and Kolda.

The development of local government in Senegal has gone through several phases since independence. The Dia government elevated all departmental capitals into full-scale urban communes, which made it possible for people in Senegal's small interior towns to elect their own mayors and municipal councils. At the same time, the Dia government established regional assemblies to represent the populations living in Senegal's 13,000 villages.

These new institutions became highly politicized and the major battleground of local clan politics. Control over jobs, honorific offices, and communal resources became the spoils of victory for successful party leaders at the local level and the source of intraparty squabbling. Contrary to the Dia government's original intentions, urban-based UPS politicians and powerful rural notables, rather than representatives of grassroots rural communities, determined the composition of the regional assemblies.

Local government regressed following Dia's political demise when Senghor took steps to reinforce the central government's control over local government institutions.[42] Senghor moved to depoliticize local government by tightening the Interior Ministry's tutelage over the administration of communal budgets, which now had to be approved by the interior minister before being executed. He also drastically reduced the flow of resources from the central government to the communes to prevent the waste of scarce national resources on expensive city halls, race tracks, and other nonproductive investments and to lower the stakes of local politics. Finally, Senghor strengthened the powers of the regional governors and expanded the scope of the territorial administration; the regional assemblies, however, survived as little more than rubber stamps for state-initiated programs. The subordination of local government to administrative control, coupled with the elimination of opposition parties, marked a sharp setback to the democratization of Senegalese politics that was not reversed until the mid-1970s.

The Administrative Reform of July 1972, which abolished the regional assemblies and provided for the establishment of the rural community (*communauté rurale*) as the basic unit of government in the countryside, set the stage for greater popular participation in local government. The philosophical underpinning of the reform derived from the ideology of African Socialism, formulated primarily by Mamadou Dia during the late 1950s and early 1960s, which saw the rural community or rural communes as the basic political units within a decentralized agrarian socialist society.[43]

The 1972 Administrative Reform called for the establishment of three to four rural communities in each *arrondissement*. Each rural community had a rural council that was granted broad powers to regulate local markets, fairs, cattle walks, and residential zoning patterns. Each council had its own small annual budget averaging approximately $40,000 to $50,000, which could be used to finance community development projects. The rural councils also had the power to allocate uncultivated land and to revise existing land tenure systems in the areas under their jurisdiction.

The reform was put into effect in the regions of Thiès and Sine-Saloum in 1974, Diourbel and Louga in 1976, the Casamance in 1978, the Fleuve in 1980, and Eastern Senegal in 1982. By the end of the 1980s, Senegal had 317 rural councils throughout the country.

Until the beginning of the 1990s, the rural communities had not realized their full potential as local government units. In most instances, the central government continued to control the rural communities through the *sous-préfèt* (subprefect), whose presence at rural council meetings intimidated council members and made it more difficult to initiate projects and policies not endorsed by the government. Morever, there were widespread charges that the *sous-préfèt* was pocketing community funds and getting kickbacks from local suppliers providing materials for community projects. Despite the paternalism of the Senegalese administrative officials overseeing the rural councils, the rural communities gradually emerged as a new force in the countryside.

During the 1980s, the role of local government expanded with the disengagement of the central government from the countryside. The rural communities thus became increasingly more involved in the construction of primary schools, health facilities, youth centers, and wells. With the development of irrigated agriculture, land with access to water became more valuable. In some instances, the rural councils have allocated land traditionally belonging to or used by other families in the community to urban politicians, bureaucrats, and expatriate firms, thus creating serious conflicts.

In 1983, the government reorganized municipal government in the Cap Vert region by creating the Communauté Urbaine de Dakar (Dakar Urban Community—CUD), a metropolitan unit of government encompassing the urban communes of Dakar, Pikine, and Rufisque. Mamadou Diop, the mayor of Dakar, was elected as the first president of the CUD council. During the late 1980s and early 1990s, his dynamic leadership led to marked improvements in city services. In the interior, however, urban government functioned much less efficiently, hampered by large numbers of superfluous and unskilled personnel, lack of sufficient resources to provide basic urban services, and the heavy-handed financial tutelage of the state.

The so-called Second Administrative Reform that preceded the November 1990 municipal and rural council elections marked a major step toward the devolution of more power to local government. The most important feature of the reform was the transfer of control over the budget and disbursement of funds from the *sous-préfet* to the president of the rural council, who was given broad executive powers. In the urban communes, a similar transfer shifted power from the municipal administrators named by the state to the elected mayors. The PS won all the seats in the November 1990 municipal and rural council elections because of the opposition parties' boycott, and as a result of internal party reforms, the victors included a large number of women and young people. In recent years, the Association of Senegalese Mayors has pressed for the transfer of more powers, especially taxing powers and control of financial resources, from the central government to the municipal governments. In January 1992, the presidents of the rural communities and other rural-based councils created a national association to promote the interests and improve the efficiency of rural local government.

The PS clearly sees local government as an important vehicle for mobilizing popular support in future elections. In April 1992, President Diouf announced that the next phase in Senegal's decentralization reforms would be the creation of elected regional councils that would have extensive powers in the realms of education, health, and other public services. The massive task of organizing the 1993 national elections diverted the government's attention from defining the legal powers, organization, and the financial resources of the regional councils. In May 1994 the government sponsored a national seminar that spelled out the broad outlines of its regionalization policy, and in 1995, it introduced a regionalization bill in the National Assembly that would become operational in 1996.[44] The main question to be resolved if local government is to become a viable institution is the extent to which the central government will transfer financial resources and taxing powers to the rural, regional, and municipal councils.

Since independence, the PS has completely dominated rural and urban local government institutions. Its natural advantage as the ruling party has been further reinforced by the opposition parties' lack of interest in local government and their boycotts of municipal and rural council elections. Senegal's political opposition will have a difficult time defeating the PS until it starts to seriously organize in the countryside and to contest local urban and rural elections outside of Dakar.

Notes

1. For example, a poll of Jeune Afrique readers had Senegal at the very top of the list of democratic countries in Africa, followed by Benin. See Jeune Afrique, No. 1628 (March 19–25, 1991): 56–59.

2. For a full account of this period, see Sheldon Gellar, "The Politics of Development in Senegal," Ph.D. dissertation, Columbia University, 1967, pp. 352–366.

3. For analyses of the evolution of Senegalese political party and government structures during this period, see Edward J. Schumacher, *Politics, Bureaucracy, and Rural Development in Senegal* (Berkeley: University of California Press, 1975), pp. 25–83; Gerti Hesseling, *Histoire politique du Sénégal: Institutions, droit et société* [Political History of Senegal: Institutions, law, and society] (Paris: Editions Karthala, 1985), pp. 237–272; and François Zuccarelli, *La vie politique sénégalaise (1940–1988)* [Senegalese Political Life (1940–1988)] (Paris: CHEAM, 1989), pp. 92–136.

4. For a major study of the liberalization process, see Robert Fatton, Jr., *The Making of a Liberal Democracy: Senegal's Passive Revolution, 1975–1985* (Boulder: Lynne Rienner, 1987). Also see Ibrahima Fall, *Sous-développement et démocratie multipartisane: L'Experience sénégalaise* [Underdevelopment and Multiparty Democracy: The Senegalese Experience] (Dakar: Nouvelles Editions Africaines, 1977), for a discussion of Senegal's multiparty regime under Senghor.

5. For the most thorough analysis of party and interest-group politics during the Diouf era, see Momar Coumba Diop and Mamadou Diouf, *Le Sénégal sous Abdou Diouf: Etat et société* [Senegal Under Abdou Diouf: State and Society] (Paris: Editions Karthala, 1990). Also see Mar Fall, *L'Etat Abdou Diouf ou les temps des incertitudes* [The Abdou Diouf Regime or Times of Uncertainty] (Paris: Editions L'Harmattan, 1986), and Christian Coulon and Donal B. Cruise O'Brien, "Senegal," in Donal B. Cruise O'Brien, John Dunn, and Richard Rathbone, eds., *Contemporary West African States* (Cambridge: Cambridge University Press, 1989), pp. 145–164.

6. For an account of Diouf's triumphant trip and general success during his first months in office, see "Les 100 jours ou le safara d'Abdou" [Abdou's First 100 Days], *Africa*, No. 130 (April 1981): 31–32.

7. For a description of the deteriorating relationships between the government and teachers and students before the conference, see Diop and Diouf, *Le Sénégal sous Abdou Diouf*, pp. 187–203. For an account of the conference itself, see *Afrique Nouvelle*, February 11–17, 1981, pp. 14–18 and 26.

8. For a discussion of the April 1981 constitutional revisions, see Hesseling, *Histoire politique du Sénégal*, pp. 290–292.

9. For an analysis of the 1983 elections, see Donal B. Cruise O'Brien, "Les élections séné-galaises du 27 février 1983" [The Senegalese Elections of February 23, 1983], *Politique Africaine*, No. 11 (1983): 7–12; and Hesseling, *Histoire politique du Sénégal*, pp. 292–298. For an analysis of the continuity in Senegalese electoral processes, see Fred M. Hayward and Siba Grovogui, "Persistence and Change in Senegalese Electoral Processes," in Fred M. Hayward, ed., *Independent Elections in Africa* (Boulder: Westview Press, 1987), pp. 239–270.

10. For a discussion of the Casamance as a serious political problem for the Diouf regime, see Mar Fall, *L'Etat Abdou Diouf ou les temps des incertitudes*, pp. 78–82.

11. For more on the police strike, see Diop and Diouf, *Le Sénégal sous Abdou Diouf,* pp. 285–293.

12. For a detailed analysis of the 1988 election and its aftermath, see Crawford Young and Babacar Kanté, "Governance, Democracy and the 1988 Senegalese Elections," in Goren Hyden and Michael Bratton, eds., *Governance and Politics in Africa* (Boulder: Lynne Rienner, 1992), pp. 57–84; and Diop and Diouf, *Le Sénégal sous Abdou Diouf,* pp. 319–354.

13. Wade claimed that he won 58.2 percent of the vote compared to Diouf's 40.8 percent. See *Sopi,* March 10, 1988, p. 1. According to Wade's figures, Diouf carried only the regions of Diourbel and Fatick.

14. For more on the Round Table, see Diop and Diouf, *Le Sénégal sous Abdou Diouf,* pp. 362–368.

15. On the role of Jean Collin in the Diouf regime, see *ibid.,* pp. 101–114.

16. For opposition attitudes concerning the reform of the electoral code, see Young and Kanté, "Governance, Democracy, and the 1988 Senegalese Elections," p. 65. For details of the provisions of the new electoral code, see *L'Unité,* No. 195 (September 1991): 4.

17. For more on Dieng's role as campaign manager, see *Le Soleil,* November 10, 1992.

18. For a brief description of Wade's electoral platform, see *Le Soleil,* December 19–20, 1992.

19. For the official results of the presidential elections, see *Le Soleil,* March 16, 1993. During the period between the February 21 elections and the proclamation of the official results by the Constitutional Council, *Le Soleil* published details of the breakdown of voting patterns at the departmental level. *Le Soleil* also provided extensive coverage of the electoral campaign, including reports on rallies and statements by opposition candidates.

20. For the official results of the May 9, 1993, legislative elections and the ruling of the Constitutional Council on charges of electoral fraud, see *Le Soleil,* May 25, 1993. For an unofficial breakdown of the vote by department, see *Le Soleil,* May 14, 1993. For a critical analysis of the 1993 national elections, see Babacar Kanté, "Senegal's Empty Elections," *Journal of Democracy,* Vol. 5, No. 1 (January 1994): 96–108.

21. For more on the Babacar Sèye affair, see Elimane Fall, "L'Etat, le juge et l'assassin" [The State, the Judge, and the Assassin], *Jeune Afrique,* No. 1700 (August 5–11, 1993): 16–18; and Geraldine Faes, "Wade au bord du précipice" [Wade on the Border of the Abyss], *Jeune Afrique,* No. 1710 (October 14–20, 1993): 18–20. For a more detailed account of the circumstances around the assassination, see Tidiane Kassé and Abdourahmane Camara, *Affaire Maitre Sèye: Enquête sur un complot* [The Judge Sèye Affair: Investigation into a Plot] (Dakar: Imprimerie Saint-Paul, 1995).

22. For a detailed analysis of the composition of the new Senegalese government, see *Le Soleil,* June 3, 1993.

23. *Le Soleil,* January 3, 1994.

24. For an account of the February 16, 1994, rioting, see *Jeune Afrique,* No. 1729 (February 24–March 2, 1994): 14–18. Also see the statement concerning the riots by Senegal's minister of the interior, Djibo Ka, in *Le Soleil,* February 18, 1994.

25. For excellent analyses of clan politics and political factionalism in Senegal, see Jonathan S. Barker, "Political Factionalism in Senegal," *Canadian Journal of African Studies* 7, No. 2 (1973): 287–303; William J. Foltz, "Social Structure and Political Behavior of Senegalese Elites," *Behavior Science Notes* 4, No. 2 (1969): 145–163; Donal B. Cruise O'Brien, *Saints and Politicians: Essays in the Organization of a Senegalese Peasant Society* (Cambridge: Cambridge University Press, 1975), pp. 149–182; and Robert Fatton, Jr., "Clientelism and Patronage in Senegal," *African Studies Review* 29, No. 4 (December 1986): 61–78.

26. For a detailed analysis of UPS party structures, see François Zuccarelli, *Un parti politique africain: L'Union Progressiste Sénégalaise* [An African Political Party: The Senegalese Progressive Union] (Paris: R. Pichon and R. Durand-Auzias, 1970).

27. For an analysis of the major support groups, see Diop and Diouf, *Le Sénégal sous Abdou Diouf,* pp. 115–148.

28. *Jeune Afrique,* No. 1472 (March 22, 1989): 36–37.

29. For a full account of this historic PS Congress, see *Le Soleil,* March 24, 25, 30, and 31, 1990.

30. For more on PDS party structures, see Christine Desouches, *Le Parti Démocratique Sénégalais: Une opposition légale en Afrique* [The Senegalese Democratic Party: A Legal Opposition in Africa] (Paris: Berger-Levrault, 1983). For analyses of the smaller opposition parties and their platforms, see Jacques Mariel Nzouankeu, *Les partis politiques sénégalais* [Senegalese Political Parties] (Dakar: Clairafrique, 1984).

31. For an extensive survey of francophone African student opinions during this crucial formative period, see Jean-Pierre N'Diaye, *Enquête sur les étudiants noirs en France* [A Survey of Black African Students in France] (Paris: Editions Realités Africaines, 1962).

32. For two major examples of Senghor and Dia's socialist ideology during the early 1960s, the period of their partnership, see Léopold Sédar Senghor, *On African Socialism* (New York: Frederick A. Praeger, 1964); and Mamadou Dia, *The African Nations and World Solidarity* (New York: Frederick A. Praeger, 1961).

33. For a discussion of the ideologies and platforms of the diverse opposition parties, see Fatton, *The Making of a Liberal Democracy,* pp. 123–153.

34. For a discussion of Diouf's use of *sursaut national* (national revitalization) as an ideological concept, see Diop and Diouf, *Le Sénégal sous Abdou Diouf,* pp. 251–281; and Fatton, *The Making of a Liberal Democracy,* pp. 123–129.

35. For the background to the development of trade union involvement in government as seen by a PS militant, see Magatte Lo, *Syndicalisme et participation responsable* [Trade Unionism and Responsible Participation] (Paris: Editions L'Harmattan, 1987). For a scholarly discussion of the evolution of the Senegalese trade union movement during the Diouf era, see Diop and Diouf, *Le Sénégal sous Abdou Diouf,* pp. 223–249.

36. For details on the September 2, 1993, general strike and the emergence of the Intersyndicale, see *Le Soleil,* September 3, 1993.

37. For an analysis of how politicians and their supporters used their state connections to enrich themselves, see Catherine Boone, "The Making of a Rentier Class: Wealth

Accumulation and Political Control in Senegal," *Journal of Development Studies* 26, No. 3 (1990): 425–449.

38. For the role of the Senegalese brotherhoods in politics, see Lucy C. Behrman, *Muslim Brotherhoods and Politics in Senegal* (Cambridge: Harvard University Press, 1970); Donal B. Cruise O'Brien, *The Mourides of Senegal: The Political and Economic Organization of an Islamic Brotherhood* (London: Oxford University Press, 1971); Cheikh Tidiane Sy, *La confrérie sénégalaise des Mourides* [The Senegalese Mouride Brotherhood] (Paris: Présence Africaine, 1969); Christian Coulon, *Le marabout et le prince: Islam et pouvoir au Sénégal* [The Marabout and the Prince: Islam and Power in Senegal] (Paris: Pedone, 1981); Jean Copans, *Les marabouts de l'arachide* [The Peanut Marabouts] (Paris: Le Sycomore, 1980); and Moriba Magassouba, *L'Islam au Sénégal: Demain les mollahs?* [Islam in Senegal: Tomorrow the Mullahs?] (Paris: Editions Karthala, 1985).

39. For a detailed analysis of Senegal's legal and governmental institutions, see Hesseling, *Histoire politique du Sénégal*, pp. 189–272. For an early major study of Senegal's judicial and governmental institutions, see Jean-Claude Gautron and Michel Rougevin-Baville, *Droit public du Sénégal* [Senegalese Public Law] (Paris: Pedone, 1970).

40. For an important study of the Senegalese Supreme Court, see Benoit N'Gom, *L'Arbitrage d'une démocratie en Afrique: Le Cour Suprême du Sénégal* [Arbiter of an African Democracy: The Supreme Court in Senegal] (Paris: Présence Africaine, 1989). For an analysis of the relations between politics and the legal system, see Serigne Diop, "Justice du politique au Sénégal" [Political Justice in Senegal] *Afrique Contemporain*, No. 156 (1990): 184–194.

41. See Francis Kpatinde, "Sénégal, L'Affaire Tavarez da Souza" [Senegal: The Tavarez da Souza Affair], *Jeune Afrique*, No. 1478 (May 3, 1989): 14–17.

42. For discussions of local central government relations following the demise of Mamadou Dia, see Clement Cottingham, "Political Consolidation and Centre-Local Relations in Senegal," *Canadian Journal of African Studies* 4, No. 1 (Winter 1970): 101–120; and Jonathan S. Barker, "Political Space and the Quality of Participation in Rural Africa: A Case from Senegal," *Canadian Journal of African Studies* 21, No. 1 (1987): 1–16. For a critique of the limitations of Senegalese decentralization efforts, see Sheldon Gellar, "State Tutelage vs. Self-Governance: The Rhetoric and Reality of Decentralization in Senegal," in James S. Wunsch and Dele Olowu, eds., *The Failure of the Centralized State in Africa: Institutions and Self-Governance* (Boulder: Westview Press, 1990), pp. 130–147.

43. See, for example, Sheldon Gellar, Robert B. Charlick, and Yvonne Jones, *Animation Rurale and Rural Development: The Experience of Senegal* (Ithaca, N.Y.: Cornell University Rural Development Committee, 1980), pp. 34–47, for an analysis of the role of the rural communities as envisaged by Mamadou Dia.

44. For details on the regionalization program, see Ecole Nationale d'Economie Appliquée, ed., *La décentralisation au Sénégal: L'étape de la régionalisation* [Decentralization in Senegl: The Regionalization Phase] (Dakar: ENEA, 1994).

3

THE ECONOMY

A T INDEPENDENCE, Senegal had one of the most advanced economies in West Africa, based primarily on one major export crop and a captive market for its industrial products. Following a short burst of growth during the early 1960s, the Senegalese economy went through a period of stagnation and decline. Despite the government's efforts to diversify, nationalize, and modernize the economy; the expansion of fishing and tourism; and large inflows of foreign aid, real per capita income has in fact declined since independence.

After fifteen years of structural adjustment programs, Senegal in the mid-1990s is still facing an uphill economic battle saddled by foreign debt, chronic government deficits, a poorly functioning banking system, and high unemployment rates, particularly among high school and college graduates. Senegal's current economic problems are by no means atypical. On the contrary, they reveal how difficult it is for low-income, energy-poor African countries like Senegal to escape the trap of underdevelopment and dependence. Until now, foreign aid has kept the national economy afloat and averted the worst catastrophes. At the same time, Senegalese urban and rural dwellers have adopted creative and complex survival strategies, which have enabled them to cope with harsh climatic, environmental, and economic conditions.

Senegal will have to rely primarily on its strategic location and the ingenuity of its people to pull itself out of the underdevelopment trap. For the next few years, the country will also need large doses of foreign aid to reduce the social costs involved in restructuring the national economy and adapting to the new economic realities created by the 50 percent devaluation of the CFA franc in 1994.

Senegalese Economic Structures:
Sahelian and Maritime Senegal

Senegal's annual per capita income is approximately $710, a figure that represents a decline in real per capita income since independence (see Table 3.1).[1] This ag-

TABLE 3.1 Evolution of Socioeconomic Indicators

Socioeconomic Indicators	1960	1977–1978	1992
GNP per capita	$150[a]	$340	$710
Life expectancy	37	42	48.3
Infant mortality (per 1,000 births)	172	N.A.	82.0
Population per doctor	22,380	15,700	13,060
Adult literacy (%)	6 (Fr)	10 (Fr)	40[b]
School-age children in primary school (%)	27	40.9	59

[a] $150 = Approximately $900 in 1992 dollars.
[b] Reflects literacy in French and national languages.
SOURCES: World Bank, *World Development Report,* 1980 (Washington, D.C.: World Bank, 1980), pp. 110, 150, 152, 154; United Nations Development Programme, *Human Development Report, 1993* (New York: Oxford University Press, 1993), pp. 140–189.

gregate figure tells one little, however, about the great disparities in income between Sahelian (the interior) and Maritime (coastal) Senegal. In Sahelian Senegal, the rural masses struggle for survival; in Maritime Senegal, the urban masses battle for a better position within a relatively modern economy.

Senegal, a country with a total area of 196,190 square kilometers, has 531 kilometers of coastline. Maritime Senegal consists of a coastal band extending about 50 miles inland. The dynamism and higher incomes of Maritime Senegal, which encompasses all of the Cap Vert Peninsula and much of the coastal band between Thiès and Saint Louis, contrast markedly with the poverty of Sahelian Senegal. Cap Vert's temperate climate and strategic location explain why Dakar has been Senegal's major development pole for nearly a century. Maritime Senegal also has one of West Africa's best natural deepwater ports, abundant fishing resources, and phosphates. It contains most of the country's modern industries, banking, and financial institutions, luxury hotels, and important international trade and conference centers. South of Dakar, coastal beaches and tourist villages located in the regions of Thiès and Ziguinchor draw large numbers of tourists seeking temporary relief from Europe's cold winters. The Niayes coastal region between Dakar and Saint Louis provides much of Senegal's expanding commercial vegetable production, and the rich fishing grounds off the Atlantic coast generate most of Senegal's fish production.

Living conditions and economic opportunities are generally much better in Maritime Senegal, particularly in Dakar, where residents have better access to doctors, pharmacies, hospitals, and maternity clinics. Most of the children living in Maritime Senegal attend public schools and tend to eat better than their cousins in the countryside. Thanks to more reliable drinking water supplies, there is less suffering from some of the endemic diseases prevalent in Sahelian Senegal. Maritime Senegal draws large numbers of young people from the interior seeking better educational and employment opportunities. During the dry season

(November to May), it also attracts thousands of seasonal workers seeking to supplement low rural incomes.

Despite its relatively favored status, Maritime Senegal cannot be classifed as middle class or affluent by Western standards. Unemployment in the formal sector is high, perhaps 40 percent, whereas the booming informal sector tends to provide low-paying jobs and opportunities for new entrants into the labor market. Despite the greater wealth of the region and the presence of an expanding Senegalese "middle class" making up 20–25 percent of Maritime Senegal's largely urban population, the majority of people living in Maritime Senegal are poor. Class structures are more complex and disparities in living standards greater than in Sahelian Senegal.[2] Dakar thus has its share of sprawling slums and shanty-towns, water shortages, pollution, and high unemployment rates, and other parts of Maritime Senegal suffer from pollution caused by phosphate mining and the giant Industries Chimiques du Sénégal (Chemical Industries of Senegal—ICS) factory. The 1994 devaluation of the CFA franc could reduce the economic gap between Maritime and Sahelian Senegal by reducing urban living standards and giving rural producers higher prices for their products.

Despite the broad differences between Maritime and Sahelian Senegal, the two regions are closely linked because of the high mobility of Senegal's rural populations and the tendency of those who have done well in Maritime Senegal to maintain their links with their home villages.

Sahelian Senegal suffers from irregular rainfall, exhausted soils, overgrazing, deforestation, and desertification. Outside of the Senegal River's alluvial floodplain, soils are not very rich. Only 27 percent of the total land surface is arable. Agriculture in the region is based largely on the cultivation of peanuts, millet, and sorghum, crops that grow quickly and require relatively little rainfall. Practically all of the rain falls during the months of June through September, and most rural Senegalese live in areas where rainfall is sparse and irregular and drought a common occurrence. Herders and farmers in the north, where the average annual rainfall varies from 10 to 20 inches (250 and 500 mm), are the most vulnerable to drought. The situation is somewhat better in central Senegal, which encompasses the country's main peanut-producing areas and where rainfall averages between 20 and 30 inches (500 and 800 mm) per year. But even in rice-producing regions like the Lower Casamance, where annual rainfall averages more than 40 inches (1,000 mm), subnormal rainfall can be a serious problem because rice requires more water than peanuts or millet. Senegal is relying heavily upon the great potential for irrigated agriculture along the Senegal River Basin made possible by the completion of the Diama and Manantali dams in the 1980s, which were built to compensate for the lack of rainfall and the low productivity of Sahelian Senegal's rainfed agriculture. Thus far, the expansion of irrigated agriculture in the Senegal River Valley has been disappointing because of high production costs, unresolved land tenure issues, and the general climate of insecurity along Senegal's northern borders with Mauritania. In the mid-1990s, less than 5 percent of the potentially 640,000 hectares of irrigable land was developed in the valley.

*Figure 3.1 The great drought of 1973: Starving cattle roam the countryside in search of food.
(Photo by United Nations/AID, R. B. Purcell)*

Sahelian Senegal's rural economy is still based primarily on the peanut, which takes up more than 40 percent of the land under cultivation.[3] This figure has declined in recent years as peasants have begun to devote more land to food crops. Agricultural productivity in Sahelian Senegal is low and insufficient to adequately feed Senegal's rural populations, let alone to generate a surplus large enough to feed the country's rapidly growing urban populations, who now make up 40 percent of the population. Population pressures on the land, shorter fallow periods, and soil erosion have reduced soil productivity in the densely populated areas of western Senegal, the first regions to cultivate peanuts as a cash crop. Except for the more recently settled pioneer zones south and east of Kaolack, where land is relatively more plentiful, landholdings have become increasingly fragmented. Even though many of Senegal's most prominent Muslim leaders own large estates, the marabouts control less than 1 percent of Senegal's farmlands. Sahelian Senegal is made up primarily of small family farms exploited chiefly by family labor. More than two-thirds of the country's farms are less than 10 acres (4 hectares) in size; only 5 percent are more than 25 acres (10 hectares).

Like most Sahelian countries, Senegal has an important livestock sector. Only a tiny fraction of Senegal's 2.8–3 million cattle are marketed on a commercial scale. Drought has periodically decimated Senegal's cattle herds. Despite the significance of cattle as a source of wealth and security, the average Sahelian Senegalese family relies more on goats and sheep for sustenance and supplementary income in hard times. Horses also play an important role in the rural economy, serving as draft animals in the peanut basin and providing rural transportation. The poultry population has also increased dramatically from 900,000 chickens in 1960 to more than 13 million in the early 1990s.

The lack of sufficient water and forestry resources also poses a dilemma for Sahelian Senegal. Few villages have safe water supplies, and polluted water sources make it difficult to check the spread of disease. During the 1980s, the Senegalese government undertook a major rural water development program and financed well and borehole construction throughout the country to provide safe water for people and livestock. Wells were also used to irrigate vegetable gardens and tree nurseries.

Deforestation caused by growing population pressures for land and the need for firewood for energy has led to a marked deterioration of the physical environment. This problem has been a growing concern for both the government and the rural populations of Sahelian Senegal.[4] Clearing for agriculture and overcutting of forests for firewood and other products has resulted in the annual loss of 60,000 hectares of forest land. The preservation of Senegal's forest resource base as a major national priority during the 1980s and 1990s sparked hundreds of small-scale reforestation projects and efforts to introduce and popularize more efficient wood-burning stoves in the rural areas. During the mid-1990s, Senegal had twenty-two active forestry projects operating throughout the country.

The government's decision to transfer 45,000 hectares of protected forestland in late April 1991 to the head of the Mouride brotherhood to be used by his followers for planting peanuts dealt a serious blow to the credibility of Senegal's environmental policy.[5] In a few weeks, thousands of Mouride *talibés* had cleared the land, a process accompanied by the eviction of 6,000 pastoralists and 100,000 animals from the Mbegue forest area. The Senegalese press and donor community sharply criticized the government's decision, which followed an old pattern dating back to colonial days when the French ceded large tracts of land to the Mourides to stimulate peanut production.

Life in Sahelian Senegal is difficult. Infant mortality remains high despite some significant gains in the 1980s due to widespread vaccination programs and improvements in water supply. Malaria and other endemic diseases afflict most of the rural population. The villages of Sahelian Senegal are not electrified and have few modern amenities. Firewood remains the sole source of energy. Life is particularly hard for women, who must spend many hours each day gathering firewood, drawing water, and pounding grain simply to meet minimal family needs. With the growing exodus of young males from the village, they also have to do more of the agricultural work. In the Senegal River Valley, children under fifteen are doing more and more of the agricultural work on nonirrigated plots.

Sahelian Senegal is generally flat, and most of the country lies less than 200 feet above sea level. This feature has facilitated the construction of roads and railroads and has made internal travel within the country relatively easy. Senegal has nearly 15,000 kilometers of roads, including nearly 4,000 kilometers of paved roads.

Senegalese Economic Structures:
From Peanut Dependency to Diversification

Although the peanut has retained a prominent position within the Senegalese economy, its relative importance has declined steadily since independence (see Table 3.2). During the 1960s, peanut products accounted for more than two-thirds of the value of Senegalese exports; by the end of the 1970s, this figure had dropped to 40 percent; and by 1990, peanut products accounted for less than 20 percent of total Senegalese exports.[6] In the 1980s and 1990s, fishing products and tourism replaced peanuts as the principal source of foreign exchange. Poor peanut crops, low world market peanut prices, and growing food shortages in the countryside, coupled with the growth of other economic sectors, such as phosphates, fishing, and tourism, have contributed to the relative decline of the peanut.

The government did little to promote the diversification of the rural economy until the late 1960s and early 1970s, when it began to promote cotton production in Eastern Senegal and the Upper Casamance and sugarcane and tomatoes in the Senegal River delta. Until then, government agricultural policy was primarily concerned with raising peanut production and productivity in the peanut basin.

TABLE 3.2 Decline of the Peanut Economy: Agricultural Production, 1960–1961 Through 1992–1993

| Years | Production in Metric Tons | | | | |
	Peanuts	Cotton	Millet/Sorghum	Rice	Maize
1960–1961	922,500	80	392,300	71,200	27,400
1965–1966	1,122,100	700	560,100	121,900	40,800
1968–1969	819,500	9,750	449,300	61,100	25,300
1972–1973	570,000	23,310	322,000	37,900	20,200
1975–1976	1,434,100	30,690	616,400	130,200	44,400
1978–1979	1,050,700	33,810	752,000	146,400	33,200
1980–1981	521,300	20,960	545,000	64,700	57,000
1983–1984	1,091,700	31,000	351,800	108,500	60,600
1986–1987	841,200	38,815	633,730	146,200	107,400
1988–1989	415,210	38,700	594,200	146,405	123,327
1990–1991	702,584	44,723	660,438	181,119	133,147
1992–1993	623,359	51,176	562,706	177,346	114,563

SOURCES: World Bank, *The World and Senegal, 1960–87* (Washington, D.C.: World Bank, 1989), p. 167; Abt Associates, *Senegal Agricultural Policy Analysis* (Cambridge, Mass.: Abt Associates, Inc., 1985), pp. 29, 31; Banque Centrale des Etats de l'Afrique de l'Ouest, "Senegal," *Note d'Information*, No. 433 (January 1994), p. 14.

Figure 3.2 Peanuts, a declining pillar of the Senegalese economy. (Photo by Michel Renaudeau)

In 1977, the government initiated a food investment strategy to promote food self-reliance by increasing millet production in the peanut basin and rice production in the Fleuve and the Casamance. By the end of the 1980s, Senegal was producing up to 750,000 tons of millet and 150,000 tons of rice paddy. Maize (128,000 tons annually) and cowpea production (41,000 tons annually) also rose sharply. Increases in food production, however, have not kept up with the growing population. Thus, despite its food self-sufficiency policies, Senegal is still producing little more than 50 percent of its total food needs, compared with 70 percent in the early 1960s.

Within the peanut basin itself, farmers are relying more on other sources of revenue—petty trade, small-scale livestock, the sale of forestry products, seasonal migration, and so on—and devoting more of their land to food crops in order to survive. Vegetable gardening has spread: In the northern peanut basin, farmers are experimenting with growing cowpeas as a food cash crop, and in the southern basin, where rainfall is more plentiful, they have focused on maize production.

Fishing products, mostly canned tuna, now compose more than a quarter of the value of Senegalese exports and provide direct and indirect employment for more than 150,000 Senegalese. The bulk of Senegal's fish production, however, is destined for the national market. Senegalese annual consumption of fish, at 26 kilograms per capita, is twice the world average.

As part of its diversification policy, Senegal became one of the first African countries to develop tourism as a major national economic activity. Tourism grew spectacularly during the middle and late 1970s and became one of the major growth industries in Senegal and the second source of foreign exchange after fishing. During the 1980s, the rate of growth slowed for various reasons—social tensions and crime in Dakar, the Casamance insurgency, the Senegalese-Mauritanian conflict, and the relatively high travel costs for European and North American tourists. Despite the slowdown, receipts from tourism attained 44 billion CFA francs in 1990. During the early 1990s, the Senegalese government sought to revitalize tourism by offering incentives to hotels to reduce costs, providing better police security, and promoting Dakar as a major international conference center. Tourism suffered a major blow following the massacre of villagers from Cap Skirring by separatist forces in 1992 and the closing of Club Med operations in the Casamance. The 1993 peace agreement signed between the government and the MFDC led to the reopening of Club Med and renewed tourist activity in that region, and the 1994 devaluation made holidays in Senegal less expensive for Europeans and sparked a sharp increase in tourism throughout the country that continued into 1995.

Thanks to protective tariffs and special tax exemptions, Senegal's manufacturing sector expanded during the 1960s, 1970s, and early 1980s. By the early 1990s, however, the manufacturing sector, particularly textiles, was in decline, generating only 13 percent of Senegal's GDP in 1990 compared with 14 percent in 1965. The 1994 devaluation, while making Senegalese manufactured products somewhat more competitive with imported goods, has thus far failed to spur industrial recovery or attract foreign investors.

From Neocolonial Dependency to Foreign Debt and Aid Dependency

Senegal provides a classic example of a dependent economy in which economic growth and prosperity are largely conditioned by external economic forces and actors.[7] Senegalese dependency under colonialism was directed toward France. The metropole determined Senegal's economic policies and pattern of development and Frenchmen controlled the leading sectors of the colonial economy. Like most colonial powers, France also discouraged nonmetropolitan investments in Senegal and oriented Senegal's foreign trade toward France and the franc zone.

A few simple statistics will suffice to illustrate the Senegalese economy's extreme dependency upon France at independence: (1) Approximately 80 percent of Senegal's foreign trade was with France; (2) nearly all of Senegal's peanut exports during the late 1950s and early 1960s were bought by France at subsidized prices 15 to 20 percent above the world market price; (3) France supplied two-thirds of Senegal's public development capital and nearly all of the foreign technical and financial assistance; (4) French investors provided more than 90 percent of the private capital and owned most of the enterprises in the capital-intensive sectors of the Senegalese economy; and (5) the French treasury covered Senegal's foreign trade deficits.

The first decade of independence brought few major changes in the old colonial patterns of dependency. Peanuts continued to provide the bulk of Senegalese exports, and France retained its dominant position as Senegal's major trade and aid partner. During this period of "neocolonial" dependency, France's European Economic Community (EEC) partners developed closer ties with Senegal and other francophone Black African states.

The first half of the 1970s was a transition period in which drought and rapidly changing market conditions moved Senegal to take steps to break out of the old colonial patterns of dependency upon the peanut and the French. In 1973 worldwide food shortages and the Arab oil embargo sparked by the Yom Kippur War drove up the price of food imports, led to a fourfold increase in oil prices, and set off a wave of inflation that had a tremendously destabilizing effect on the Senegalese economy. The 1972–1973 drought sharply reduced Senegalese peanut exports, increased the need for food imports, and led to record trade deficits. Shortly afterward, however, dramatic increases in the world market price of phosphates and peanuts gave the Senegalese some hope for the future. To take advantage of this favorable economic conjuncture, the Senegalese government became the majority shareholder in the country's phosphate mining companies and established a state-controlled corporation charged with handling all Senegalese peanut exports. It also counted upon the profits generated by high peanut and phosphate prices to finance several large-scale projects designed to diversify the economy and reduce Senegal's great dependency on the peanut. At the same time, the government borrowed heavily in international private capital markets at relatively high interest rates with the hope that world peanut and phosphate prices would remain high, thus allowing Senegal to keep its foreign debt at a manageable level.

Unfortunately, peanut and phosphate prices dropped sharply, thus depriving Senegal of the revenues needed to repay its loans and finance its major development projects. Senegal's financial difficulties were further aggravated by the return of drought to Senegal during the late 1970s and another round of OPEC-inspired steep increases in oil prices. This combination brought the Senegalese economy to the brink of bankruptcy by the end of the 1970s.

At the beginning of the 1980s, the Senegalese economy was more than ever hostage to external economic forces.[8] Dependency upon the peanut and upon France had steadily diminished, but new forms of dependency had emerged. During the 1960s, oil imports had accounted for no more than 5 percent of Senegal's total import bill. In 1970, the oil bill was only 2.5 billion CFA francs; in 1980 it was 50 billion CFA francs. Even more alarming was the spectacular rise in foreign debt, from $103 million in 1970 to nearly $2 billion in 1982. Senegal's debt service also rose, from a manageable 5–6 percent of exports during the mid-1970s to more than 20 percent by the beginning of the 1980s.

In December 1979, then Prime Minister Diouf announced an IMF-inspired five-year (1980–1985) economic recovery program (*plan de redressement*) designed to cut government spending, promote economic growth, and reduce

TABLE 3.3 The Dependency Trap: Foreign Aid and Foreign Debt (millions of $)

Year	Total Aid	Grants	Loans	External Debt	Debt Service
1970	41.7	N.A.	N.A.	103	2
1978	271	N.A.	N.A.	587	31
1980	267.6	199.8	67.8	N.A.	N.A.
1982	291	173.5	117.5	1,906	N.A.
1984	380.2	241.4	138.8	2,114	190
1986	599.7	283.5	316.2	3,184	339
1987	679	337.8	341.2	4,360	403
1988	599.6	330.1	269.4	3,068	341
1990	788	N.A.	N.A.	3,745	N.A.
1991	577	N.A.	N.A.	3,522	N.A.

SOURCES: USAID Senegal, *Official Development Assistance (ODA) to Senegal, 1980–1989* (Dakar: USAID Program Office, 1991), pp. 18–26; Club du Sahel, *From Aid to Investment . . . to Financial Support* (Paris: Club du Sahel/CILSS, January 1990), pp. 6–9; World Bank, *World Development Report, 1980* (Washington, D.C.: World Bank, 1980), pp. 134, 136, 138; World Bank, *World Development Report, 1993* (Washington, D.C.: World Bank, 1993), p. 276.

Senegal's trade deficit and foreign debt. During the early and mid-1980s, Senegal's external debt continued to climb, reaching more than $4.3 billion in 1987. That same year, Senegal's debt service burden surpassed $400 million. During the late 1980s and early 1990s, the foreign debt and debt service burden tapered off, thanks to a combination of stringent financial policies and the rescheduling or cancellation of part of Senegal's foreign debts by diverse donors. By the end of 1992, Senegal's foreign debt had declined to $3 billion and its debt service burden to $200 million. The devaluation of the CFA franc in January 1994, however, automatically doubled Senegal's foreign debt, thus canceling out most of the earlier reductions (see Table 3.3).

External aid was probably the most successful "growth industry" for Senegal during the 1980s.[9] In 1989, per capita aid to Senegal was $92, nearly three times the average for sub-Saharan Africa. For most of the decade, aid grew at an annual rate of 14 percent and averaged more than $500 million a year. During this period, external aid, in the form of grants and loans, represented close to 20 percent of Senegal's national income and financed nearly all of its public investments.

In the early 1990s, donors put greater pressure on Senegal to cut back government spending. In 1993, an election year, the IMF and the World Bank refused to release funds to the Senegalese government until it would bite the bullet and sharply reduce the amount of money allocated to public-sector salaries. Faced with the prospects of not having sufficient funds to meet its payroll, the government launched the Sakho-Loum emergency economic recovery plan in August 1993 to convince donors to resume giving financial and economic aid to Senegal. The donor community, led by the IMF, also placed great pressure on Senegal (which had been one of the major opponents to the devaluation of the CFA franc) to accept the inevitable, which came in January 1994. Donors like the World Bank continued to put pressure on Senegal by not releasing credits until the government showed that it would implement promised structural adjustment reforms. During the last quarter of 1994, the World Bank and France provided sufficient funding to keep the government afloat and to partially alleviate the heavy social costs resulting from the devaluation.

Africanization, Nationalization, and Privatization

Since independence, Senegal has undergone considerable changes concerning the control of key sectors of the economy. With the exception of the state's efforts to take control of the peanut trade, Africanization of the economy proceeded very slowly during the first decade of independence.[10] In 1960 the Dia government established a state-controlled Senegalese development bank (Banque Sénégalaise de Développement—BSD) and an agricultural marketing board (Office de Commercialisation Agricole—OCA) to break the hold of the French banks and trading companies over the financing of the peanut *traite*. The BSD extended credit to the OCA, which in turn extended credit to the newly created state-sponsored cooperative movement. In 1966, the government established the Office National de Coopération et d'Assistance au Développement (National Cooperative and Development Assistance Office—ONCAD), which took over most of the marketing functions previously exercised by the OCA. Shortly afterward, the government decreed that all peanuts had to be marketed through the cooperatives, thus eliminating Senegalese private traders. The "nationalization" of the peanut trade did little to promote the African private sector as the state rather than African businesses replaced the European trading companies as the main economic force in the countryside.

Throughout the 1960s, Senghor firmly resisted pressures to nationalize other sectors of the Senegalese economy or to accelerate the pace of Africanization in the private sector. Senghor insisted that Senegal did not yet have the capital or technical expertise to undertake large-scale nationalizations and maintained that such measures would frighten potential foreign investors. Senghor worked very closely with French investors, who benefited from the tariff barriers put up by the Senegalese government to protect local French-owned industries against "foreign" competition. Little effort was made to attract non-French foreign capital or to encourage the expansion of the African private sector.

The May–June 1968 crisis reflected widespread dissatisfaction with the slow pace of Africanization and the fact that after nearly a decade of independence, the French and, to a lesser extent, the Lebanese continued to control the leading sectors of the modern economy and to prosper while most Senegalese were suffering from declining living standards. Senegalese trade unions demanded the immediate nationalization of the French-owned water and electricity companies and rapid Africanization of positions still held by skilled European workers and lower- and middle-management employees; African businessmen demanded that certain sectors of the economy, particularly those dominated by the Lebanese, be reserved exclusively for Senegalese Africans; and students and younger Senegalese cadres demanded a reduction in the number of French technical assistance personnel.

Senghor responded to these pressures by stepping up the pace of Africanization. Foreign firms were pressed to Africanize their personnel and asked to submit plans for "Senegalization." Africanization proceeded most rapidly in jobs previously held by the French working-class *petits blancs* who had flocked to Senegal during the post–World War II boom. By the end of the 1970s, nearly all of the French skilled workers, mechanics, foremen, and sales clerks had been replaced by Senegalese, and even Lebanese shopkeepers who traditionally relied on family labor had been obliged to hire Africans. The Africanization of managerial positions progressed much more slowly. By the mid-1970s, foreigners still held nearly half the executive positions and 9 percent of middle-management positions. By the end of the decade, however, the traditional preference of French firms for hiring French nationals was declining, partly because of government pressures but also because an expatriate manager cost the company three to five times as much as a Senegalese holding the same job.

Under the direction of the younger and more nationalist technocrats, the government launched a drive to nationalize important sectors of the Senegalese economy during the early and mid-1970s. These measures included taking over the water and electric utilities, which had become glaring symbols of neocolonialism, and exercising direct control over other key sectors of the economy by becoming the majority shareholder in the companies dominating these sectors. Thus, the state bought 50 percent of the shares in the mining companies that produced Senegalese phosphates and created the Société Nationale de Commercialisation des Oléagineux du Sénégal (Senegalese National Oilseed Marketing Corporation—SONOCOS) to gain full control over the manufacturing and marketing of Senegalese peanut oil and oilcake exports. This wave of nationalizations took place at a time when world market prices for phosphates and peanuts were at their height.

During the 1970s, the government also took steps to expand the number of parastatal agencies in the country. Between 1970 and 1975, seventy new parastatal companies were created, primarily to stimulate investments in sectors neglected by private capital. By 1975 parastatal agencies controlled more than 40 percent of the value added in the modern sector and employed about one-third of the workers in the modern wage sector. Foreign donors provided much of the financing for the parastatals during the 1970s.

By the end of the decade, Senegal's parastatal agencies came to be seen more and more as a cause of Senegal's economic problems rather than a solution. Western donors, led by the World Bank, criticized the inefficiency of the parastatals and their drain on public financial resources, and the political opposition accused the regime of using the parastatals to pillage the country. ONCAD was the largest state agency and the target of frequent criticism.[11] At its height, it had more than 4,000 state employees and an annual turnover of more than 100 billion CFA francs. The state used ONCAD to control the rural economy through its marketing functions and distribution of credit, seeds, fertilizer, and equipment to the rural populations. The agency also provided jobs and patronage for loyal party supporters and siphoned off resources from the rural sector to the urban sectors, thanks to the relatively low prices paid the peanut farmer during the late 1960s and early 1970s. Over the years, ONCAD became increasingly unpopular with the peasantry. Mismanagement and widespread corruption undermined its credibility with the Senegalese public and foreign donors. On August 20, 1980, the Senegalese National Assembly voted to abolish ONCAD, which left a staggering debt of more than 100 billion CFA francs.

During the 1980s, the government came under heavy pressure from donors to streamline, liquidate, or privatize costly and inefficient public enterprises as part of its structural adjustment program.[12] Privatization generally entails the transfer of functions previously carried out by the state to the private sector or the sale of public enterprises to private individuals or firms. Although it agreed to initiate a privatization program, the Senegalese government insisted that it retain control over key sectors of the economy that had been nationalized during the 1970s, such as phosphates, peanut oil, water, and electricity.

In 1985 Diouf spelled out the elements of a privatization strategy that included the divestiture of public enterprises with little or no public service function. In 1986 the government signed a structural adjustment loan (SAL) agreement with the World Bank in which it promised to privatize twenty-seven enterprises by the end of the year. This did not happen. By mid-1994, only sixteen public enterprises earmarked for privatization had been sold off, and these were generally small-scale operations that brought little money to the state's coffers. In summer 1994, Diouf promised that Senegal would make a greater effort to revitalize its flagging privatization program.

Although attempts to Africanize employment and nationalize leading sectors of the economy controlled by foreigners during the 1960s and 1970s were designed to reduce foreign economic domination, the resistance to privatization and the slow pace at which it took place during the 1980s and early 1990s had little to do with fear that foreigners would gain too much control of the economy. In the first place, foreign investors had little interest in taking over unprofitable Senegalese state enterprises unless they were virtually given away. Second, the government placed restrictions on the number of shares that foreigners could acquire. Finally, the government was determined to maintain its control of the leading sectors of the economy, which had been previously dominated by foreigners. Despite more liberal investment codes and the establishment of an Industrial Free Zone (IFZ) in Dakar in 1976, Senegal during the 1980s and early 1990s attracted very little new foreign private capital. By the end of the 1980s, the IFZ had attracted only eight firms employing a total of fewer than 500 people. Foreign capital tended to leave the country as unprofitable enterprises like the huge Bata shoe factory in Rufisque closed their doors. Although several large-scale, predominantly foreign-owned enterprises involved in sugar, cement, textiles, and oil refining maintained privileges from the 1960s that enabled them to make profits, these firms constituted a drain on the Senegalese treasury and national economy. Mimran, for example, maintained its monopoly of sugar production and distribution in Senegal, thus keeping Senegalese sugar prices well above the world market level. In 1993, the government decided to stop sharing revenues earned on taxing sugar imports with Mimran, which had previously received 40 percent of the income generated by the sugar tax. During the mid-1990s, Senegalese private-sector associations like UNACOIS and the GES were demanding that the state stop giving monopoly privileges to certain large-scale enterprises. Following the 1994 devaluation, the Senegalese government assured donors that it would dismantle state monopolies in certain areas. At the same time, it attempted to woo French investors back to Senegal.

Senegalese Economic Policy: From African Socialism to Economic Liberalism

During the Senghor era (1960–1980), African Socialism was Senegal's official ideology. Formulated by Mamadou Dia and Leopold Senghor, the doctrine stressed building a socialist society based on traditional African communitarian values and modern economic planning. Socialism in the countryside was to be achieved through the development of the cooperative movement and the regrouping of Senegalese villages into self-governing rural communes. Dia's blueprint for implementing African Socialism in the countryside called for the revitalization of Senegal's 13,000 villages through the Rural Animation program (Animation Rurale), initiated by the state to democratize village institutions and local power structures and to mobilize the rural populations for developmental activities. The village-based, multifunctional cooperative constituted the basic economic unit of the agrarian socialist society originally envisaged by Dia and Senghor.

During the early 1960s, the government established a vast network of more than 1,600 cooperatives. Most were peanut marketing cooperatives. Dia's plan to expand the role of the cooperatives to conform with his socialist vision was dropped after his fall from power. During the mid-1960s, the cooperatives assumed responsibility for marketing Senegal's entire peanut crop and became primarily channels for marketing peanuts and distributing agricultural credit and inputs in accordance with government-initiated programs. Most cooperatives came under the control of local party bosses, rural notables, or marabouts, who used the cooperatives for their own ends. The credibility of the cooperative movement was also undermined by the widespread corruption within ONCAD and the growing indebtedness of the cooperatives to the state. The peasants came to perceive the cooperatives as instruments of oppression rather than liberation and themselves as captives of the coop movement. Efforts by some of the younger Socialist cadres in the government and the ruling party to reform the cooperative movement by creating smaller and more financially autonomous coop units at the village level during the late 1970s and early 1980s failed to revive the movement.[13]

As an ideology, African Socialism affected Senegalese economic policy in four important ways. First, it discouraged the emergence of large-scale capitalist enterprises in the countryside and fostered the development of rural cooperative structures rather than private plantations. Second, it led to the 1964 Loi sur le Domaine National (National Land Tenure Law), which gave the state proprietary rights over all rural land and in theory abolished rents paid to absentee landlords. Under this arrangement, the state would become the steward of the land and allocate land rights only to those who worked it. Third, African Socialism's emphasis on the stewardship of the state was used to justify massive state intervention in regulating and controlling key sectors of the Senegalese economy. Senghor regarded the state as the principal instrument for building the nation and a socialist society. Fourth, African Socialism was flexible enough to maintain that there was an important place for foreign capital and the Senegalese private sector, provided that their activities were compatible with national development goals.

Senghor's stress on dialogue, international cooperation, and the complementarity of civilizations emptied Senegalese African Socialism of the strident nationalist content found in other hyphenated socialist ideologies. The identification of Senegal's national leaders with the principles of the more pragmatic, European-style democratic socialism since joining the Socialist International made it easier for the regime to justify its growing collaboration with foreign capital and the Senegalese private sector.

A belief in the efficacy of national economic planning was another crucial component of African Socialism. During the early years of independence, the Senegalese four-year plans incarnated the mystique of development promoted by the government. The First Plan (1961–1964) was elaborated under the supervi-

Figure 3.3 M'Bao oil refinery, Cap Vert. One of Senegal's first basic industries. (Photo by Michel Renaudeau)

sion of Mamadou Dia after more than two years of careful study and preparation and laid the groundwork for Senegalese economic policies during the 1960s. Primarily concerned with qualitative goals and structural change, the First Plan stressed such goals as ending the isolation of the so-called peripheral regions and their integration into the market economy, diversification of agriculture, exploitation of Senegal's mineral wealth, the promotion of several basic industries—such as oil refineries, textiles, and so on—and the establishment of innovative state rural development agencies designed to mobilize the rural populations and provide them with technical assistance.

After ousting Dia in the middle of the First Plan, Senghor promised that Senegal would continue the priorities laid down by Mamadou Dia, except more efficiently. During the course of the First Plan, peanut production rose substantially, road-building projects made the Fleuve and the Casamance more accessible during the rainy season, and the state established a rural development bureaucracy that reached much of the country. However, little was done to diversify agriculture, and industrial growth was hampered by the loss of Senegal's former West African markets.

The Second Plan (1965–1969) was more project-oriented and placed much greater emphasis on raising production and productivity. In contrast with the frequent references to socialism in the First Plan, the Second Plan hardly mentioned the word. During the rest of the 1960s, the Senghor government adopted a more "productionist" approach to rural development and downgraded the role to be played by some of the rural development institutions—Rural Expansion Centers, Rural Animation, and the cooperative movement—established under Dia to promote African Socialism and development. Instead, French technical assistance agencies were given the primary responsibility for raising productivity in the peanut basin and introducing cotton as a cash crop. Little was done to promote food crops outside the peanut basin, but generous tax breaks and high tarriff barriers were created to protect Senegal's largely French-owned import-substitution industries.

During the 1970s, the plan lost much of its mystique and force as a guide to development strategy and became primarily a shopping list of development projects that might be financed by foreign donors. The 1970s, a period of chronic drought, convinced the government to make a greater effort to diversify the economy and reduce its vulnerability to drought. This was to be done through a series of *grands projéts* (large-scale projects) that would permit the economy to once and for all break out of its dependency on the peanut. This new approach required a massive influx of foreign aid and capital and centered around the following major projects: (1) the creation of a customs-free industrial zone to promote export-oriented industries; (2) the development of a giant oil refinery and petrochemical industry to service all of West Africa; (3) the rapid expansion of Dakar's port facilities to accommodate giant tankers and the establishment of a tanker-repair industry (Dakar-Marine); (4) the expansion of Senegalese phosphate production and exports, intensification of the search for oil, and the exploitation of iron ore reserves in Eastern Senegal; and (5) the establishment of a major tourism industry.

During the 1970s, the state's rural development bureaucracy rapidly expanded with the emergence of specialized regional development agencies (RDAs) responsible for introducing new technology and raising productivity throughout rural Senegal—peanuts and millet in the peanut basin; cotton in Eastern Senegal and the Upper Casamance; rice in the Fleuve; and rice and corn in the Casamance. Toward the end of the decade, more emphasis was also placed on raising food production. The government put its main hope into developing irrigated agriculture all along the Senegal River Valley in collaboration with Mali and Mauritania and sought massive funding to build the Diama anti-salt dam in Senegal and the Manantali dam in Mali.

When Abdou Diouf became president in 1981, the Senegalese economy was still foundering under the weight of a rapidly deteriorating rural economy and massive foreign debt. Few of the *grands projéts* had been fully implemented. Only the tourist industry had come close to fulfilling expectations. Senegal's customs-free industrial zone had attracted few foreign investors; phosphate production and exports climbed slowly because of sluggish world market prices; the fall of the Shah of Iran had dampened Senegalese plans to build a giant oil refinery and petrochemical industry; Senegal's oil and iron resources were far from being exploited; and the expansion of Dakar's port and ship repair facilities had to be scaled down with the reopening of the Suez canal.

The agricultural sector did not fare much better. The inefficient RDAs were far from reaching their production targets, and the cooperative movement was moribund. Moreover, rice production, though rising along the Senegal River, was proceeding very slowly, and high production costs prevented Senegalese rice from being competitive with imported rice.

During the 1980s, the World Bank, the IMF, and other major donors put pressure on the Diouf government to radically change its economic policies. In 1980, Senegal became one of the first African countries to adopt a structural adjustment program (SAP).[14] Over the course of the decade, Senegal moved away from the statist economic policies of the late 1960s and 1970s and toward greater economic liberalization. Diouf himself coined a new slogan—"*moins d'état, mieux d'état*" (a smaller government, a better government)—that reflected the state's disengagement from key sectors of the economy.

The IMF and the World Bank stressed stabilization and economic growth as the major objectives of policy reform and proposed a wide range of measures to achieve these goals, presenting them as conditions that the Senegalese government had to meet in order to receive SALs and rescheduling of its foreign debt. Stabilization meant reducing state budgetary deficits, foreign debt, and the rate of inflation. These goals were to be reached by cutting or slowing government spending, reducing the size of the bureaucracy, instituting more stringent credit policies, and promoting exports. Sound financial policies would thus avert state bankruptcy and create a sounder business climate, which would stimulate investments in the private sector. Economic stabilization would, in theory, be followed by or accompanied by higher economic growth rates.

Senegal was most successful in achieving the macroeconomic stabilization goals set by the IMF. By 1988, Senegal had reduced its budgetary deficit from 8.8 percent of GDP to 2.5 percent and the external current account deficit from 18.4 percent of GDP to 10.2 percent. The inflation rate dropped from 9 percent to 2.5 percent. By the end of the 1980s, government expenditures as a share of GDP had fallen from 32 percent in 1981 to 21 percent. The Senegalese economy, however, experienced very modest growth rates during the 1980s and showed few signs of entering a higher growth path during the early 1990s. In 1993, the annual economic growth rate was −2.1 percent, and in 1994, the rate rose to an estimated 1.5 to 2 percent.

Although the Diouf government accepted the need for economic liberalization, it also had to face the political consequences when economic policies were detrimental to key political groups within Senegalese society, such as state bureaucrats, trade unionists, employers, and low-income urban dwellers. Under pressure from its constitutents, the government often failed to implement donor-imposed conditions or proceeded very slowly. For example, it often delayed liquidating or scaling down the size of RDAs, and many state employees remained on the public payroll long after their agency had been abolished.

In 1984, the Diouf government introduced what was heralded as the Nouvelle Politique Agricole (New Agricultural Policy—NPA), which called for the progressive disengagement of the state from activities in agricultural production, processing, and marketing to the profit of the private sector.[15] As part of this program, the government dissolved two RDAs, reduced the number of personnel in the surviving RDAs, and reoriented them toward extension and research functions. The rural credit program, which had been used to finance the distribution of seed, fertilizer, and other agricultural inputs through the cooperative movement, was dismantled, fertilizer subsidies gradually eliminated, and fertilizer distribution privatized. The elimination of the state agricultural credit program and fertilizer subsidies resulted in a sharp drop in the use of fertilizer in the peanut basin as well as lower peanut and millet yields. During the late 1980s and early 1990s, the government reiterated its commitment to the broad lines of the NPA but warned that it had to move cautiously in order to avoid possible negative effects on the agricultural sector. In 1992, Prime Minister Habib Thiam declared that fertilizer subsidies might have to be reestablished to prevent further drops in peanut and millet production and to provide incentives to farmers who could not otherwise afford to use fertilizer. This position put the Senegalese government into conflict with the World Bank and other donors who had long fought for the suppression of fertilizer subsidies. Peanut farmers continued to receive low prices for their peanuts but began to seek other sources of income. It remains to be seen whether the 1994 devaluation of the CFA franc, which theoretically should make local millet and rice more competitive with imported grains and peanut products and cotton more competitive in international markets, will spur agricultural production.

In February 1986, the government launched the Nouvelle Politique Industrielle (New Industrial Policy—NPI) with the objectives of sharply reducing state ownership and management in the industrial sector, forcing Senegalese industries to become more competitive by lowering tariffs on imported goods, and providing incentives to industry through export subsidies and changes in the Labor Code to give employers greater freedom to lay off workers.[16] Between 1986 and 1988, Senegal lowered the basic customs duty for final goods from 40 percent to 10 percent. The reduction led to a sharp decline in customs receipts, threatened the survival of Senegal's textile industries, and led to a drop in the country's industrial workforce. In August 1989, with IMF approval, the financially strapped government raised the basic customs rate from 10 to 15 percent and backtracked from the more radical tariff reforms introduced only a few years before.

The NPI drew sharp criticism from Senegal's industrialists, who claimed that the government did not consult them in formulating the reforms, and from Senegalese trade unions, who argued that the changes in the Labor Code would lead to massive layoffs and higher unemployment. Lower tariffs and import liberalization, however, stimulated the growth of Senegal's informal sector by providing cheaper goods, primary materials, and spare parts. These measures also provided benefits to Senegalese consumers by sharply reducing inflation rates and contributing to price stability.

During the early 1990s, the short-run prospects for Senegal's industrial sector remained bleak. An overvalued currency, relatively high labor and energy costs, and fierce competition from other world producers indicated that Senegal might have to go through a difficult transitional period of "deindustrialization" before becoming more competitive. Although the 50 percent devaluation of the CFA franc in January 1994 will provide an opportunity for Senegalese export industries to become more competitive, it is not certain that Senegalese industrialists will be able to take advantage of the situation. The benefits of devaluation could well be canceled out by higher labor costs, soaring energy prices, inflationary pressures on the price of local raw materials, and the lack of investment capital to modernize Senegalese factories.

Development for Whom?

During the colonial era, the Senegalese economy was developed primarily for the benefit of the *métropole* and expatriate companies involved in the colonial economy. The gap between the material benefits accruing to expatriates working in Senegal and those earned by Senegalese workers in the modern sector was enormous. Non-Africans earned three times the wages and salaries of Senegalese holding similar kinds of jobs[17] and nearly all the profits generated by Senegal's largest firms went to foreigners.

The Africanization and nationalization programs of the late 1960s and 1970s favored a small number of Senegalese businessmen; managers, and professionals in the private sector; influential politicians; government ministers; university professors; and Senegalese cadres working for the parastatals. This group was predominantly male, highly educated, politically well-connected, and able to afford European-style living standards—that is, cars, modern appliances, nice villas or apartments, good schools, and higher education for their children, and opportunities to travel abroad.

Although Africanization and nationalization policies led to a modest shift in income distribution from foreigners to Senegalese nationals, the gap between the Senegalese elite and the masses has probably widened since independence. On the whole, postcolonial development policies have failed to raise living standards for most Senegalese or to redistribute wealth and services in favor of the poor. The structural adjustment programs of the 1980s and early 1990s have helped to lower the living standards of many Senegalese civil servants and salaried workers. During this period, government salaries and minimum wages in the private sector have not kept up with inflation. Between 1985 and 1990, the official minimum wage remained unchanged at 183.75 CFA per hour; in the early 1990s this figure rose slightly, reaching 201.60 CFA per hour. During the second half of 1993, the government announced that it would reduce government salaries by 15 percent, provoking a fierce reaction from public-sector employees. The January 1994 devaluation of the CFA franc raised the specter of sharp price increases for imported food, clothing, and other essential commodities without a corresponding rise in salaries or farm prices to prevent a drop in living standards.

In January 1994, the National Assembly gave Diouf extensive emergency powers to control wages and prices for a three-month period. Failure to prevent hyperinflation would wipe out the competitive advantages to be gained by a devalued currency. In its fight against inflation, the government had to face growing demands by the trade unions for wage increases to compensate for the loss in purchasing power caused by the devaluation. Diouf responded by canceling the wage cuts called for in the Sakho-Loum plan and negotiating a relatively modest 15–20 percent average increase in wages in both the public and private sectors. Although the devaluation theoretically would stimulate the recovery of Senegalese industries, in fact it was accompanied by a sharp increase in layoffs and requests for reducing the industrial work force. By mid-1994, an additional 1,000 jobs in the industrial sector had been eliminated and the government was no longer putting up much resistance to firms requesting further layoffs. Although the government made an effort to hold down price increases of basic commodities and the reduction of customs duties, the purchasing power of most Senegalese declined sharply as the general price index quickly jumped more than 30 percent. The inflation rate for 1994 turned out to be 40 percent, a figure that demonstrated that Senegal had managed to avoid hyperinflation. Government officials predicted that inflation would be held to 8 percent in 1995.

State patronage and clientelist relations have helped create a small new class of wealthy Senegalese who have used their political connections to get loans, import licenses, tax exemptions, and other special privileges from state-run banks and government agencies regulating national and international commerce.[18] One of the principal reasons for the near collapse of Senegal's banking system was the nonrepayment of large loans taken by prominent religious leaders, politicians, and their families—the so-called "untouchables." The Senegalese elite have also used their access to state resources to invest in the private sector, especially in the Cap Vert region where civil servants, politicians, and businessmen have invested in real estate, commerce, and agriculture. In some parts of the rural hinterlands of the Cap Vert region, city dwellers own as much as 70 percent of the land. The so-called "*jardiniers de Dimanche*," or "Sunday farmers," have invested in truck farms, orchards, and cattle-fattening operations.

Corruption has also contributed to the growing gap between the Senegalese elite and the masses. Shortly after becoming president, Abdou Diouf launched a major campaign against government corruption (*l'enrichissement illicite*) that led to the arrest and prosecution of several high-ranking officials. The liberalization of the economy, tighter donor surveillance over Senegal's public finances, and anti-corruption campaigns during the 1980s and early 1990s have to some extent reduced the opportunities for high-level government corruption and increased the possibility and costs of getting caught. Corruption and fraud were particularly widespread in the customs service. Despite anticorruption measures and the trend toward greater transparency in government operations, it remained difficult to prove to a skeptical Senegalese public that corruption had declined significantly in the 1990s.

In the countryside, rural development policies did little to alleviate poverty despite the government's efforts to raise production and productivity through the diffusion of modern agricultural equipment and technology. Thus far, the main beneficiaries have been the bureaucrats, managers, technicians, and foreign technical assistance personnel involved in rural development agencies and programs and a small number of marabouts, rural notables, and relatively wealthy farmers with enough land and labor to take advantage of the modern equipment, technology, and access to easy credit offered by the government. Since the mid-1980s, the NPA has adversely affected many middle-level bureaucrats who are losing their jobs with the reduction in RDA activities. Farmers who no longer have easy access to credit to purchase fertilizer, seed, and other farm inputs have also suffered.

The real incomes of most Senegalese farmers have dropped since the mid-1960s. Depressed peanut prices and drought contributed to a drastic decline in rural incomes during the late 1960s and 1970s, and despite government efforts since the mid-1970s to shift more resources to the rural areas, rural incomes have not kept up with inflation. Producer prices for peanuts, rice, cotton, and other cash crops remain relatively low. The situation in the densely populated western peanut basin has become especially critical for young farmers because of land shortages and deteriorating soil conditions. As a result, the rural exodus towards Dakar and other towns has accelerated.

Despite this gloomy picture, Senegal's rural populations are making a valiant effort to survive under extremely difficult conditions.[19] The disengagement of the state has been accompanied by a remarkable proliferation of community-based associations and groups that have organized to protect the environment and find new ways of supplementing their meager rural incomes. Women and youth, the least privileged groups in Senegalese society, have spearheaded the drive to revitalize the village economy through reforestation projects, small livestock raising, vegetable production, and other small-scale rural activities. Forced to rely more on their own resources, the rural populations are beginning to shed the "*mentalité d'assisté*" (dependency syndrome) characteristic of state-peasant relationships during the 1960s, 1970s, and early 1980s. International and Senegalese-based nongovernmental organizations (NGOs) have provided technical and financial assistance to hundreds of community-based associations. Since the 1980s, donors have been channeling more of their development assistance funding to the NGOs.

In the cities, particularly in Dakar, the informal sector has been providing employment and income for many Senegalese who cannot find jobs in the formal sector.[20] The informal sector also provides inexpensive goods and services for Senegal's urban poor who cannot afford to pay for the goods produced by Senegal's formal industrial sector. For example, an enormous market exists for cheap used clothing, which is often smuggled illegally into the country and permits Senegalese families to clothe their children at relatively little cost.

Strong ties of solidarity between those living in Dakar, other Senegalese towns, and abroad and their home villages have facilitated the flow of resources from urban to rural areas. Urban-based hometown associations often collect money from their members to construct mosques, wells, schools, dispensaries, and modern housing in the villages; they also support young villagers coming to town looking for work. Traditional social values continue to oblige wealthy urban Senegalese to play the role of patron and redistribute some of their wealth to family, friends, and their villages of origin. Social solidarity and patron-client relations somewhat diminish the intensity of class conflicts.

In view of the negative growth rate in real per capita income since independence, it is rather remarkable that the living standards of Senegal's urban and rural masses have not fallen more than they have. During periods of drought, the misery of the rural masses has been partially alleviated through large-scale food relief programs. During the 1980s and early 1990s, health conditions improved in the countryside, thanks to the expansion of potable water supplies and widespread vaccination and mother and childcare campaigns. Foreign aid has also provided the government with much-needed resources to prevent further declines in mass living standards and to temporarily compensate civil servants who lost their jobs as a result of donor-induced austerity programs.

It remains to be seen whether the Senegalese masses can move beyond survival and whether the structural adjustment programs and recent devaluation will create the basis for a healthy economy that will support higher growth rates and better living standards for Senegal's rapidly growing population.

Structural Adjustment and Devaluation: Economic Recovery or Pauperization?

In 1988, the IMF pointed to Senegal as a success story of an African country that enjoyed "adjustment with growth."[21] Unfortunately, this evaluation proved to be overly optimistic and inaccurate. Elliot Berg, the author of the famous report that shaped World Bank aid policy to Africa in the 1980s, sharply criticized the IMF assessment.[22] In the first place, the IMF claims were based on unreliable statistics. Thus, the modest growth rates obtained by Senegal during the late 1980s, which averaged a little over 4 percent from 1986 through 1988, were due more to favorable rain conditions, which led to increased agricultural production from a depressed agricultural base, than to structural adjustment policies. Second, Berg argued, Senegal had not taken the tough measures needed to fully implement structural adjustment policies. Instead, it had played the game to obtain higher levels of aid than most African countries. With 1.5 percent of the population of sub-Saharan Africa, Senegal received 4.8 percent of the total public aid to that region during the 1980s. Senegal's success in getting aid enabled the government to refrain from making the hard decisions needed to turn the economy around.

Berg also rejected arguments that claimed that structural adjustment policies led to increased suffering. Using data showing that life expectancy rose from forty years in 1970 to forty-eight years by 1987, that infant mortality declined, and that the number and percentage of school age children in Senegal expanded, Berg maintained that Senegal's modest structural adjustment policies had not hurt the poor. The main losers were the state bureaucrats and wage earners in the private sector.

Senegalese critics have attacked Senegal's structural adjustment program for its high social costs and failure to achieve economic recovery and have rejected the arguments made by proponents of structural adjustment.[23] Thus, the reduction in Senegal's balance-of-payments deficits during the late 1980s derived more from external factors, such as the sharp drop in world market prices for oil and rice, two of Senegal's major imports, than from the implementation of structural adjustment policies.[24] Moreover, the lowering of tariffs called for in the IMF-inspired New Industrial Policy led to deindustrialization and a sharp rise in imports, which would lead again to higher foreign trade deficits. Finally, the decline in state budgetary deficits resulted primarily from higher indirect taxes on consumer goods such as oil and rice rather than from rigorous austerity policies.

Critics further argued that the structural adjustment programs had heavy social costs.[25] Although the percentage of Senegalese children in school may have increased, the quality of education declined with the introduction of double session and multigrade classes in 1986, the rise in student-teacher ratios, the lowering of standards in hiring teachers, and the growing difficulty for students of modest means to attend private schools. Moreover, although life expectancy may have increased and infant mortality may have declined, the quality and quantity of medical care deteriorated, as reflected in the decline in hospital beds and medical personnel per capita, the lack of medicines in public health facilities, and the appalling conditions of public hospitals.

According to Senegalese critics of structural adjustment, the chronic economic crisis adversely affected not only the poor but all segments of Senegalese society, with the exception of the elite in power and their allies in the private sector, and had led to pauperization.

The Sakho-Loum emergency economic recovery plan presented in August 1993 indicated that the Senegalese government was finally willing to take decisive measures to drastically cut government spending.[26] By cutting public-sector salaries by 15 percent, taking other austerity measures to reduce state spending, raising taxes on gasoline, and increasing customs receipts, the government argued that it had saved 13,400 positions that otherwise would have had to be eliminated. President Diouf declared that he would cut his own salary by 50 percent and that ministers' salaries would be reduced by 25 percent.

Widespread strikes in September and October 1993 (conducted under the slogan "Don't touch my salary!") did not move the government to back down. The November payroll reflected the 15 percent cuts in salaries. To soften the blow, the government slightly reduced the prices of certain basic commodities.

The January 1994 devaluation presented the government with a new crisis. IMF and World Bank officials declared that the 50 percent devaluation of the CFA franc would revitalize agricultural production, promote the interests of the rural populations, and spur exports, thus sparking economic recovery and growth in the depressed African economies.[27] The trade unions bitterly denounced the devaluation as "the recolonization of Africa" and attacked France for betraying its promise to maintain the parity of the CFA franc.[28]

While Diouf and other Senegalese government officials put on a brave face, the devaluation dealt a major blow to their efforts to keep the economy afloat while maintaining social peace. To prevent high inflation rates from canceling out the benefits of the devaluation and provide some relief for Senegalese consumers, the government restricted price increases on basic commodities such as grains, vegetable oils, sugar, and gasoline and on public services such as water, electricity, transportation, and telephone and temporarily froze rent levels.[29] To encourage farmers to produce more, the government raised the price of peanuts from 70 CFA to 100 CFA per kilo; cotton from 85 CFA to 110 CFA per kilo; and rice from 85 CFA to 90 CFA per kilo.

Senegalese government sources claimed that Senegal would receive more than $500 million in foreign aid in 1994.[30] In fact, Senegal received less than this figure because of delays by key donors in releasing funds. Much of this aid was earmarked to help wipe out Senegal's foreign and domestic debt and to provide budgetary support to the Senegalese government during the difficult transition to a postdevaluation economy. It remains to be seen whether devaluation will have the desired effects. In the short-run, it seemed clear that the devaluation would depress Senegalese urban living standards and heighten social tensions.

Notes

1. It is extremely difficult to accurately estimate Senegal's per capita income and to translate this figure into dollars. Sharply fluctuating exchange rates play havoc with such attempts. The official currency of Senegal is the CFA franc, which is tied to the French franc (1 French franc = 50 francs CFA). During the 1980s and early 1990s, the value of the CFA franc in relation to the dollar fluctuated between 230 and 480 francs CFA to the dollar. At the end of 1993, the dollar was worth about 290 francs CFA. The January 1994 devaluation of the CFA franc changed the ratio (1 French franc = 100 francs CFA) so that the dollar doubled in value, hovering around 580 CFA shortly after the devaluation. Efforts to compare changes in per capita income over time are further complicated by unreliable economic data, changes in official population statistics, and inflation.

2. For a Marxist analysis of Senegal's class structures, see Majhemout Diop, *Histoire des classes sociales dans l'Afrique de l'Ouest: Le Sénégal* [History of Social Classes in West Africa: Senegal] (Paris: François Maspero, 1972). Little has been done to trace the recent evolution of Senegalese class structures.

3. For a detailed description of agrarian structures in Sahelian Senegal, see Paul Pélissier's monumental study, *Les paysans du Sénégal: Les civilisations agraires du Cayor à la Casamance* [Peasants of Senegal: Agrarian Civilizations from Cayor to the Casamance] (Saint-Yrieix: Imprimerie Fabreque, 1966); and Valy-Charles Diarrasouba, *L'évolution des*

structures agricoles du Sénégal [The Evolution of Senegalese Agricultural Structures] (Paris: Editions Cujas, 1968). For a broader sketch of the difficulties facing Sahelian countries, see Jacques Giri, *Le Sahel au XXIè siècle* [The Sahel in the 21st Century] (Paris: Editions Karthala, 1989).

4. For a detailed inventory and analysis of Senegal's shrinking natural resource base, see Gerold Grosenick et al., *Senegal Natural Resources Management Assessment: Final Report* (Washington, D.C.: DEG/Louis Berger International, Inc., Institute for Development Anthropology, June 1990).

5. For a detailed analysis of the Mbegue fiasco, see Karen Schoonover Freudenberger, "Mbegue: The Disingenuous Destruction of a Sahelian Forest," Occasional Paper No. 21 (London: IIED, September 1991).

6. Most of the statistics presented in this chapter are taken directly or indirectly from official Senegalese sources, UN statistical yearbooks, and donor reports. For more recent official Senegalese statistical data see the quarterly reports on Senegalese economic indicators published by the Banque Centrale des Etats de l'Afrique de l'Ouest (Central Bank of West African States—BCEAO). Also see the French weekly *Marchés Tropicaux* for current news about the Senegalese and other francophone African economies.

7. For an analysis of the patterns of colonial dependency, see Sheldon Gellar, *Structural Changes and Colonial Dependency: Senegal, 1885–1945* (Beverly Hills, Calif.: Sage Publications, 1976). For a useful collection of essays on Senegalese postcolonial dependency, see Rita Cruise O'Brien, ed., *The Political Economy of Underdevelopment: Dependence in Senegal* (Beverly Hills, Calif.: Sage Publications, 1979). See also Samir Amin, *L'Afrique de l'Ouest bloquée* [The Blocking of West African Development] (Paris: Editions de Minuit, 1971).

8. For a bitter critique of Senegalese economic policies on this point, see Mamadou Dia, *Le Sénégal trahi: Un marché d'esclaves* [Senegal Betrayed: A Market of Slaves] (Paris: Selio, 1988).

9. For data on aid to Senegal during the late 1970s and 1980s, see Club du Sahel/CILSS. *From Aid to Investment . . . to Financial Support* (Paris: Club du Sahel/CILSS, January 1990).

10. For a detailed discussion of Dia's measures to nationalize the peanut trade, see Edward J. Schumacher, *Politics, Bureaucracy, and Rural Development in Senegal* (Berkeley: University of California Press, 1975), pp. 131–149.

11. For the best analysis of the rise and fall of ONCAD, see Nim Casswell, "Autopsie de l'ONCAD: La politique arachidière du Sénégal, 1966–1980" [Autopsy of ONCAD, Senegalese Peanut Policy, 1966–1980] *Politique Africaine,* No. 14 (1984): 38–73.

12. For a pungent critique of Senegal's reform efforts, see Elliot Berg, *Adjustment Postponed: Economic Policy Reform in Senegal in the 1980s* (Bethesda, Md.: Development Alternatives, Inc., October 1990).

13. For an analysis of the evolution of the cooperative movement from 1960 to the mid-1980s, see Sheldon Gellar, "Circulaire 32 Revisited: Prospects for Revitalizing the Senegalese Cooperative Movement in the 1980s," in John Waterbury and Mark Gersovitz, eds., *The Political Economy of Risk and Choice in Senegal* (London: Frank Cass, 1987), pp. 123–159.

14. For studies of the impact of structural adjustment programs on Senegalese policy, see Gilles Duruflé, *L'ajustement structurel en Afrique: Sénégal, Côte d'Ivoire, Madagascar* [Structural Adjustment in Africa: Senegal, the Ivory Coast, Madagascar] (Paris: Editions

Karthala, 1988); World Bank, *The World Bank and Senegal, 1960–1987* (Washington, D.C.: World Bank, 1989); and Berg, *Adjustment Postponed.* Also see Gilles Duruflé, *Le Sénégal peut-il sortir de la crise? Douze ans d'ajustement structurel au Sénégal* [Can Senegal Break Out of the Crisis? Twelve Years of Structural Adjustment in Senegal] (Paris: Editions Karthala, 1994).

15. For an analysis of the disengagement of the state in the countryside, see Cheikh Tijiane Sy, ed., *Crise du développement rural et desengagement de l'etat au Sénégal* [The Crisis of Rural Development and the Disengagement of the State in Senegal] (Dakar: Nouvelles Editions Africaines, 1988); and Pierre Jacquemot, "State Disengagement: The Case of Senegal," *Africain Environment* 7, Nos. 1–4 (1990): 153–164.

16. For an analysis of the NPI and customs reforms, see Berg, *Adjustment Postponed*, pp. 111–146; and Jim Lowenthal, Gerard Chambas, John Lewis, and James T. Smith, *A.I.D. Impact Evaluation Report No. 77: A.I.D. Economic Policy Reform Program in Senegal* (Washington, D.C.: U.S. Agency for International Development, September 1990).

17. For a detailed discussion of wage differentials during the 1960s, see Guy Pfefferman, *Industrial Labor in the Republic of Senegal* (New York: Frederick A. Praeger, 1968). For a more recent analysis of labor markets in Senegal, see Katherine Terrell and Jan Svejnar, *The Industrial Labor Market and Economic Performance in Senegal* (Boulder: Westview Press, 1989).

18. For an analysis of this phenomenon, see Catherine Boone, "The Making of a Rentier Class: Wealth Accumulation and Political Control in Senegal," *Journal of Development Studies* 26, No. 3 (1990): 425–449 and Catherine Boone, *Merchant Capital and the Roots of State Power in Senegal, 1930–1985* (New York: Cambridge University Press, 1992).

19. For discussions of the rural crisis and peasant survival strategies, see Philippe Bonnefond and Philippe Couty, "Sénégal: Passé et avenir d'une crise agricole" [Senegal: Past and Future of an Agricultural Crisis] *Revue Tiers Monde* 29, No. 114 (April–June 1988): 319–340; and Abdoulaye-Bara Diop, "Les paysans du bassin arachidier: Conditions de vie et comportements de survie" [The Peasants of the Peanut Basin: Living Conditions and Survival Behaviors] *Politique Africaine*, No. 45 (March 1992): 39–61.

20. On Senegal's informal sector, see Meine Pieter van Dijk, *Sénégal: Le secteur informel de Dakar* [Senegal: The Informal Sector of Dakar] (Paris: Editions L'Harmattan, 1986).

21. See the IMF *Survey* of May 1988 cited by Berg, *Adjustment Postponed*, p. 209.

22. Berg has presented the most cogent critique of Senegalese economic policy reform from the right. His view is summarized in the title of his report—*Adjustment Postponed: Economic Policy Reform in Senegal in the 1980s.*

23. For a recent critique of Senegal's structural adjustment program that attempts to refute Berg's assertion that it has not harmed the poor, see Makhtar Diouf, "La crise de l'ajustement" [The Adjustment Crisis], *Politique Africaine*, No. 45 (March 1992): 62–85.

24. Ibid., pp. 66–73.

25. Ibid., pp. 73–84.

26. For details of the Sakho-Loum plan, see *Le Soleil*, August 18, 1993.

27. For references to donor optimism, see *Le Soleil*, January 17, 1994.

28. *Marchés Tropicaux*, January 21, 1994, p. 118.

29. See *Le Soleil*, January 24, 1994, for a full list of government measures to deal with the devaluation.

30. *Le Soleil*, January 28, 1994.

4

■■■■■■■■

SENEGAL
AND THE WORLD

SENEGAL'S SMALL POPULATION and lack of wealth have not deterred it from becoming one of the most active and influential Black African countries on the international scene.[1] Despite some minor setbacks in the late 1980s due to difficulties with some of its neighbors, Senegal's diplomatic efforts have been remarkably successful in giving the nation a place of honor in various regional and international organizations. Thus, Senegal hosted the Third International Francophone Conference in Dakar in May 1989. And in December 1991, when the Organization of the Islamic Conference (OIC) held its sixth summit conference in Senegal, it was the first time that such a summit had been held in a Black African country since the founding of the OIC in 1971.

Since coming to power in 1981, Abdou Diouf has continued Senghor's pro-Western, outward-oriented foreign policy while strengthening Senegal's ties with the Islamic world and its role as a tribune for Black Africa within Muslim circles. Under Diouf Senegal has maintained its special relationship with France while building closer ties with the United States, Canada, and other Western countries. Like his predecessor, Diouf has pursued an activist policy in African continental and regional politics—opposing Libyan intervention in Chad and Soviet and Cuban intervention in Angola, supporting Morocco in the Western Sahara, sending Senegalese troops to Gambia to save the Jawara regime in 1981, and promoting West African regional economic integration. Acting as a nonaligned nation, Senegal has consistently backed anticolonial and national liberation movements in Africa, supported the Palestine Liberation Organization (PLO), and opposed superpower intervention in Vietnam, Angola, and Afghanistan. In recent years, Senegal has also enhanced its international reputation by being one of Black Africa's small number of functioning, multiparty democracies and hosting several major international conferences on democracy and human rights.

The French Connection

After more than three decades of independence, Senegal's special relationship with France remains one of the pillars of Senegalese foreign policy. The French connection is deeply rooted in modern Senegalese history. French political, economic, and cultural institutions were implanted in Senegal as far back as the seventeenth century with the establishment of Saint Louis as the capital of French Senegal. Senegal's privileged position within the French colonial system and the involvement of Senegalese intellectuals and politicians in metropolitan politics and culture during the colonial period have left cultural and emotional bonds that are not easily broken. Senegalese intellectuals still read *Le Monde,* and French opinion journals regularly and closely follow French politics. Opposition leader Abdoulaye Wade often attempted to use the French press to discredit the Diouf regime through articles and interviews. Diouf, like his predecessor, often responds angrily to French critics of his economic policies and of flaws in Senegalese democratic practices in public press conferences.

Senegal's special relationship with France during the Senghor era (1960–1980) was reinforced by Senghor's personal loyalty to France and his acceptance of most of the premises of Gaullist foreign policy.[2] Like the French, Senghor thus opposed the domination of world politics by the two major superpowers, regarded France as the natural leader of an independent Europe and a champion of Third World interests, and saw an alliance between Europe and Africa as the best hope for providing a "Third Force" to counteract superpower domination. While still in office, Senghor worked closely with France to promote a *trilogue* among Europe, Africa, and the Middle East. Senghor was also one of the chief proponents of a loose commonwealth of French-speaking nations—*la francophonie*—joined together by common cultural and linguistic bonds.[3] During the 1980s and early 1990s, Senegal's special relationship with France continued, thanks to Diouf's close political ties with French President François Mitterrand and the French Socialist party.

Since independence, Franco-Senegalese relationships have gone through four phases. The first phase was dominated by the presence of Charles de Gaulle, who insisted upon maintaining paternalistic relationships with Senegal and other former French Black African colonies remaining in the French orbit. De Gaulle promised to provide generous financial and technical assistance in exchange for fidelity to France and to protect the new francophone states against internal subversion and hostile neigbors. During the Gaullist years (1958–1969) Senegal did little to reduce its economic dependency upon France or to nationalize French-held sectors of the economy. On the contrary, Senghor often criticized the reluctance of metropolitan firms to invest in Senegal and expressed the fear that French public opinion was succumbing to Cartierism[4] and becoming less supportive of aid programs to France's former colonies.

The upheavals of May–June 1968 that rocked France and the Gaullist regime also affected Senegal. The agitation and unrest in Dakar during this period was in large part triggered by popular resentment over French political, economic, and cultural domination. France stood by Senghor during the crisis. Although both de Gaulle and Senghor survived the upheavals, the end of the Gaullist era was near. De Gaulle's departure from the political scene in April 1969 signaled the beginning of a new phase in Franco-Senegalese relationships.

Under Georges Pompidou (1969–1974), de Gaulle's successor, France showed more flexibility and less paternalism in dealing with the francophone African states.[5] Senegal continued to enjoy warm relations with France, abetted by Senghor's longtime friendship with Pompidou dating back to the 1920s, when both men had been students at the prestigious Louis Le Grand Lycée in Paris. The 1974 revisions of the postindependence Franco-Senegalese cooperation agreements reduced the size of the French military contingent in Senegal, transferred Senegalese military bases from French to Senegalese sovereignty, and stepped up the Africanization of the University of Dakar. Senegalese nationalists had long demanded such measures, and their implementation provided tangible signs of the evolution away from the paternalism of the past.

The election of Valery Giscard d'Estaing to the French presidency following Pompidou's death in 1974 opened a third phase in Franco-Senegalese ties.[6] Giscard continued to pursue a Gaullist policy in Africa and to make the Franco-African summits that had been initiated by Pompidou in 1973 an annual event. During the late 1970s, Senegalese foreign policy became more intertwined with that of France. Thus, Senegal supported French military intervention in Chad, applauded France's role in ousting the Bokassa regime in the Central African Empire, permitted France to use Senegalese air bases, and joined forces with France and Morocco in sending troops to Zaire to defend Shaba Province against invasion by rebel forces opposing the Mobutu regime. Senegal's growing friendship with the Islamic world during this period also made Senegal a valuable asset to France, coinciding with Giscard's efforts to increase French influence and insure secure oil supplies in the Middle East through the *trilogue.*

The defeat of Giscard d'Estaing and the coming of power of François Mitterrand and the French Socialists opened a fourth phase in Franco-Senegalese relationships.[7] The Diouf regime welcomed the unexpected Socialist victory in the 1981 French elections. As a member of the Socialist International, the PS had established close ties with Mitterrand and other French Socialist leaders. Senegal enthusiastically supported Mitterrand's pro–Third World foreign policy and commitment to increase French aid to Africa. For its part, the French Socialist regime warmly praised Senegal's human rights record and efforts to promote democracy and regarded Senegal as one of its staunchest and most reliable allies in Black Africa.

As pragmatic politicians who both led Socialist parties affiliated with the Socialist International, Diouf and Mitterrand were natural allies. Though maintaining close ties between France and francophone Africa, they sought to alter the neocolonial links that characterized Franco-African relations during the 1960s and 1970s. Mitterrand thus sought to expand France's influence in Anglophone

Figure 4.1 Abdou Diouf with French president François Mitterrand. (Photo courtesy of Le Soleil)

and Lusophone Africa and adopted a more Third World–oriented foreign policy in which the former French colonies received a relatively smaller share of French largesse. For his part, Diouf sought to expand Senegal's visibility and ties beyond the French and francophone African orbit by developing closer political ties with the United States and the Muslim world. Senegal continued to loyally back France's foreign policy agenda and military presence in Africa, and France promoted Senegalese aspirations for greater international stature. Thus, France supported the choice of Dakar as the site of the Third International Francophone Conference in 1989 and backed Abdou Diouf as vice president of the Socialist International in the early 1990s. Mitterrand has also recruited President Diouf as an important ally in his efforts to have France play a leading role in revitalizing the North-South economic dialogue. At the 1989 conference, Mitterrand announced that he was canceling the poorest francophone African countries' public debt to France, including that of Senegal. During the early 1990s, Mitterrand's efforts to use French aid as a lever to promote democratic reforms in France's former African colonies also bolstered Senegal's image within francophone Africa.

    The decisive defeat of the Socialists in the 1993 French national legislative elections by the French right and the emergence of Edouard Balladur as prime minister raised some concern in Senegal that Franco-Senegalese relations might not continue to be as warm as in the past. The current French government's antiforeigner campaign threatens thousands of Senegalese now working legally or illegally in France. Moreover, Balladur, unlike Mitterrand, who stressed the importance of democratization as a condition for French aid in the early 1990s, insisted that French economic aid be tied more to economic policy reforms and compliance with IMF guidelines. The Balladur government's support for the devaluation of the CFA franc in January 1994 marked the end of an era in francophone Africa and caused much resentment of France in Senegal. In late July 1994, Prime Minister Balladur made an official visit to Senegal in which he took great pains to reiterate France's close ties with Senegal and praised Senegal as a beacon of democracy courageously meeting the challenges of devaluation.

Jacques Chirac's victory in the May 1995 French presidential elections meant that France would once again be led by a president with a fondness for Francophone Africa. Unlike his former rival Balladur, Chirac is more likely to pursue a more personal, flexible, and generous policy toward Senegal and other Francophone countries.

Economic dependency is another crucial factor underlying Senegal's special relationship with France. Although France no longer monopolizes Senegalese foreign trade and aid as it did at independence, the former metropole remains Senegal's principal trading partner and most important source of financial and technical assistance. France still provides approximately 20 percent of all aid to Senegal and has been willing to finance projects in areas that other donors have not been willing or able to enter. And when the Senegalese government finds itself in a serious financial bind, it usually turns to France for help. In exchange, Senegal continues to give preferential treatment to French banking and commercial interests operating in Senegal.

Senegal's membership in the franc zone ties its currency to the French franc. For many years France and the African nations in the franc zone resisted pressures from the IMF, the World Bank, and the United States to devaluate the inflated CFA franc. On January 11, 1994, the fourteen African states in the franc zone meeting in Dakar announced a 50 percent devaluation of the CFA franc.[8] Experts estimated that the Senegalese CFA franc had been overvalued by 41 percent. Although it made Senegal's export products more competitive, the steep devaluation was also likely to increase social tensions in Senegal because it would induce a sharp increase in the cost of living. France moved to mitigate some of the negative effects of devaluation by creating a special development fund to generate more employment and promising to cancel part of the francophone African states' debt to France.

Although Senegal's special relationship with France continues, the French presence in Senegal has been declining steadily since independence.[9] Thus, the number of French living in Senegal dropped from 50,000 on 1960 to fewer than 18,000 by the beginning of the 1980s. The drastic reduction in the number of French administrative and military personnel immediately after independence; Senegal's stagnant economy; greater opportunities for Europeans in the Ivory Coast, Cameroon, and Gabon; and the Africanization of skilled-labor and managerial jobs in the private sector were all factors contributing to the decline. By the mid-1990s, there were fewer than 15,000 French living in Senegal.

Senegal and Africa

During the Gaullist 1960s, Senegal's inter-African foreign policy focused primarily on its relationships with its immediate neighbors and other francophone states in North and Black Africa. In the 1970s and 1980s, Senegal dramatically expanded its diplomatic horizons and became much more involved in continental African politics as it developed close ties with Zaire, Egypt, and other African states traditionally outside the French sphere of influence. During the 1990s, the growing movement toward multiparty democracy in francophone Africa enhanced Senegal's prestige. Senegal has capitalized on this by hosting conferences on democracy and supporting fledgling democratic regimes. The early 1990s also saw Senegal taking the lead in promoting greater West African regional economic integration. In 1991 Diouf set up a special ministry for economic regional integration within his new government to promote this objective. At the October 1992 Libreville Franco-African summit, Diouf presented a report spelling out the need for greater regional cooperation in Africa.

Despite its extensive involvement in inter-African politics and its diplomatic successes, Senegal has experienced the most difficult diplomatic relations with its immediate neighbors—most recently with Mauritania, Guinea-Bissau, and the Gambia.[10] During the 1960s and 1970s, political and ideological differences were at the heart of Senegal's poor relations with Guinea and Mali. During the 1980s and 1990s, economics, territorial disputes, and interethnic violence undermined Senegal's relations with other immediate neighbors.

Senegal's relations with Mali hit bottom during the early 1960s after the collapse of the Mali Federation in August 1960. Mali broke its ties with Senegal and rerouted its trade through the Ivory Coast even though the Dakar-Niger railroad provided the most economical way of shipping goods in and out of landlocked Mali. Relations between the two countries began to improve when Mali agreed to cooperate with Senegal in plans to develop the Senegal River basin. The 1968 military coup led by Moussa Traoré overthrew the more radical Malian nationalist regime led by Modibo Keita and facilitated political rapprochement between Senegal and Mali. Economics brought the two countries closer together during the 1970s when both countries realized that they had to cooperate in order to attract the tens of millions of dollars needed to finance the Diama and Manantali dam projects. Senegal saw the dams as a safeguard against drought and an instrument for achieving national food self-sufficiency whereas Mali expected to benefit from the Manantali dam because it would provide hydroelectric power and an outlet to the sea for the landlocked country.

During the 1980s, relations between the two countries were cordial. After the 1989 break between Senegal and Mauritania, President Moussa Traoré's efforts to mediate the Senegalese-Mauritanian conflict failed. Despite Diouf's past good relations with the Traoré regime, Senegal immediately recognized the new regime that overthrew Traoré in March 1991 and supported its efforts to establish a democratic multiparty system in Mali, a goal the regime attained in 1992. Despite being invited, Diouf did not attend Mamadou Konaré's inauguration as president of Mali, however. Instead, he sent Amath Dansonko, PIT party leader and minister, to represent Senegal.

During the Senghor era, Senegal's relations with Guinea were frequently stormy. As one of the leaders of the radical camp in Africa, Guinea clashed with Senegal on many issues concerning the pace of decolonization in Africa. Led by the fiery Sékou Touré, Guinea invariably took a more militant, anticolonialist position than Senegal, which it often accused of being an instrument of French neocolonialism. Another major source of conflict arose from the fact that Senegal gave political refuge to tens of thousands of Guineans fleeing their country. Relations between Senegal and Guinea deteriorated rapidly after Touré smashed an unsuccessful attempt to overthrow his regime by an invasion launched from Portuguese Guinea in November 1970. Shortly afterward, the two countries launched vitriolic radio attacks on each other's regimes. The "battle of the airwaves" continued for several years, reaching its peak in 1973 when Senegal broke off diplomatic relations with Guinea.

Senegalese-Guinean relationships improved dramatically following Touré's rapprochement with France in 1978. That same year, a reconciliation between Touré and his two arch-rivals, Senghor and Houphouët-Boigny, took place in Monrovia. Relations between Senegal and Guinea continued to improve during the early 1980s as Touré took steps to liberalize his regime, move closer to France, and become more active in the Islamic Conference. Common development problems also brought the two countries together. In 1981 Guinea joined the Organisation de Mise en Valeur du Fleuve Gambie (Organization for the Development of the Gambia River Basin—OMVG), which had been created in 1978 by Senegal and Gambia.

The military coup that followed Touré's death in 1984 did not lead to any dramatic changes in Senegal's relations with Guinea. Although Senegal recognized the new regime, Diouf did not develop close ties with its leaders. Economic liberalization and the Peulh commercial networks operating in Senegal and the Fouta Djallon in Guinea sparked an increase in informal trade between the two countries. However, the maintenance of Guinea's national currency discouraged greater economic integration between the two states. In 1991 Senegal angered President Lansana Conté by giving shelter to Alpha Condé, a leading critic of the regime, who had returned to Guinea from Paris in May 1991 to organize a new political party in preparation for the announced transition to a civilian regime. Despite the incident, Senegal continues to enjoy correct if not warm relations with Guinea.

Senegal's most serious difficulty with an immediate neighbor concerns Mauritania. During the early 1960s, Senegal and other francophone Black African states supported Mauritania in the face of Moroccan claims that Mauritania was an integral part of Morocco. Senghor saw Mauritania as a buffer state between Senegal and North Africa. Senegalese-Mauritanian relations cooled during the mid and late 1960s when Mauritania began to loosen its ties with the francophone African bloc and move closer to the Arab world. Mauritania joined the Arab League in 1973 and the Mahgreb Union with Algeria, Morocco, Tunisia, and Libya in February 1989.

As Senegal itself developed closer ties with the Islamic world, relations between the two countries again improved. Senegal supported Mauritania's claim to that part of former Spanish Sahara that it had annexed in 1975 and backed both Mauritania and Morocco in their conflict with the Polisario Liberation Movement. Relations again cooled after the military government that took power in Mauritania in 1978 made its peace with the Polisario in 1979 while Senegal continued to support Morocco. In early 1981, an unsuccessful attempt at a military coup launched by Mauritanian exiles and backed by Morocco led to charges by Mauritania that Senegal had been involved in the plot. President Diouf denied the charges and expelled Mauritanian opponents of the regime living in Senegal.

During the late 1980s, relations deteriorated, exacerbated by the growing dissatisfaction of large segments of Mauritania's Black African minority concentrated along the Senegal River with the Arabization programs imposed by the Moorish majority since independence. Perhaps even more crucial was the decision of the Moor-dominated government to nationalize the land along the Senegal River, which had become increasingly more valuable since the establishment of the Diama and Manantali dams in 1985 and 1987, respectively. In May 1988, the Mauritanian government abolished the rights of customary landholders in Boghé and gave their land to wealthy Moors from Nouakchott. In precolonial times, Black Africans owned land on both sides of the Senegal River. The expropriation of their Mauritanian lands by Moors from the north angered farmers on the Senegalese side of the border, who organized self-defense committees. Tensions grew between the two countries. On April 8, 1989, Mauritanian soldiers killed two Senegalese in the village of Diawara. The incident touched off bloody massacres on both sides of the border, the mass departure of Senegal's Moorish population, and the forced expulsion of thousands of Black African Senegalese and Mauritanian farmers from their traditional lands along the Senegal River.[11]

Efforts to mediate the conflict by Mali and the Organization of African Unity (OAU) under the leadership of Hosni Mubarak in 1989 and 1990 failed. Tensions increased as Senegal accused Mauritania of providing Iraqi arms and other support to insurgents in the Casamance secession movement. In turn, Mauritania accused Senegal of backing antigovernment movements like the Forces de Libération des Africains de Mauritanie (African Liberation Forces of Mauritania—FLAM) and Black African military officers allegedly involved in plots to overthrow the Ould Taya regime. Both countries also took different sides in the Gulf War. Mauritania enthusiastically supported Iraq, whereas Senegal sent troops to Saudi Arabia.

In 1990 Senegal called for a revision of existing borders based on a 1933 French colonial decree that would give Senegal control over both sides of the Senegal River.[12] The present border is in the middle of the Senegal River. However, Senegal has been reluctant to press this point because of its acceptance of the principle of the inviolability of borders inherited from the colonial period.

Tensions eased somewhat with the attendance of Mauritania at the December 1991 Islamic Conference and the restoration of diplomatic and communications links between the two countries. However, the situation remains a potentially explosive one despite the reestablishment of official diplomatic relations in 1993, the creation of a special commission to look into refugee and transhumance issues, and a cordial meeting between high-ranking Mauritanian and Senegalese officials in Senegal in July 1994. Relations continued to improve in 1995.

Chronic drought has sedentarized the majority of Mauritania's formerly nomadic Moorish population and led them to move south to the Senegal River, where the region's black population, formerly slaves, till the land for them. The Black Africans living on the banks of the Senegal River have not taken kindly to Moorish efforts to force them off their traditional lands. The presence of thousands of Black African Mauritanian refugees on the Senegalese side of the border provides the material for militant irredentist movements.

Senegal's relations with Guinea-Bissau have also been mixed. For many years, they were colored by Senegal's stance toward Portugal and the liberation forces during the long war for national independence (1963–1974). When the armed struggle led by Amilcar Cabral and the Partido Africano da Independência da Guiné e Cabo Verde (African Independence Party of Guinea and Cape Verde—PAIGC) broke out in 1963, Senegal at first supported a rival group. As the war intensified, thousands of refugees crossed the border into the Casamance. Portugal's raids and shelling of Senegalese border villages severely strained relations between Senegal and Portugal during the late 1960s and early 1970s as Senegal condemned Portugal's violation of its national sovereignty. Although sympathetic to the liberation struggle, Senegal moved to restrict the movement and training of Guinean freedom fighters on Senegalese soil to avoid Portuguese reprisals. These measures did not endear Senegal to Cabral and the PAIGC. However, when Guinea-Bissau declared its independence in 1974, Senegal was one of the first African states to recognize the new regime. Because of Guinea-Bissau's own internal political problems and preoccupation with rebuilding its war-torn economy, Senegal's initial concern that the more radical Bissau regime might encourage autonomist movements in the Casamance proved to be unfounded. When Joao Vieira overthrew the Luiz Cabral government in November 1980, Senegal moved quickly to recognize the new regime.

Relations between the two countries deteriorated during the mid-1980s with the emergence of the separatist movement in Casamance and a territorial dispute over rich fishing waters and potentially rich oil deposits in the maritime areas along the borders. In 1985, Senegal and Guinea-Bissau agreed to submit their dispute to arbitration in an international tribunal in Geneva. When the tribunal ruled in Senegal's favor in 1989, Guinea-Bissau rejected the decision and insisted that the case be taken to the International Court of Justice in the Hague. In 1990, the two countries were close to military conflict when Senegalese forces moved across the border into Guinea-Bissau territory. The Senegalese withdrew, however, and Presidents Diouf and Vieira pledged to seek a peaceful solution to the dispute. Relations steadily improved during the early 1990s following a cease-fire between the Senegalese government and the Casamance rebels and Guinea-Bissau's reiteration of its desire to find a compromise that would satisfy Senegal. Although the International Court of Justice ruled in Senegal's favor, the Senegalese government in October 1993 made a goodwill gesture by agreeing to share fishing and mineral rights with Guinea-Bissau in the contested areas, thus ending the long-standing dispute. For its part, Guinea-Bissau agreed to no longer provide the Casamançais rebels sanctuary.

When Gambia obtained its independence from Great Britain in 1965, many observers felt that the tiny Gambian enclave would soon be absorbed by its larger neighbor. To date, Gambia has resisted Senegalese efforts to integrate it into its economic orbit because of the English-speaking elite's fear of being swallowed up by Senegal. During the late 1960s and early 1970s, Senegal accused Gambia of "economic aggression" because of the large-scale smuggling that took place across borders. At that time, many Senegalese peanut farmers unhappy with the low peanut prices in Senegal sold their peanuts in Gambia. Smuggling of consumer goods such as transistor radios, watches, and textiles deprived the Senegalese government of revenues derived from taxes levied on imported goods. Senegal's infant textile industry also suffered from the large volume of cheap Asian textiles smuggled into Senegal from Gambia.

During the late 1970s, the two countries began to move closer together, especially in the area of economic cooperation and foreign policy. In 1978 Senegal and Gambia formed the OMVG to jointly develop the Gambia River Basin. Like Senegal, Gambia, under the leadership of Sir Dawda Jawara, intensified its links with the Islamic world, and it adopted many similar stances on international issues. In November 1980 Senegal sent troops to Gambia at the request of the Gambian government, which reported that Libya was financing efforts to recruit Gambian nationals in Gambia and Senegal and establish Islamic republics. On July 30, 1981, while President Jawara was in London, left-wing elements seized power and proclaimed the establishment of a Marxist-Leninist regime in Gambia. When Jawara asked for help, Senegal responded immediately by sending troops. The rebellion was crushed after several days of bloody fighting in the Gambian capital of Banjul. With Jawara restored to power, the two governments began negotiations to establish a confederation, and by the end of the year, the Gambian and Senegalese governments had ratified a treaty establishing the Senegambian Confederation. The treaty went into effect on February 1, 1982.[13]

Throughout the 1980s, Gambians dragged their feet in accepting further political and economic integration with Senegal. Smuggling remained Gambia's main industry, and Senegal claimed to lose 20 billion CFA in lost revenues to the practice each year. Gambia also stalled in building an international bridge across the Gambia that would facilitate economic integration with Senegal. The Mandinka who dominated Gambian politics and the ruling Progressive People's Party (PPP) feared that a formal federation with Senegal would reduce their power and lead to the Wolofization of their country. In 1989 matters came to a head when President Jawara suggested that the presidency of the Senegambian Confederation be rotated annually. The 1981 agreement had specified that Senegal would always hold the presidency. Diouf reacted to the proposal in August 1989 by ordering the withdrawal of the Senegalese troops who had been in the Gambia since the aborted 1981 coup. The Senegambian Confederation was formally dissolved on September 30, 1989. Relations deteriorated as Senegal placed restrictions on the import of certain commodities from Gambia while Gambian officials harassed Senegalese at the Gambia River border crossings. Relations improved during the early 1990s. By the end of 1991, the two countries had signed a new "Friendship Treaty." In September 1993, however, Senegal temporarily closed its borders with Gambia to shut down the flow of smuggled goods that was costing the Senegalese treasury millions of dollars in lost customs revenues.

When a junta of young military officers, led by Yaya Jammeh, overthrew the Jawara government in July 1994, the Senegalese did not intervene to put Jawara back in power. Instead, Senegal gave the deposed president political asylum and recognized the new Gambian government, which promised to restore civilian rule in 1996.

During the first fifteen years of independence (1960–1975), a permanent feature of Senegal's foreign policy was its effort to build a coherent bloc of moderate francophone Black African states strong enough to play a major role in African continental politics. During the 1960s and early 1970s, Senghor and Houphouët-Boigny of the Ivory Coast continued their old rivalry and vied for the leadership of the moderate francophone African states regrouped within the Organisation Commune Africaine et Malgache (Joint African and Malagasy Organization— OCAM). Houphouët saw OCAM primarily as a political instrument to combat the influence of radical states within the Organization of African Unity (OAU), whereas Senghor looked to OCAM to promote economic cooperation and new markets for Senegalese exports. Because of the Ivory Coast's economic prosperity and dominant position within the Conseil de l'Entente (Entente Council), which grouped the Ivory Coast, Benin, Upper Volta, and Niger, Houphouët-Boigny was in a much better position to assert a leadership role within OCAM than was Senghor.

During the early 1970s, OCAM lost its cohesiveness as a unified, pro-French political bloc as several francophone states withdrew from the group. While OCAM was fragmenting, Senghor and Houphouët-Boigny patched up their differences and formed a Dakar-Abidjan axis to isolate Sékou Touré's Guinea. The Ivoirean leader also supported Senghor's plan to establish a Communauté

Economique de l'Afrique de l'Ouest (West African Economic Community—CEAO) of francophone states in 1973 to facilitate trade. At this time, Senegal also joined the Comité Inter-Etats de Lutte contre la Sécheresse dans le Sahel (Permanent Sahelian Anti-Drought Inter-State Committee—CILSS), established that same year to devise a common strategy for overcoming the desertification of the region. Senegal joined the Economic Community of West African States (ECOWAS) in 1975 despite its fears that Nigeria would dominate the organization. From the mid-1970s through the mid-1990s, the Franco-African summits replaced OCAM as the main vehicle for francophone African bloc politics.

Since independence, Senegal has been both a rival and a partner of Nigeria on the African political scene.[14] During the 1960s, Senghor, Houphouët and de Gaulle sought to develop a francophone counterweight to Nigerian influence in West Africa. Although Senegal officially supported the Nigerian government during the Biafra war, it also showed much sympathy for the Biafran cause. During the early and mid-1960s, however, Senegal and Nigeria were part of the moderate Monrovia bloc of African states that opposed the more radical Casablanca bloc of African states within the Organization of African Unity. Nigeria's oil wealth during the 1970s enabled the country to expand its role in African affairs and to offer Senegal aid and cheaper oil prices.

Senegal and Nigeria have often found themselves on different sides in foreign policy issues concerning South Africa and the Marxist government in Angola. In contrast with Senegal, Nigeria took a hard line toward South Africa and gave strong diplomatic support to the MPLA regime in Angola. During the late 1980s and early 1990s, Senegal and Nigeria drew closer together and coordinated efforts to promote West African regional cooperation and end the civil war in Liberia. Prodded by Nigeria, Senegal sent a contingent of troops to Liberia as part of the Economic Community of West African States Monitoring Group (ECOMOG) forces seeking to restore order to that war-torn country. During his term as president of ECOWAS in 1991–1992, Diouf worked for greater regional economic integration and continued to support ECOMOG's efforts to end the Liberian civil war. In late 1993, Diouf withdrew Senegal's military contingent from Liberia.

During the late 1970s and throughout the 1980s, Senegal played an increasingly active role in francophone African politics and developed close ties with the Mobutu regime in Zaire. Senegal denounced the 1976 invasion of Shaba Province and sent a battalion of Senegalese troops to Zaire in June 1978 as part of an African peacekeeping mission. In 1992, it unsuccessfully attempted to mediate the conflict between Mobutu and the political opposition and to find an acceptable formula for the transition to multiparty democracy. Senegal also took the lead in promoting a nonaggression mutual defense pact among CEAO members. The pact was signed in Abidjan in 1977. Senegal consistently supported French military intervention in Chad during the 1980s to stop the Libyans, and it has played a leadership role at the annual Franco-African conferences that have taken place on a regular basis since 1973. During the 1980s, Senghor's 1979 call for the creation of a French-speaking commonwealth that would rival the English-speaking commonwealth in influence and prestige and serve as a bridge between the industrialized and developing countries became a reality with three major francophone conferences held in Paris, Montreal, and Dakar. Diouf was also an ardent supporter of the francophone commonwealth and paid tribute to his mentor and predecessor at the opening of the French-language Leopold Sédar Senghor University in Alexandria in November 1992.[15]

With the emergence of Afro-Marxist regimes in Burkino Faso and Benin, the decline of the Ivoirean economy, and growing internal criticism of the one-party Ivoirean regime, Houphouët-Boigny's influence in francophone African affairs waned in the 1980s. Sékou Touré's death in 1984 also removed one of francophone's Africa's most prestigious leaders from the scene and gave Abdou Diouf the opportunity to exercise an increasingly important leadership role in francophone and continental African politics. Diouf's participation at the 1981 Islamic Conference held in Taif, Saudi Arabia, established him as a leading spokesman for Sahelian interests. As president of the OAU in 1985–1986, Diouf drew attention to Africa's growing economic plight resulting from the debt crisis. He also presided over the 1989 Francophone Conference held in Dakar. And in 1992, Senegal hosted the African Cup championship matches and the annual OAU summit.

Throughout the decade, Senegal continued to strongly back liberation movements in southern Africa while vigorously opposing Cuban troops in Angola and Ethiopia. In the Angolan civil war, Senegal clearly favored the UNITA forces headed by Jonas Savimbi over the MPLA Marxist-led central government. The demise of Afro-Marxist regimes and the move toward multiparty political systems throughout Africa during the early 1990s enhanced Diouf's prestige as one of Africa's most internationally respected national leaders.

Senegal is tied to North Africa by history, religion, and culture. While president, Senghor often cited the many contributions of Berber and Arab culture to Black African civilization and the need for Black Africa to maintain close ties with its White African neighbors. During the first decade of independence, Senegal was primarily concerned with its relationships with Algeria, Morocco, and Tunisia. Since the mid-1970s, Senegal has also become increasingly involved with Libya and Egypt.

Senegal has maintained cordial relations with Tunisia since independence, largely because of the similarities of the two regimes in political organization and foreign policy orientation. The two countries worked together closely as leading members of the Inter-African Socialist International, cofounded by Senghor during the late 1970s. With the institution of liberal, multiparty reforms following Ben Ali's rise to power in 1987, Tunisia's political system is again very close to that of Senegal.

Senegal and Morocco have remained close allies since the mid-1960s when the latter renounced its claims on Mauritania and left the radical bloc of the OAU.

Figure 4.2 OAU president Hosni Mubarak of Egypt greeting Abdou Diouf in Cairo at 1992 OAU summit. (Photo courtesy of Le Soleil)

Senegal applauded Franco-Moroccan military intervention in Zaire and later supported Morocco in its attempts to put down the Algerian-backed Polisario movement during the late 1970s and early 1980s. Since then, Senegal has tried to promote a peaceful settlement to the conflict. Senegal's Tijani brotherhood originated in Morocco, and the two countries have extensive commercial ties. Both also played prominent roles in the Islamic Conference, with Morocco heading the Committee to Liberate Al Quds (Jerusalem). Senegal felt somewhat let down when King Hassan II did not attend the December 1991 OIC summit in Dakar.

Senegal and Algeria have often found themselves in opposite camps. One of the leaders of the radical camp within the OAU, Algeria was committed to radical social revolution at home and supported armed struggle by national liberation movements in southern and Portuguese Africa during the 1960s and 1970s. Senegal also supported national liberation movements, but it advocated more conciliatory approaches that stressed negotiations rather than armed struggle.

During the late 1970s, Senegal and Algeria continued to take sharply different positions on several major issues. Thus, Senegal deplored the presence of Cuban troops on Angolan soil, refused to recognize the pro-Soviet regime in Angola, and resisted efforts by Algeria, Angola, and Cuba to push the nonaligned Third World bloc into the Socialist camp.

Relations with Algeria improved during the 1980s and early 1990s as Algeria took an increasingly less ideological stance in African and Third World politics. Morocco's rapprochement with Algeria, joint U.S.-Soviet efforts to find a solution to the Angolan civil war, Namibian independence in 1990, and de Klerk's release of Nelson Mandela and legalization of the African National Congress in the early 1990s were all factors that reduced tensions between moderate and radical states like Senegal and Algeria. Although Senegal and Algeria found themselves on different sides during the Gulf War crisis, they continued to retain good relations. In 1992, when the Algerian government nullified the results of its national elections and crushed the fundamentalist Muslim movement that would have taken power, Senegal was one of the first Black African countries to receive an Algerian delegation seeking to explain Algeria's position and enlist understanding for this setback to democracy. More recently, Senegalese intellectuals and artists have openly protested the systematic killing of prominent Algerian intellectuals by fundamentalist terrorists.

During the late 1970s and throughout the 1980s, Senegal's involvement with Libya and Egypt in inter-African politics grew considerably. Throughout much of this period, Senegal and Libya were bitter enemies. Senegalese-Libyan relationships deteriorated because of Libyan intervention in Chad and the Kaddafi regime's backing of Ahmed Niasse's movement to establish a radical Islamic republic in Senegal. Libya also reportedly supported leaders of the 1981 putsch in Gambia that was crushed by Senegalese military intervention. That same year, Senegal led a diplomatic offensive against Libya throughout francophone Africa and pressured France to take a stronger position against Libyan expansionism in Black Africa. Relations were not helped by Abdoulaye Wade's frequent trips to Libya during the early and mid-1980s or the arrest of Libyan nationals in 1988 who were accused of attempting to smuggle in explosives to disrupt the 1988 Senegalese national elections. Relations improved following the resumption of formal diplomatic ties between the two countries and a state visit by Kaddafi to Senegal in 1989. For the 1991 Islamic Conference, Libya lent Senegal a 750-room floating hotel to lodge delegates for the duration of the meetings.

Senegal drew closer to Egypt during the late 1970s, backing Anwar Sadat's Middle East peace initiatives, and maintained its friendship with Egypt when that nation became increasingly isolated in the Arab world following the signing of the Camp David agreements. Under Sadat, Egypt regarded Senegal as a valuable ally. Senegal helped Egypt to gain new friends in Black Africa and a more sympathetic view for Egypt's positions on the Middle East within the European-dominated Socialist International.

After Sadat's assassination in 1981, Diouf continued Senegal's strong ties with Egypt and worked closely with President Hosni Mubarak on inter-African and Middle East issues. Senegal worked discreetly behind the scenes to facilitate a reconciliation between Egypt and the moderate Arab states. During the early 1990s, Senegal supported Egypt's position in the Gulf crisis and its efforts to initiate peace negotiations in the Middle East between Israel, the Palestinians, and the Arab states.

Senegal and the Islamic World

Despite its special relationship with France and its advocacy of a French-speaking commonwealth, Senegal has managed to establish its credentials as a prominent actor in the Islamic world. Senegal's close ties with both the West and Islam continue patterns found in Senegal's precolonial past. During the colonial period, France carefully controlled Senegal's relations with the Islamic world outside the French empire. With independence, it was natural that Senegal would attempt to broaden its ties with the Muslim world.

During the early years of independence, Senegal's relations with the Arab Middle East reflected internal concerns. Senegal quickly established diplomatic relations with Saudi Arabia to facilitate the pilgrimage for several thousand Senegalese who travel to Mecca each year to fulfill their religious obligations. Senegal's ties with Lebanon were initially motivated by the presence of a large Lebanese community, which numbered 20,000 at independence.

In the early and mid-1960s, Senegal did not take sides in the Arab-Israeli conflict. It enjoyed excellent relations with Israel, which was then widely regarded in Black Africa as a small, courageous developing country willing to share its technical expertise with the Third World. After the Six Day War in 1967, Senegal's friendship with Israel cooled and its foreign policy tilted toward the Arab side. When Israel rebuffed Senghor's peacemaking efforts as head of an OAU-sponsored mission to the Middle East in 1971, Senegalese relations with Israel steadily deteriorated. In February 1973, Senegal permitted the PLO to open its first office in Black Africa, located in Dakar. And in October 1973, Senegal joined several other Black African states in formally breaking diplomatic relations with Israel less than a month after the outbreak of the Yom Kippur War.

Under Senghor, economic considerations were another major factor spurring Senegal to strengthen its ties with the Islamic world. Hard-pressed by drought and soaring oil prices following the 1973 Arab oil boycott, Senegal welcomed the financial assistance offered by the oil-rich Arab nations to Black Africa. Senegal appealed to Muslim religious solidarity in developing close ties with Saudi Arabia and Kuwait, conservative Muslim countries committed to promoting Islam throughout Black Africa. During the 1970s, the Arabs set up multilateral financial institutions like the Arab Bank for Economic Development in Africa and the Islamic Development Bank to disburse aid to friendly Muslim African states and to those supporting the Arab position in the Middle East.[16]

Under Senghor Senegal did not limit its Islamic ties to the Arabs; it also sought the patronage of the Shah of Iran. Senegalese-Iranian relations expanded rapidly after Senghor attended the twenty-five hundredth anniversary of the Persian Empire in 1971.[17] Senegal's blossoming relationship with Iran was further reinforced by Senghor's ties with Sadat, who also was a close friend of the shah's. The partnership collapsed suddenly in 1979 when the Iranian Revolution led by Ayatollah Khomeini drove the shah into exile. As a result, the grandiose projects to build a $1 billion petro-chemical industry and an ultra-modern port in Senegal with Iranian financing never materialized. On the contrary, Senegalese-Iranian relations deteriorated rapidly.

Senegal's role as a prominent actor in the Islamic world increased dramatically following Diouf's coming to power in 1981. Diouf enhanced his prestige at home and throughout the Middle East following a visit to Saudi Arabia to attend the Islamic Conference held in Taif in late Janaury 1981. Upon returning home, Diouf announced that he had obtained a $50 million grant from Saudi Arabia and $40 million from Iraq for the Senegal River Basin development project.

Since the late 1970s, Senegal and Guinea have been Black Africa's two main recipients of Arab aid to Black Africa. The Arab aid, however, far from compensates for the huge trade imbalance that exists between Senegal and the Arab countries or the higher oil prices following the 1973 and 1979 crises. During the early 1990s, Senegal was importing more than 230 billion CFA annually from the Arab world but exporting only 8 billion to Arab countries.

During the 1980s, Senegal forged a close alliance with Saudi Arabia and Kuwait, which provided generous aid to Senegal. Although Senegal did not take sides when Iraq invaded Iran in 1981, it tended to be more sympathetic to Iraq. By the end of the decade, relations with Iraq had cooled considerably because of Iraq's support of Mauritania in the Senegalese-Mauritanian conflict in 1989.[18] As for Iran, the Senegalese government kept its distance from the Khomeini regime because of its militant religious radicalism. During the mid-1980s, relations with Iran worsened because of Iran's attempt to foster radical fundamentalist movements in Senegal. In January 1984, Senegal expelled Iranian diplomats from the country and broke diplomatic ties, which were not resumed again until February 1989, just a few months before Ayatollah Khomeini's death. By this time, Iran under President Rasanjani had reduced its efforts to export its revolution to Black Africa in general and to Senegal in particular.

During the 1980s and early 1990s, Senegal remained a loyal friend of the PLO and the Palestinian independence struggle, acting as a strong advocate for Palestinian rights within the United Nations. During the late 1980s, Senegal was one of the first Black African countries to recognize Palestine as an independent state and gave Yassar Arafat full state honors during his not infrequent visits to Senegal. Senegal also worked quietly to discourage other Black African states from resuming diplomatic ties with Israel.[19] Shortly after the PLO signed an agreement with Israel on principles for making peace in September 1993, Senegal once again warmly received Arafat as head of Palestine and strongly backed the peace process. In August 1994, Senegal and Israel resumed diplomatic relations.

Following the Iraqi takeover of Kuwait in summer 1990, Senegal condemned the invasion. In November 1990, Diouf visited King Fahd in Saudi Arabia and pledged to send a military contingent of 500 Senegalese troops to fight in the Gulf

War. In a tragic airplane accident, ninety-three Senegalese soldiers lost their lives in Saudi Arabia following Iraq's crushing defeat. The Gulf War had delayed the Islamic Conference, which had been slated to be held in Dakar in 1990. With the end of the war, the conference finally took place, in Dakar in December 1991.[20] Senegal formally took over the presidency of the OIC from Kuwait, which had hosted the previous conference. Iraq boycotted the conference because of its condemnation of its invasion of Kuwait. Saudi Arabia and Kuwait had financed most of the multi-million dollar infrastructure that had been built to host the conference. Seeking to enhance Iran's status in the Muslim world, President Rasanjani attended the conference and praised Senegal's role as host. Iran also lent Senegal four helicopters to help with security.

At the conference, Saudi Arabia announced that it was going to cancel the public debts of the poorest African countries that were members of the OIC. In 1992, Saudi Arabia formally canceled the loans that it had given Senegal during the early and mid-1980s as part of the World Bank's structural adjustment program. Kuwait also promised that Senegalese labor would be given an important role in the reconstruction of its war-torn country.

Senegal and the Third World

During the 1980s, Senegal's Third World relations became a relatively less important part of Senegalese foreign policy as leaders concentrated more on Africa and the Islamic world. As a result, Senegalese diplomacy paid less attention to Latin America and Asia than it had in earlier decades.

Since independence, Senegal's Third World policy had been based on principles of peaceful coexistence with different forms of political and economic systems. In dealing with Asia, Senegal has taken great pains to maintain good relationships with Communist regimes in the People's Republic of China, North Korea, and Vietnam and has astutely avoided taking sides in disputes involving contending Asian countries. Senegal thus has maintained good relations with both North and South Korea, China and Vietnam, and Pakistan and Bangladesh. Despite Senegal's strong Islamic connections, it maintains good relations with India and the Philippines, which both have often-dissatisfied Muslim minorities. Senegal has collaborated with India in sponsoring Third World economic fora like the 1968 UN Conference on Trade and Development (UNCTAD) held in New Delhi and in participating in North-South dialogues, most recently the one initiated by François Mitterrand in summer 1989. Senegal also hosted the G-15 conference of Third World states in November 1992.

In 1990 Diouf became the first African leader to visit the Philippines since Aquino became president in 1986 following the fall of the Marcos regime. During that visit, President Aquino asked Diouf to evaluate the situation of the 5 million

Figure 4.3 Abdou Diouf with the late King Faisal and other Saudi leaders. With Diouf as president, Senegal has become one of Saudi Arabia's closest African allies. (Photo by Michel Renaudeau)

Muslims in her country and to use his influence as future president of the Islamic Conference to prevent the conference from recognizing the Moro National Liberation Front (MNLF), a Muslim separatist group waging bloody guerrilla warfare in the southern Philippines.[21]

Senegalese diplomacy has been traditionally less active in Latin America than in Asia. Senegal has attempted to expand its economic and cultural ties with larger Latin American countries such as Brazil and Mexico. In 1982, Senegal discreetly permitted the British to use Dakar-Yoff airport as a staging post for their retaking of the Falkland Islands following the Argentine takeover. Relations with Argentina improved following the demise of the military regime and the establishment of a democratic system. Senegal's relations with Cuba have been poor since the latter's military involvement in Angola and Ethiopia. With Cuba's withdrawal of troops from the African continent during the early 1990s and the end of the Cold War, relations between the two countries are likely to become less confrontational.

Senegal's Third World policy centers more around active participation in international organizations and institutions like the United Nations than on bilateral relations with Third World states. Senegal often seeks to present itself as a voice for Third World aspirations in these organizations. During the 1970s, Senegal ardently spoke in favor of a New International Economic Order (NIEO) and called for improved terms of trade for Third World primary products, preferential treatment for Third World manufactured goods, and increased financial aid from the industrialized countries. In 1978, Senegal sent a small contingent of troops to Lebanon as part of a UN peacekeeping operation.

During the global Third World debt crisis of the 1980s, Senegal frequently called upon the richer countries and international institutions like the IMF and the World Bank to reschedule debt repayment timetables and reduce the debt burden that was crippling many Third World countries' development programs. During the 1980s and early 1990s, Senegalese officials came to hold important managerial positions within international financial institutions like the IMF, the World Bank, and the African Development Bank.

Senegalese diplomats have been active in the UN and other international organizations. A Senegalese, Amadou Moktar M'Bow, was secretary-general of the United Nations Educational, Scientific, and Cultural Organization (UNESCO) from 1974 until 1990, when he was forced to resign under pressure from the United States and other Western countries in the midst of charges of mismanagement and nepotism. Senegal gained another prominent UN post when Jacques Diouf was chosen as the new director of the UN Food and Agriculture Organization (FAO) in 1993. During the late 1980s and early 1990s, Senegalese diplomats, government officials, and scholars continued to actively speak out in UN and other international fora and conferences presenting Third World positions on such timely topics as human rights, women's rights, democracy, and the environment.

Senegal and East-West Relationships

One consistent aim of Senegalese foreign policy since independence was to prevent the United States and the Soviet Union from using Africa as a battleground in the Cold War. Although clearly pro-Western in orientation, Senegal carefully avoided taking a position in the political struggle between the two superpowers. Thus, although Senegal condemned the Soviet invasion of Afghanistan, it refused to follow the lead of the United States in boycotting the 1980 Olympic games held in Moscow on the grounds that sports should not be used as a pawn in the Cold War. Closer to home, Senegal both denounced the stationing of Cuban troops and Soviet military advisers in Angola and Ethiopia and chided the United States for dragging its feet in seeking to end white minority rule in South Africa. This policy persisted through the mid-1980s.

During the late 1980s and early 1990s, the collapse of Soviet and Eastern European communism, the decline of Soviet and Chinese influence in Africa, the fall of the Mengistu regime in Ethiopia, and the withdrawal of Cuban and South African troops from Angola marked the end of the Cold War in Africa and radically altered the nature of Senegal's relationships with Eastern Europe. For example, Senegal used to enjoy warm relations with the Communist regimes in Rumania and Yugoslavia, which pursued relatively independent foreign policies and played a not insignificant role on the international political scene as nonaligned nations. Rumania had close ties with both the Arab countries and Israel, and Yugoslavia had been one of the leaders of the nonaligned bloc. The fall of the Ceausescu dictatorship in Rumania and the disintegration of Yugoslavia into warring republics meant that these two countries were now too preoccupied with internal problems to continue an active foreign policy in Africa and the Third World. With German reunification, East Germany no longer existed. The Soviet Union, which had been the center of communism and had supported Afro-Marxist regimes and Marxist-Leninist parties throughout Africa, also ceased to exist. Senegal no longer had to worry about Soviet adventurism in Africa or Soviet support of radical opposition Marxist parties and movements operating in Senegal. Moreover, the former Soviet Union was no longer an ideological opponent of moderate regimes in Africa or a major player in inter-African politics because of its own internal political and economic problems. Ironically, however, the demise of the Soviet Communist bloc raised fears that Western aid would be diverted to Eastern Europe and the former Soviet Union at the expense of Africa.

Senegal's diplomatic ties with the United States date back to the early 1960s. Senegal was one of the first African countries to accept U.S. Peace Corps volunteers, and it enjoyed especially good relations with the United States during the Kennedy era (1961–1963). Relations between the two countries cooled somewhat during the next decade as a result of Senegal's criticism of U.S. involvement in Vietnam and racial unrest in the United States.

U.S. interest in Senegal increased after the establishment of the Sahel Development Program in 1973 as the United States stepped up its food and economic aid to Senegal and other Sahelian countries. By the end of the 1970s, Senegal was receiving approximately $30 million a year in U.S. aid. Senegal's flourishing tourist industry also attracted many Americans; by the beginning of the 1980s, approximately 12,000 U.S. tourists were visiting Senegal each year.

Under Diouf, Senegal moved closer to the United States. The Reagan and Bush administrations valued Senegal as an important ally in their eforts to minimize Soviet and Cuban influence in Africa. Senegal's alliance with the moderate Arab states and fear of radical Muslim regimes in Libya and Iran also coincided with U.S. strategic interests. Senegal and the United States were, of course, on the same side in the Gulf War. Senegal's movement toward a more liberal, market-based economic system during the 1980s, and its status as an island of democracy in a continent of one-party and military regimes, also won praise from the United States. U.S. aid to Senegal reached $50 million a year by the beginning of the 1990s but began to taper off in the mid-1990s. With the November 1994 election of a conservative Republican Congress seeking to cut government spending, Senegal will need to muster all of its diplomatic skills to avoid further aid reductions in the future.

Americans and American culture became popular in Senegal during the Diouf era. The Senegalese appreciated the fact that Peace Corps volunteers spoke the local languages and understood Senegalese African traditions. During the 1980s, many Senegalese, including two of Abdou Diouf's children, went to study in American universities. Hundreds of Senegalese flocked to learn English at the American Cultural Center, and many Senegalese went to America to seek their fortune. In the mid-1990s, an estimated 6,000 Senegalese were living in the United States. Diouf himself visited the United States in 1994 to receive an honorary doctorate from the University of Connecticut and to seek more postdevaluation financial support from Washington.

During the 1970s and 1980s, Senegal reinforced its ties with Canada, which has channeled much of its Third World aid toward francophone Africa. Canadian bilateral aid to Senegal sometimes surpassed that of the United States. The relatively large Canadian presence in Senegal is one of the by-products of Senegal's championing the francophone commonwealth.

While maintaining its special relationship with France, Senegal has steadily increased its bilateral and multilateral ties with Europe. During the 1960s, Senegal dealt primarily with the European Economic Community (EEC), which then consisted of the "six"—France, West Germany, Italy, Belgium, the Netherlands, and Luxembourg. Senegal's association with the EEC facilitated an influx of non-French consumer goods and provided a new source of development loans and grants from the European Development Fund, which partially compensated for a drop in French aid and the loss of French subsidies for Senegalese peanut exports to France. Senegal and other francophone countries counted upon France to champion their cause within the EEC by lobbying for more aid and preferential tariff treatment for the associated African states.

The expansion of the EEC during the 1970s and 1980s to include Great Britain and other Western European countries was accompanied by the widening of Senegal's European contacts. During this period Senegal reinforced its bilateral ties with Great Britain, West Germany, and Italy and signed economic and cultural agreements with the Scandinavian countries, Switzerland, Spain, and Portugal. Senegal's extensive links with Western Europe enhanced its reputation and increased the number of Senegal's aid and trade partners. Senegal also benefited from the provisions of the four Lomé Conventions signed between the EEC and the associated African countries between 1975 and 1989. In addition to receiving grants and loans from the European Development Fund (EDF), Senegal also received some compensation for falling peanut prices from STABEX, the EEC's export stabilization fund. The 1993 unification of European markets may have adverse effects on Senegal and other primary commodity exporters to Europe who now receive stabilization funds and preferential tariffs for their products. These advantages may fall by the wayside with the further liberalization of trade within the EEC.

Diouf, like Senghor, has made frequent state visits to European capitals and has capitalized on PS membership in the Socialist International. During the 1980s, Italy emerged as one of Senegal's most important bilateral aid partners, and smaller European countries such as Switzerland and the Netherlands also stepped up the volume of aid to Senegal. Europe continued to be Senegal's main aid and trading partner, with French aid playing a relatively smaller role than during the Senghor era.

During the 1980s and early 1990s, Senegal developed closer economic relations with Japan. Japanese vehicles took a larger share of Senegal's automobile market, and by the early 1990s Japan had become one of Senegal's major bilateral donors on a par with Italy, Germany, and the United States. In 1994 Japan offered Senegal a 22 billion CFA grant to help offset some of the negative consequences of the devaluation of the CFA franc.

Despite some setbacks in the late 1980s due to difficulties with its immediate neighbors, Senegal in the early 1990s enjoyed a remarkably high reputation as an important African actor on the international scene. The OAU called on Senegal to replace Togo as the host of the June 1992 OAU summit when it became evident that the explosive political situation in Togo would make a summit meeting there inopportune. Senegal had in 1991 been the first Black African country to host the Islamic Conference and in 1989 was the first Black African country to host the international Francophone Conference. Senegal's status as one of Black Africa's few democratic regimes and a model for other francophone African states also enhanced its prestige in the West.

To sum up, Senegalese diplomacy since independence has remained more or less constant in following the basic pillars of foreign policy established by

Senghor, who sought to: (1) maintain the French connection and promote the French-speaking commonwealth of nations; (2) increase Senegal's influence in francophone African and inter-African relations while keeping the Cold War out of Africa; (3) establish Senegal as an important player in the Islamic world as a moderate Islamic state; (4) champion African and Third World interests in international fora and institutions; and (5) diversify and expand Senegal's political, cultural, and economic ties with the West.

Notes

1. For the most comprehensive discussion of Senegal's foreign policy during the 1960s, see W.A.E. Skurnik, *The Foreign Policy of Senegal* (Evanston, Ill.: Northwestern University Press, 1972). For one of the most thorough analyses of Senegalese foreign policy in the 1970s, see Pierre Biarnés, "La diplomatie sénégalaise" [Senegalese Diplomacy], *Revue Française d'Etudes Politiques Africaines*, No. 149 (May 1978): 62–78. Much of the material and analysis in this chapter was culled from French-language periodicals and the Senegalese press.

2. For a detailed description of Gaullist foreign policy and attitudes toward Africa, see Dorothy S. White, *Black Africa and De Gaulle: From the French Empire to Independence* (University Park: Pennsylvania State University Press, 1979).

3. For more on the Francophone Commonwealth, see the special May 1989 issue of *Ethiopiques* devoted to that subject, especially Léopold Sédar Senghor's article, "De la Francophonie" [Concerning the Francophone Concept], pp. 7–26.

4. Cartierism was the name given to a movement begun in France during the late 1950s to reduce the amount of aid going to France's overseas colonies in order to have more capital to invest in the metropole. French journalist Raymond Cartier launched the movement with a series of articles appearing in *Paris Match* in August 1956 arguing that the colonies did not pay. Similar sentiments are expressed today in France under the rubric of "Afro-pessimism."

5. For France's Africa policy under Pompidou, see Kaye Whiteman, "Pompidou and Africa: Gaullism After de Gaulle," *The World Today* (1970): 241–249.

6. For detailed accounts of Giscard's Africa policy, see J. R. Frears, *France in the Giscardien Presidency* (London: George Allen & Unwin, 1981), pp. 104–127.

7. For Mitterrand's Africa policy, see Jean-François Bayart, *La politique africaine de François Mitterrand* [The African Policy of François Mitterrand] (Paris: Editions Karthala, 1984). For a summary of French policy in Black Africa since African independence, see Sheldon Gellar, "All in the Family: France in Black Africa, 1958–1990," *Asian and African Studies* 26, No. 2 (July 1992): 101–117.

8. For the French presence in Senegal, see Rita Cruise O'Brien, *White Society in Black Africa: The French of Senegal* (Evanston, Ill.: Northwestern University Press, 1972).

9. For more details about the devaluation, see *Le Monde*, February 13, 1994, pp. 1, 14, 15.

10. For Senegal's stormy relations with its neighbors in the late 1980s, see Sennen Andriamirado, "Sénégal: Abdou Diouf dans la tourmente" [Senegal: Abdou Diouf in Torment], *Jeune Afrique*, No. 1497 (September 11, 1989): 29–31. For a more detailed scholarly analysis, see Momar-Coumba Diop, ed., *Le Sénégal et ses voisins* [Senegal and Its Neighbors] (Dakar: Sociétés-Espaces-Temps, 1994).

11. For an analysis of the conflict, see Ron Parker, "The Senegal-Mauritania Conflict of 1989: A Fragile Equilibrium," *The Journal of Modern African Studies* 29, No. 1 (1991): 155–171. For a description of the early months of the crisis, see *Jeune Afrique*, "Comment Nouakchott et Dakar ont géré la crise" [How Nouakchott and Dakar Managed the Crisis], No. 1491 (August 2, 1989): 34–44.

12. For background to Senegal's border claims, see Jean Devisse, Abdourahmane Ba, Claire Bernard, and Brigitte Bougerol, "Fleuve Sénégal: La question frontalière" [The Senegal River: The Border Question], *Afrique Contemporaine*, No. 154 (February 1990): 65–73.

13. For a recent analysis of the demise of the Senegambian confederation, see Arnold Hughes, "The Collapse of the Senegambian Confederation," *Journal of Commonwealth & Comparative Politics* 30, No. 2 (July 1992): 200–222.

14. For Senegalese-Nigerian relations, see Bamitale Omole, "Bilateral Relations Between Senegal and Nigeria, 1960–1980: Cooperation and Conflicts," *Génève-Afrique* 25, No. 2 (1987): 80–101.

15. *Le Soleil*, November 6, 1990.

16. For a detailed analysis of Arab aid to Senegal, see Charbel Zarour, "La coopération arabo-sénégalaise" [Arab-Senegalese Cooperation], *Afrique et Développement* 11, Nos. 2–3 (1986): 261–287.

17. For more on Senegal-Iran economic ties under the Shah, see *Marchés Tropicaux*, May 5, 1975.

18. For Iraqi involvement in Mauritania and other African countries, see François Soudan, "L'Offensive africaine de Saddam Hussein" [Saddam Hussein's African Offensive], *Jeune Afrique*, No. 1516 (January 22, 1990).

19. For Senegal's role in Israeli-African relations, see Sennen Andriamirado, "Israel tente d'opposer Le Zaire au Sénégal" [Israel Attempts to Build Up Zaire in Opposition to Senegal], *Jeune Afrique*, No. 1273 (May 29, 1985): 24–37.

20. For extensive coverage of the Islamic Conference, see editions of *Le Soleil*, from December 8–14, 1991.

21. *Marchés Tropicaux*, June 8, 1990, p. 1603.

5

CULTURE
AND SOCIETY

SENEGALESE SOCIETY AND CULTURE are in rapid flux and undergoing severe social strains. During the 1980s, Senegal, which had been remarkably free of the ethnic, racial, and religious strife plaguing other African nations, found that it was
not immune to such problems. Insurrection in the Casamance, the anti-Moor rioting and mass exodus of Moors in 1989, and the opposition of much of the
Muslim community to an official visit by the Pope in summer 1985 were all signs
of a more turbulent and less tolerant Senegalese society. Fundamentalist Islamic
currents have also emerged to challenge the Senegalese brotherhoods' religious
authority and the legitimacy of the secular state.

Rapid population growth and changing demographics have affected Senegal's
social structures.[1] At independence, Senegal's population was slightly more than 3
million. By the mid-1990s, it had surged to more than 8.5 million (see Table 5.1).
Although the estimated annual population growth rate is 2.7 to 3 percent, the
number of Senegalese under fifteen years of age is growing by 3.8 percent a year.
By the mid-1990s, nearly 60 percent of the population was under twenty. Rapid
growth is placing heavy strains on Senegal's natural resource base and pushing
young people into the towns.

Senegal is rapidly becoming urbanized. At independence in 1960, only 22 percent of the population lived in urban areas; by the mid-1990s, more than 40 percent of the population lived in the towns, with nearly 20 percent of Senegal's total
population living in the greater Dakar area. Confronted with limited employment
opportunities, Senegalese youth are restless, apprehensive about their future, and
less willing than previous generations to accept the authority of their elders.
Student strikes, which used to be limited primarily to Dakar and Saint Louis, have
spread to other parts of the country. The elders complain about alcoholism, drug
abuse, and the degradation of morals.

TABLE 5.1 Population Trends in Senegal

Year	Total Population	Annual Growth Rate (percent)	Rural (percent)	Urban (percent)
1904	1,130,000	N.A.	97	3
1926	1,358,000	N.A.	95	5
1936	1,773,000	1.6	90	10
1945	1,872,000	1.8	85	15
1960	3,000,000	2.2	78	22
1976	5,000,000	2.7	66	34
1988	6,900,000	2.9	61	39
1995	8,500,000 (est.)	N.A.	58	42
2001	11,000,000 (est.)	N.A.	56	44
2015	16,000,000 (est.)	N.A.	44	56

SOURCES: Ruth Schachter-Morgenthau, *Political Parties in French-Speaking West Africa* (Oxford: Clarendon Press, 1964), p. 129; Mohamed Mbodj, Babacar Mané, and Waly Badiane, "Population et 'développement': Quelle politique?" in Momar Coumba Diop, ed., *Sénégal* (Paris: Editions Karthala, 1992), pp. 177–204; and Souleymane Bachir Diagne, Guy le Moine, and Paul Ndiaye, *Etude Prospective: Sénégal 2015* (Study of the Future: Senegal in the Year 2015) (Dakar:Ministère du Plan et de la Coopération, July 1989), pp. 50–57.

Social strains can also be felt in the countryside, where deteriorating environmental conditions have made it increasingly difficult for the people to live off the land. Rural youth have less access to good farming land than their parents had and look to the cities for other employment activities. Those who remain want a greater voice in village affairs. Rural women are demanding relief from the tedious chores of hauling wood, drawing water, and pounding millet and are becoming more active in politics and local self-help groups.

Despite the strains, Senegalese society remains remarkably vibrant and resilient. Although Dakar youth have rioted in the streets, they have also spontaneously organized vigorous campaigns to clean up the Senegalese capital and to fight crime. Self-help groups that have sprung up throughout the country have demonstrated great ingenuity in delivering basic public goods and services and undertaking small-scale development projects. The multiple networks of social solidarity that bind Senegalese together have provided a safety net that has kept many Senegalese from falling into abject misery in difficult economic times.

Popular culture and the arts are also thriving. Senegalese writers, artists, filmmakers, and musicians have gained international fame. The press has expanded rapidly during the past decade, and TV programming has become more varied and sophisticated.

Islam in Senegal

Since the implantation of French colonial rule, Islam has made steady progress. At the turn of the century, less than half of Senegal's population was Muslim. Today, more than 90 percent of the people embrace the religion. Since independence. Islam has become an ascendant force in Senegalese society, thanks to the Muslim brotherhoods' ability to adapt to changing social and political conditions, the spread of Koranic primary schools, and Senegal's strong ties with the rest of the Islamic world.

During the colonial period, Muslim brotherhoods were the main vehicles for spreading the Sufi form of Islam and organizing the faithful. Today, most Senegalese Muslims are affiliated with one of Senegal's three principal brotherhoods—the Mourides, the Tijaniyya, or the Qadiriyya (see Table 5.2).[2] Each brotherhood, or *tariqa* ("the Way" in Arabic), is distinguished by slight differences in rituals and codes of conduct.

The Qadiriyya is the smallest as well as the oldest brotherhood in Senegal. Missionaries from Mauritania and the Niger Bend introduced the Qadiriyya or-

TABLE 5.2 Major Senegalese Islamic Brotherhoods

Order	Founder	Ethnic Groups	Location
Qadiri	Abu Bounama Kunta (1780–1840)	Wolof, Moor, Mandinka, Fulbe, Sarakollé, Lebu	Cap Vert, Thiès, Casamance, Fleuve
Mouride	Amadou Bamba M'Backé (1850–1927)	Wolof, Serer	Cap Vert, peanut basin
Tijani	Umar Tall (1794–1864)		
Tijani dynasties			
Sy	Malick Sy (1855–1922)	Wolof, Serer	Cap Vert, Thiès, Sine-Saloum
Niasse	Abdoulaye Niasse (1850–1922)	Wolof, Serer	Sine-Saloum
Tall	Seydou Nourou Tall (1879–1980)	Tukulor	Dakar, Fleuve

der in Senegal during the eighteenth and early nineteenth centuries. Its main influence is in the Dakar-Thiès metropolitian areas and in parts of the Casamance.

The Mourides constitute the most tightly organized and influential brotherhood in Senegal with well over a million members.[3] During his tenure as Grand
Khalife (1968–1989), Abdoul Lahat Mbacké strengthened the brotherhood after
taking office following the death of his brother Falilou Mbacké. Abdoul Lahat reiterated the gospel of work preached by Amadou Bamba, urged the Mourides to
return to the land and adopt modern agricultural methods, and defended the interests of Wolof farmers in the peanut basin vis-à-vis the state bureaucracy.
Mouride influence has been growing, especially in areas adjacent to Mouride
population centers in the peanut basin, where many Serers have undergone
"Mouridization." Thanks to their ability to provide capital, jobs, and economic security for their members, the Mourides have also won many new followers in urban areas, including many university students.

Abdoul Lahat's piety, financial probity, and efforts to reform and modernize the
brotherhood enhanced his popularity among the faithful and won much respect
from non-Mourides as well. He transformed Touba, the Mouride capital, from a
tiny religious outpost in the wilderness to a bustling town of more than 150,000
people. Though he maintained his distance from the state while Senghor was president, he became a staunch backer of President Abdou Diouf's during the 1980s.

When Abdoul Lahat died in June 1989 at the age of seventy-seven, his brother
Abdoul Khadre, who had close ties with Abdoulaye Wade, succeeded him.
However, Abdoul Khadre died in May 1990 and was succeeded by Saliou Mbacké,
who does not seem to have the same political influence over the Mouride rank
and file as Abdoul Lahat.

One of the most visible signs of Mouride preeminence is the huge attendance
at the annual Magal, the religious festival held in Touba to commemorate the anniversary of Amadou Bamba's return from exile. Each year, hundreds of thousands
of Senegalese crowd the roads to make the pilgrimage to Touba. Representatives of
the government, other religious communities, and the diplomatic community
also attend.

Although the Mourides are the most influential brotherhood in Senegal, there
are more Senegalese who consider themselves to be Tijanis. Most Senegalese
Tijani owe their allegiance to one of three prominent maraboutic houses. The
oldest Tijani house traces its roots back to Umar Tall, the Tukulor warrior and
empire builder. Until his death in 1980 at the venerable age of 101, Seydou
Nourou Tall, Umar's grandson, headed the Tall dynasty. He was succeeded by his
son, Mountaga Tall, who played an active role in calling on the Senegalese government to defend the land tenure rights of Tukulor farmers living on both sides of
the Senegal River during the 1989 Senegal-Mauritania conflict.[4] The Tall dynasty's
influence has been primarily political and ethnic. In general, Tukulor Tijanis do
not display the same kind of reverence and blind obedience to their religious
leaders as do the Mourides.

Figure 5.1 The great mosque at Touba, religious capital of the Mourides. (Photo by Michel Renaudeau)

The most prominent Tijani house in Senegal is based in Tivaouane and traces its origins to El Haj Malick Sy. The current Grand Khalife is Abdoul Aziz Sy, who has headed the Sy dynasty since the 1950s. The Sy Tijanis tend to place more emphasis on Islamic education than the Mourides. Since independence, they have promoted the rapid spread of Koranic schools in the region of Thiès and have set up Koranic schools for girls, a marked departure from past traditions of reserving education for the boys. Like the Mourides, the Sy dynasty has a large following among the Wolof in the peanut basin in what used to be the precolonial state of Cayor, in the new pioneer zones to the east that were originally settled by followers of Malick Sy, and in urban centers.

The third major Senegalese Tijani dynasty has its capital in Kaolack and was founded by Abdoulaye Niasse, a marabout of blacksmith origins. Less influential in Senegal than the other Tijani dynasties, the Niasse dynasty has had the most ties with the broader Muslim world and claims to have millions of followers in Nigeria, Ghana, and other West African countries. Unlike the heads of the other brotherhoods, the Niasses have not had good relationships with the Senegalese government. Ibrahim Niasse, head of the dynasty until his death in 1975, had little love for Senghor. One of his sons, Ahmed, popularly known as the "Ayatollah of Kaolack," founded Hizboulahi, the "Party of God," in 1979. The party was immediately banned by the government because religious parties are forbidden by the Senegalese constitution.[5] In 1984, Ahmed's younger brother, Sidy Lamine, started *Wal Fadjri* (The Dawn) an Islamic newspaper dedicated to promoting an Islamic Republic in Senegal.

The position of the Niasses, however, is a minority one within Senegal's brotherhoods. For the most part, Muslim leaders see radical and reformist currents and demands for an Islamic state as a threat to their own authority and privileged relationships with the Senegalese state. Nevertheless, the marabouts have become part of Senegal's Islamic revival movement in pressing for greater Islamic content in public school curricula and the expansion of Islamic educational institutions. The Tijanis and Mourides have also established their own university groups to mobilize Senegalese students to their cause.

Senegal's Islamic revival since independence has been accompanied by the phenomenal expansion of Muslim religious and cultural associations in the Cap Vert region and a growing interest in Islamic theology, philosophy, and the Arabic language. Arab countries like Saudi Arabia, Kuwait, Egypt, and Libya have supported this trend by contributing funds to Islamic institutes and the study of Arabic and providing scholarships for Senegalese to study abroad.

Since independence, the governing party has attempted to check and control religious radicalism by supporting moderate reformist movements like the Féderation des Associations Islamiques au Sénégal (Federation of Islamic Associations in Senegal—FAIS) and the Union pour le Progrés Islamique au Sénégal (Union for the Advance of Islam in Senegal—UPIS), preserving its close ties with the powerful brotherhoods, and carefully monitoring the efforts of revolutionary Islamic states like Libya and Iran to finance and foster Senegalese radical religious movements. Under Diouf, the government has also shown greater responsiveness to Muslim religious opinion. For example, in 1989 the government banned the sale and distribution of Salman Rushdie's *Satanic Verses* following denunciations of the book by Senegalese religious leaders like Abdoul Aziz Sy.

Most of Senegal's political and intellectual elite remain committed to a secular democratic state.[6] Nevertheless, some political leaders, such as the late Boubacar Guèye, formerly head of the MRS, and Babacar Niang, head of the Parti pour la Libération du Peuple (People's Liberation Party—PLP), have called for an Islamic Republic; others, such as Mamadou Dia, have maintained close ties with radical reformers like Cheikh Touré, founder of the Union Culturelle Musulmane (Muslim Cultural Union—UCM) and editor of *Etudes Islamiques* (Islamic Studies). Religious fundamentalism has been clearly on the rise in Senegal, sparked, in part, by a deteriorating social and economic climate.

With the resurgence of Islam in Senegal, Senegal's small Christian community, which accounts for less than 5 percent of the population, feels somewhat apprehensive about the future, especially since the departure of Senghor, a Roman Catholic, from the presidency.[7] In the past, relationships between Senegal's Muslim and Catholic communities have been very good and characterized by mutual tolerance and respect. However, the golden era of good relations may be over. In 1984, when the bishop of Thiès sought permission to rebuild a ruined church in Tivaouane, the capital of the Sy dynasty, he touched off a controversy that was not resolved until 1986 when the Catholics agreed to close down the diocese of Thiès and turn over the church to the state to prevent its destruction by the local Muslim community. In 1985, a planned visit by Pope John Paul II had to be canceled because of opposition to his visit by various Muslim dignitaries. With the rise of Islamic triumphalism in some Senegalese circles, it is not surprising that the Christian community staunchly supports Senegal's survival as a secular state in which all religions will be given equal status.

One should not, however, proclaim the demise of good relationships between the Catholic and Muslim communities. Pope John Paul II found a warm welcome and was well received by Muslim leaders when he visited Senegal in February 1992 as part of a tour of several African countries. Moreover, Elizabeth Diouf, the president's popular wife, is Catholic and has played an increasingly visible role in public affairs in recent years. Two Catholics, Robert Sagna and Jacques Baudin, held prominent positions in the new government formed after the May 1993 legislative elections, and Senegal forcefully and successfully promoted a Catholic as Senegal's and Black Africa's candidate to head the FAO in 1993. Despite the small size of Senegal's Catholic community, Senegal has produced Cardinal Thiandoum, one of Black Africa's few cardinals within the Catholic church.

Nearly all of Senegal's Christians are Catholics, and two-thirds live in towns. They are most strongly concentrated in Dakar, Thiès, Mbour, and the lower Casamance. As a group, they have been more exposed to Western-style education and values than the Muslims, Thanks to mission schools, literacy rates in predominantly Catholic areas of rural Senegal are much higher than in the Muslim areas. The most renowned of Senegal's intellectuals, Senghor himself, was a product of Catholic mission school education.

Interethnic Relationships and Conflicts

Until recently, race and ethnicity have not been major sources of political and social conflict in Senegalese society. Race has not been a major issue in Senegalese politics since the early colonial period. After independence, French and Lebanese residents, if they wished, had the option of adopting Senegalese citizenship. For the most part, Senegal has also been tolerant of non-Senegalese Africans coming to live and work in the country. Senegal has thus received and absorbed tens of thousands of Guineans who fled the Sékou Touré regime. With the notable exception of the Moors in 1989, there have been no mass expulsions of "stranger" populations in Senegal despite high unemployment and growing economic problems and the fact that the Senegalese themselves have been victims of such policies in countries like Zaire and Zambia.

After more than two decades of interethnic peace, however, Senegal experienced two major upheavals during the 1980s—the armed separatist insurrection against state authority in the Casamance beginning in 1982 and the slaughter of Moor shopkeepers and the departure of nearly the entire Moor community from Senegal following the widespread massacres of Black Africans in Mauritania in 1989.

Senegal's precolonial traditions and long colonial history have helped forge a strong sense of Senegalese national identity among the majority of the people, particularly among urban youth. The sense of Senegalese national identity is particularly strong among the populations north of the Gambia River, who share similar hierarchical social structures and Islamic traditions, and weakest among the Diola populations of the forest areas of the Casamance.

The Wolof, who account for 43.7 percent of Senegal's total population according to the 1988 national census, are the largest and most influential ethnic group in the country.[8] They also have the most highly developed sense of Senegalese nationality. Their language, particularly in the urban areas, is in the process of becoming a national one that is already understood by 71 percent of the population.

The Serer, who once had the reputation of being staunch traditionalists who kept to themselves, have been undergoing rapid Islamization and Wolofization since independence. Thus, Serer migrating to Dakar are assimilating into the dominant Wolof urban culture and many rural Serer in the peanut basin have been adopting Wolof lifestyles and agricultural practices after converting to Islam and joining predominantly Wolof brotherhoods. The Serer, who comprise slightly less than 15 percent of the population, have a reputation for being a hard-working and industrious people and are particularly skilled in traditional farming methods.

The Lebu, a small but influential people closely related to the Serer and living almost exclusively in the Cap Vert region, have long been Wolofized. Lebu notables own a good deal of valuable real estate in Dakar and Rufisque because of their status as the original inhabitants of Cap Vert. Lebu fishermen also tend to dominate Senegal's ocean fishing industry. Although the Wolof-speaking Lebu retain their own ethnic identity, they tend to identify themselves as primarily Senegalese. Together, the Wolof, Serer, and Lebu constitute well over half of Senegal's total population.

In the Casamance, the Diola, Mandinka, and other small ethnic groups have been developing a strong regional Casamançais identity in conflict with the Senegalese national identity. During the nineteenth century, the Diola fiercely resisted Islamization and French rule. Their region was the last to be "pacified" by the French. For many years, the Casamance, divided from northern Senegal by the Gambia River, was governed by France as a distinct administrative entity from the rest of Senegal. Casamançais migrating to Dakar spoke of "going to Senegal" when they went north. During the 1950s, autonomist movements emerged which eventually were absorbed into Senghor's BDS.

The Casamance rebellion began in December 1982 when a group of Casamance separatists led a demonstration for independence in Ziguinchor, burned the

Senegalese flag, and attacked the local radio station.[9] This event marked the beginning of the predominantly Diola-led rebellion against the central government which continued into the mid-1990s. Organized by the Mouvement des Forces Démocratiques de la Casamance (Casamance Movement of Democratic Forces— MFDC) and led by Augustine Diamoune Senghor, a Diola Catholic priest, the rebellion was sparked by three major factors: (1) the feeling of many Casamançais that the Casamance had been discriminated against in terms of allocation of national development resources and government jobs; (2) resentment against the growing power and influence of non-Casamançais emigrants and government officials living and working in the region, many of whom had received land from the state; and (3) the resurgence of traditionalist values among the Diola, who saw their sacred forests being destroyed and their traditional way of life being undermined by the more Islamized northerners. The uprising was confined to the region of Ziguinchor, where the Diola are the most important ethnic group.

The government's efforts to crush the rebellion by force or to settle the crisis through negotiations and promises to devote more resources to the Casamance were unsuccessful for many years. A negotiated cease-fire in 1993, coupled with a French declaration supporting Senegal's legal claims to the region, brought peace to the Casamance. However, in early 1995, tensions rose again when dissident rebels killed several Senegalese soldiers in clashes with Senegalese security forces.

During the 1980s, the rapid expansion of irrigated agriculture on both sides of the Senegal River contributed to the intensification of interethnic conflicts in Mauritania and Senegal.[10] Moor discrimination against the Black African populations—Wolof, Tukulor, Peulh, and Soninké—living on the Mauritanian side of the Senegal River, coupled with efforts by the Moor majority to expropriate farmlands traditionally owned by the Black African inhabitants, heightened tensions along the river. On April 9, 1989, Mauritanian soldiers killed two Senegalese in the village of Diawara in the Bakel area and touched off what became full-blown pogroms in both countries. Shortly afterward, rioters in Nouakchott, the Mauritanian capital, killed scores and wounded hundreds of Senegalese and black-skinned Mauritanians. Enraged by eyewitness reports of Mauritanian atrocities, Senegalese mobs went on a rampage, looting Mauritanian shops and looking for Moors to kill in revenge. The carnage went on for days before a mutual exchange of populations was arranged. At least 60,000 Senegalese were deported or fled from Mauritania and 120,000 Moors were obliged to leave Senegal.

Until the 1989 outbreak of violence, the Moors had been an integral part of the Senegalese economy, controlling much of the small-scale retail trade in urban communities. Moor shopkeepers could be found in nearly every urban neighborhood in the Dakar-Thiès metropolitan area. Many Senegalese did not like doing business with the Moors, who were often depicted as tight-fisted and greedy merchants. For their part, the lighter-skinned Moors often looked down on the Senegalese. After the Moors left, the Senegalese, many of Guinean origin, took over nearly all of the estimated 17,000 shops abandoned by the Moors. With improvements in relations between Senegal and Mauritania, some Moors cautiously returned to Senegal in the mid-1990s.

The Puular-speaking populations of the Middle Senegal River Valley have been affected the most by the expansion of irrigated agriculture and the Moors' expropriation of their lands on the right bank of the Senegal River. More than any other ethnic group in Senegal, the Tukulor have supported movements in Mauritania to overthrow the present regime there and spurred the Senegalese government to defend their traditional land tenure rights. Reputed to be the most pious of Senegal's ethnic groups, the Tukulor do not look favorably upon the great influence exercised by the predominantly Wolof brotherhoods in the country's political and religious life. Tukulor traditionalists deplore the Wolofization process that is taking place among the Tukulor living in Dakar and other major urban areas. They also fear an influx of non-Tukulor populations coming into the Senegal River Valley with the further development of irrigated agriculture.

The Peulhs, who in the past led a seminomadic life, have become increasingly sedentarized. Drought, the development of the Diama and Manantali dams, which submerged former grazing lands, and the takeover of their traditional grazing areas by Wolof farmers seeking new land to cultivate have all contributed to the decline of their old way of life.

Senegal's non-African population, mostly French and Lebanese, has dropped sharply since independence, with more than 90 percent living in the Cap Vert region. The French population has declined from 50,000 to fewer than 15,000. A reduced French military presence, Africanization of the private and public sectors, and the dismal state of the Senegalese economy have all been major factors underlying the shrinking size of the French community in Senegal.

Approximately 30,000 to 35,000 Lebanese live in Senegal.[11] The overwhelming majority of these are Shiite Muslims who have their own cultural and religious institutions. Unlike the French, most of the Lebanese who came to Senegal learned Wolof and tried to develop friendly ties with prominent Senegalese political and religious personalities, to whom they look for protection. Since independence, the Senegalese government has refrained from launching anti-Lebanese campaigns or nationalizing Lebanese firms despite complaints from Senegalese businessmen who see the Lebanese as blocking their entry into many areas of business. Although the majority of Lebanese have taken Senegalese citizenship, they nevertheless remain a vulnerable group because they are still regarded as foreigners by most Senegalese. During the 1980s, the situation of well-educated young Lebanese professionals became more problematic. It was difficult for them to find employment because of the economic crisis and the Senegalization policies of the government. As a result, a growing number of young Lebanese professionals left Senegal to establish themselves in Europe and North America during the late 1980s and early 1990s.

Relations among different Senegalese ethnic groups are generally good despite some ethnic rivalry between the Wolof and the Tukulor, between the northerners and the Casamançais, and between older Dakar residents and newcomers. The

Afro-European *métis* population, which once played a vital role in Senegal's political, economic, and cultural life, has declined, and many of the children of the old Afro-European elite have departed for France, where they have been integrated into French society. In the mid-1990s, Senegal no longer had any Afro-European personalities with the stature of an André Guillabert, who served as ambassador to France and held high party and government posts under Senghor, or a Jean Diallo, who headed the Senegalese army for many years.

Senegal has its own brand of ethnic politics operating at both the national and local levels. The national government thus attempts to give representation to the major ethnic groups in the government, and government ministers often tend to choose their closest collaborators from their own ethnic groups. The constitution outlaws ethnic political parties, however, and the PS has discouraged the establishment of ethnic caucuses within local party units.

Solidarity Networks
and Self-Help Associations

One of the most striking features of Senegalese society is the individual's membership in numerous solidarity networks, which provide a modicum of economic and social security and a safety net even for the poorest of the poor. The pathetic person in Senegal is not the one with no material means but the one without social networks. Communal values stressing helping those in need coupled with membership in diverse solidarity networks explain how the Senegalese have been able to cope during the current economic crisis.

Senegalese individuals and communities rely on their social ties to meet certain needs or to resolve specific problems.[12] These ties include family, friends, ethnic groups, neighborhood associations, religious brotherhoods, political parties, work associates, trade unions, age sets, old boys networks, nongovernmental organizations (NGOs), various social and professional associations, hometown networks, sports and cultural associations, and contacts with influential foreign individuals and organizations such as Peace Corps volunteers and expatriate NGOs.

The Senegalese, like the Americans, are a nation of joiners. Nearly every Senegalese is a member of several organizations. The Western-educated urban elite belong to modern international organizations like the Rotary Club, Soroptimists, and Amnesty International. Senegal also has many modern and traditional organizations to deal with the poor and needy. The Muslim brotherhoods and the Catholic church have their own charitable institutions. The imam of the Grande Mosquée of Dakar distributes alms each Friday.[13] The beggars themselves are well organized, laying claim to various locations within the capital as their own personal turf. The blind and handicapped have formal associations that receive recognition and some financial support from the government.

During the 1980s, a remarkable proliferation of local self-help associations sprang up in urban neighborhoods and villages throughout Senegal. Several fac-

Figure 5.2 Urban Koranic school. (Photo by Michel Renaudeau)

tors fostered this movement: (1) the crisis in public finances, which reduced the amount of state funds available for public goods and services and small-scale development activities; (2) a decline in the so-called *mentalité d'assisté* (dependency syndrome) on the part of members of the Senegalese population, who were forced to take more initiative to meet their needs; and (3) the growing involvement of expatriate NGOs in development activities as donors distributed more of their aid through these organizations.

Village-based parent-student associations have played an increasingly important role in financing school construction and providing school supplies and materials in the rural areas. In a a similar manner, village health committees have been organized to build maternity and village health centers and to manage the distribution of simple medicines. Neighborhood associations have also been organized in Dakar to deal with garbage collection and other sanitation problems.[14]

In the countryside, associations have been formed to plant village woodlots and to manage other natural resources. In the Senegal River region, peasants associations like the Association des Agriculteurs du Walo (Walo Farmers' Association)[15] and the Féderation des Soninkés (Soninké Federation) have organized the local farmers to launch their own irrigated agricultural projects and to reject the tutelage of the Société d'Aménagement et d'Exploitation des Terres du Delta (Corporation for the Development and Exploitation of Delta Lands—SAED), the state water development agency. Donors and expatriate NGOs have helped to finance these small-scale development activities. Various hometown associations

led by elites working in Dakar or abroad have also sent funds to their villages to finance projects such as mosque construction, wells, improved housing, motor
pumps for irrigation, and the like.

The establishment of various self-help associations has been an integral part of
Senegalese community development and survival strategies. The associations
provide a training ground for local populations to manage their own affairs, and
in time, they will evolve into forceful advocates for local community interests vis-
à-vis the national government and provide a new generation of locally based political leadership. For example, Abdoulaye Diop, the founder of the Walo Farmers'
Association, has already become a prominent political figure in the Senegal River
delta region where he started his group.

Women

One of the most significant developments in Senegalese society since independence has been the change in the role and status of women.[16] Greater participation by women in Senegalese politics has been promoted by greater access to education and government policies instituted since the mid-1970s to advance their
welfare in general and to reduce their traditional workload in the rural areas. In
1982, as part of its response to the UN Decade for Women, the Senegalese government launched a National Action Plan to improve the status and condition of
women in Senegal. For their part, Senegalese women now have greater expectations for a larger voice in society.

Throughout most of the colonial period, Senegalese women were confined
largely to traditional roles and had little access to formal education. As late as
1965, fewer than 1 percent of Senegalese women could speak or write in French.
During the colonial period, Muslim girls rarely went to public school and few attended school as frequently as boys. However, since independence, there has been
a sharp increase in the number and percentage of Senegalese girls in school. In
1961 the ratio of boys to girls attending primary schools was more than 2 to 1; by
the beginning of the 1990s, girls composed 42 percent of the primary school population and their numbers had grown from 41,000 in 1961 to more than 300,000.
The number and percentage of Muslim girls attending Koranic schools has also
risen dramatically.

Before 1946, Senegalese women, even residents of the Four Communes, were
not allowed to vote. In the postwar period, women were given suffrage and were
active in Senegalese politics, but they held no major public office. Women were
absent from the National Assembly until 1963 when Caroline Diop became
Senegal's first woman deputy. Fifteen years later, however, all three parties contending the 1978 legislative elections had several women candidates on their list.
After the elections, Caroline Diop and Maimouna Kane became the first women
to attain ministerial rank in the Senegalese government. Both women have played

a highly visible role in national and international women's politics and have used their office to vigorously promote the status of women.

During the 1980s and early 1990s, the involvement of women in politics increased. Senegal's first woman mayor was elected in 1984, and changes in election rules assured that at least one woman would be elected as a rural councillor in every rural community. One of the most interesting recent developments has been a direct appeal for women's support by the PS and the PDS and other opposition parties. In 1992, government-controlled television presented a long program on the role of women in politics featuring women representatives of several major political parties taking part in a debate. Moreover, leaders of the women's wings of the main parties received more attention in party functions and meetings during the 1993 presidential and legislative campaigns. Following the May 1993 elections, ten women held seats as deputies, a record number.

Senegal's educated women have also begun to make their mark on the intellectual and cultural life of the nation. Women constitute one-third of the University of Dakar's total enrollment. Senegal has produced distinguished women writers like Mariama Ba and Aminata Sow Fall, whose novels have won prizes in Senegal and Europe.[17] A small number of Senegalese women now teach at the University of Dakar or, like Fatou Sow, conduct research at the prestigious Institut Fondamental d'Afrique Noire (Basic Research Institute of Black Africa—IFAN) and present papers at international conferences. Marie-Angelique Savané, in addition to editing *Famille et Développement,* a Dakar-based magazine widely read throughout francophone Africa, has been at the forefront of Senegal's feminist movement. And despite women's generally second-class status within Islam, Senegalese female Muslim intellectuals have organized women's study groups and seminars discussing various religious themes. Western-educated Senegalese women have been openly critical of the rise of fundamentalist currents in Senegal and their implication for women's rights, and leading Senegalese female Muslim intellectuals and teachers have rejected demands by some fundamentalists that they wear the veil as not in accordance with African traditions.

Change has proceeded rapidly in Dakar, where women have been entering the labor market as secretaries, typists, sales clerks, maids, and unskilled workers in textile mills and tuna-canning factories. Four thousand women worked as farm laborers for a fruit and vegetable export firm before its collapse in late 1979.[18] Morals and mores are also evolving rapidly in the urban areas, where the elders complain about a shocking rise in teenage sexual promiscuity and many middle-class women are beginning to advocate family planning—a dramatic change in a country where women have an average of 7.2 children each. Senegal's 1972 Family Code, which provides legal protection for women, has had a much greater impact in the towns than in the countryside.

The rural areas have also experienced a surge in women's consciousness and organizations. Senegal was one of the first African countries to establish a rural development agency—Animation Feminine—designed specifically to organize village women so that they could begin to take steps to improve the quality of family and village life and to involve them more actively in the development process. A government ministry devoted to women's issues was created in 1976. Since then, the ministry has organized hundreds of women's associations at the village level. In 1987, 2,500 of these groups joined to form a national federation. By the mid-1990s, there were more than 3,500 women's groups in the federation.

Rural women have become increasingly involved in managing village forestry resources and operating mechancial millet and rice mills. They play a prominent role on village health committees and in prenatal and postnatal programs. Women's groups have also organized various economic projects—such as vegetable gardens, small livestock raising, and the like—to supplement individual, family, and community income.

Access to formal education and rural animation programs is steadily transforming the traditional attitudes of rural women. Despite the changes in the countryside, however, there is still a wide social and cultural gap between the better-educated and more sophisticated women of Dakar and their sisters in the countryside that reflects the general social and cultural gap between the capital and the interior. And despite their gains in the political arena, women remain largely outside the inner circles of the powerholders in government and in Senegalese political parties.

Youth

The future of Senegal's youth has become a matter of growing concern for Senegal's national leaders. Urban youth have become increasingly restless and alienated from the regime and more prone to violence. The main participants in the post-1988 election riots and the 1989 rampage against the Moors were angry and disaffected urban youths. During the early 1990s, student unrest was growing owing to deteriorating conditions at the university and frustration at the lack of employment opportunities after graduation. Students of the newly opened Saint Louis University launched a strike in early 1992 and took some university officials hostage before settling. Student strikes also took place in secondary schools throughout the country. In Tambacounda, unemployed local youths blocked the roads to protest the fact that the government was bringing in Senegalese laborers from outside the region to work on road projects.

Like youth in many developing countries, Senegalese youth are embracing new values and becoming increasingly restless about the future. They are the main force underlying the demand for *Sopi*, which means "change" in Wolof.

Urban violence by Senegalese youth has not been the only response to difficult economic times, a deteriorating environment, and alienation from the political establishment. In 1990, Dakar's youth launched spontaneous neighborhood clean-up campaigns (*Set-Sétal*), mobilizing thousands of youngsters in the capital.[19] In addition to physically cleaning up the city, the *Set-Sétal* campaign sparked an explosion of artistic expression as young people painted hundreds of wall murals and other artwork on buildings throughout the city. The murals portrayed health and environmental themes; Senegalese historical figures, such as Lat Dior, Blaise Diagne, and Lamine Guèye; religious leaders, such as Malick Sy and Amadou Bamba; black heroes, such as Nelson Mandela and Martin Luther King; and traditional Senegalese symbols and motifs, including the lion and the prankster rabbit (*leuk-le-lièvre*).

Providing jobs and a productive place in society for the rising tide of Senegalese youth entering the job market each year has become one of the most difficult tasks facing the country. Nearly all of the 100,000 new people entering the labor force each year are under twenty-five. By the end of the 1980s, there were 25,000 secondary and university graduates seeking first-time employment with only 4,000 to 5,000 jobs open in the modern sector. Because of the poor employment prospects, Senegalese university students often stay in school as long as possible, especially when monthly stipends and scholarships provide them with a decent standard of living. The steady expansion of the student body from 1,000 in 1960 to 10,000 in 1980 and to nearly 20,000 in the 1990s has put severe strains on Cheikh Anta Diop University's physical plant. Although students constitute a privileged group within Senegalese society, student unrest may eventually pose a serious threat to the stability of the regime, especially if large numbers of students fail to find work in the government or private sector. Structural adjustment programs have reduced opportunities for government employment to absorb graduates.

The less educated urban youth are also restless. Juvenile delinquency, drug use, prostitution, and AIDS have become major concerns in recent years. Religious leaders have attacked the degradation of values and the decline of tradition and morality. Secular opposition intellectuals blame government corruption and neo-colonial economic policies for fostering greed and unemployment and appeal to Senegal's urban youth to reject the regime. The government has tried to solve some of these problems through the Youth and Sports Ministry, which provides jobs and athletic facilities for urban youth. During the late 1980s, the government organized a special agency, the Agence d'Exécution des Travaux d'Intérêt Public Contre le Sous-Emploi (Implementation Agency for Public Works Projects Fighting Underemployment—AGETIP), financed by the World Bank, to provide employment outlets and training for unskilled urban youth.

Although their lifestyles and educational levels are markedly different from those of urban youth, Senegal's rural youth share similar kinds of concerns. In many densely populated areas of rural Senegal, land shortages are obliging young unmarried males to migrate to the pioneer zones or go to the towns to look for jobs. Even where land is available, the unremunerative nature of Senegalese agriculture has spurred a large-scale rural exodus. Many young Senegalese have gone abroad, and there are an estimated 200,000 Senegalese living outside the country. Approximately 60,000 of these work in France as janitors, street-cleaners, and un-skilled laborers; others work as traders and artisans throughout Black Africa. Their earnings help support the families they leave behind. When they return, they often bring with them new ideas and values.

Senegalese rural youth are less attached to traditional values than their elders and more individualistic. They have fewer caste biases and are more willing to marry outside their ethnic groups. Lower-caste youth are also less willing to ac-cept orders from the traditional nobility. One of the major concerns of Senegalese youth is the high cost of the bride-price, which prevents many men from getting married before their mid-thirties. Like their urban brothers, young men in rural areas enthusiastically support government efforts to put an official ceiling on the bride-price.

Rural youth groups and associations attempting to find new and improved ways for young people to make a living have sprung up throughout the country since the beginning of the 1980s. The village elders have strongly backed the emerging groups, which they hope will stem the rural exodus. The government has also stepped up its efforts in recent years to provide more incentives for rural youth to stay in the countryside. It has sponsored special training programs for young artisans, farmers, and herders; provided land in sparsely populated areas; and established rural youth centers and athletic facilities in the rural communities.

The lowering of the voting age to eighteen and a serious government voter reg-istration campaign put tens of thousands of young Senegalese on the electoral roll for the first time. The PS, PDS, and other opposition parties campaigned hard to win the support of these new voters in the 1993 presidential and legislative elec-tions. Despite their desire for change, Senegalese young people did not turn out to vote in large numbers in the 1993 national election. Their failure to vote dashed the hopes of the opposition for a better showing and reflected youth's widespread alienation from the political system.

Popular Culture and the Arts

Senegal's popular culture is rich and vibrant, covering an astounding range of African, Islamic, and Western motifs and modes of expression. The development of a new popular art form—glass paintings, which depict religious and historical scenes and personalities—is only one example of Senegalese artistic creativity. Senegalese goldsmiths, weavers, and tailors, using a combination of traditional and modern techniques, also produce some of West Africa's most exquisitely de-signed jewelry, carpets, and clothing.

The *griots* are the main repositories of traditional Senegalese culture. The older ones are generally illiterate and attended neither European nor Koranic schools. The *griot* prepares for his profession as oral historian and musician by doing

practical exercises to develop his memory, by learning the genealogies and histo-
ries of the great families, and by learning to compose songs and play traditional
musical instruments.[20]

In precolonial Senegal, *griots* lived off the generosity of the kings and nobles
whom they served. Although becoming increasingly rare, one can still find
Senegalese families, particularly among the Tukulor nobility, who have retained
their family *griots* and continue to support them financially. The *griots* have kept
alive the traditional folk wisdom, which they transmit in the form of stories and
proverbs that provide moral lessons and truths for the listener to ponder.[21]

Some talented *griots* today earn an excellent living as publicists for political
parties and prominent politicians. These *griots* compose and sing songs praising
the merits of their patrons or ridiculing their rivals. They are an important part of
every major political rally. Abdou Diouf's *griot* has his own radio program; other
griots have learned how to play modern musical instruments, such as the electric
guitar, and to manage complicated sound equipment. Many have organized their
own bands that play an eclectic blend of traditional African music and modern
Black American style jazz and rhythm and blues as well as West Indian reggae.
Some bands even have their own female vocalists.

The government has encouraged the preservation of traditional Senegalese music and dance by establishing a national Senegalese ballet company and organizing
regional dance troupes and competitions. The Senegalese national ballet company
has traveled abroad frequently, enjoying much praise from Western critics.
Performing traditional dances is still one of the most popular forms of recreation
in the rural areas, and children learn to dance almost as soon as they learn to walk.

The music industry has become one of Senegal's major growth sectors. Senegal
even has its own world-class recording studio—Studio 2000. Unfortunately, however,
the country has more musical talent than it can support. In order to make big money,
the best known and most talented have to seek markets outside of Senegal and rely on
European and American recording studios. During the 1980s and early 1990s,
Senegalese singers like Youssou Ndour and Baaba Maal emerged as international
stars. Many musicians, however, cannot afford the cost of electronic instruments and
sound equipment. Some have complained about the small royalties they get and the
loss of income due to pirating of their cassettes. In 1990, Senegalese musicians organized the Association Nationale des Métiers de la Musique (National Association of
Musical Professions—ANAMM) to promote and protect their interests.

Senegalese music speaks to youth and provides a vehicle for expressing traditional values and critiques of contemporary Senegalese society while integrating
Senegalese youth into world culture. In a newspaper poll taken in Dakar in
January 1995, Youssou Ndour emerged as the most-admired Senegalese of 1994,
coming well ahead of Abdoulaye Wade and Abdou Diouf. Ndour, whose music
expresses the African urban experience, had recently won a European gold record
award for one of his songs and returned to Senegal a hero. Another Senegalese
world culture star, Baaba Maal, uses his more traditional music to raise consciousness. Senegalese rappers, who preach their social messages on television and

Figure 5.3 Youssou Ndour, Senegalese singer and world music star. (Photo courtesy of Le Soleil)

radio programs, have also become increasingly well known in the country. Senegalese musicians, among the best in Africa, work with American and European artists. Together, they have put on major concerts in Africa, Europe, and North America.

Senegal has also produced successful filmmakers, the most prominent being Ousmane Sembène, the Senegalese novelist whose films have won him international acclaim. Through his films, Sembène has provided a powerful critique of colonialism (*Camp de Thiaroye*), the marabouts (*Ceddo*), and the corruption of Senegal's nouveau riche bourgeoisie (*Xaala*).

The Senegalese are enthusiastic sports fans. One of the most popular sports is the traditional Senegalese version of wrestling, or *"la lutte,"* which combines theatrics with wrestling skills and provides marvelous entertainment for the spectators. Professional Senegalese wrestlers usually come from lower-caste backgrounds and serve as champions of their respective ethnic group or region. Much of the excitement takes place before the match actually begins as each wrestler tries to psych the other out by boasting of his prowess and past deeds. Each wrestler has his own entourage of drummers and praise-singers to build him up and intimidate the opponent. The wrestlers also wear many *gris-gris,* or talismans, to give them extra strength and protection.

Introduced by the French around World War I, soccer is the most popular modern sport in Senegal, especially among urban youth. But its popularity has spread to the rural areas, where each village has its own youth team. Senegal has the equivalent of a soccer major league where teams representing different regions in the country play regular schedules and vie for the national championship.[22] In January 1992, Senegal hosted the African Soccer Cup matches. Although Senegal was touted by many observers as a possible winner, its hopes were dashed by a defeat by Cameroon in the semifinals. Diouf had hoped that a victory would bolster the nation's morale and win the regime more popularity since sports and politics are intimately connected in Senegal.[23]

Although French is the official language of the country and the main language of instruction in the schools, it has not become an integral part of popular culture. Even the most educated Senegalese are far from being "Black Frenchmen" culturally. Most Senegalese prefer to speak their first language at home and among friends. The Dakar Wolof dialect, which absorbs or Africanizes many French words and European concepts into its vocabulary, is in the process of becoming Senegal's unofficial national language, even for the country's non-Wolof populations, especially in the urban areas where youth communicate primarily in Wolof.

The liberalization of the regime during the early 1980s, urbanization, and the development of television and radio programming have all contributed to the growing importance of the modern mass media in Senegal's political and cultural life. In recent years, television has become increasingly accessible to the Senegalese masses. In 1980, there were only 8,000 TV sets in the country; by the beginning of the 1990s, this figure had climbed to more than 250,000. Radio still remains the most important medium, especially in the countryside. Nearly every Senegalese family has at least one radio. In 1990, Senegalese owned more than 800,000 radio sets.

During the 1980s, the number of newspapers and magazines in Senegal increased dramatically. In addition to the government-controlled daily *Le Soleil* (The Sun), Senegal has two other daily newspapers, a vigorous opposition press, two satirical journals that poke fun at the government and the political parties, independent investigative journals that provide excellent and well-documented analyses of diverse political, economic, and social issues, and an Islamic press. At the present time, these publications are geared to the urban, Western-educated reader. Although some newspapers print an occasional article in Wolof, the basic language of the press is French. Adult literacy programs in Senegal's other six official national languages—Wolof, Puular, Serer, Diola, Mandinka, and Soninké—remain sparse and have not yet produced a broad audience for newspapers in the national languages.[24] The devaluation of the CFA franc in 1994 posed a serious threat to the viability of the Senegalese print media because it doubled the cost of newsprint. The devaluation also priced imported books and periodicals beyond the reach of all but the wealthiest Senegalese.

During the mid and late 1980s, the Diouf regime put pressure on offending journalists to restrain themselves in their critique of the regime and attacks on leading government personalities by taking them to court. For example, in 1990, the editor of *Sopi* was given a six-month prison sentence for publishing an article that claimed that the Supreme Court had falsified the 1988 election results. Government control of the courts, in effect, encouraged journalists to impose limits on their attacks on the regime and placed subtle restrictions on press freedom. In July 1994, *Jeune Afrique* was banned for a year following a court decision finding the Paris-based weekly guilty of libel for implying that a high-ranking Senegalese civil servant had been removed from his post for trying to obtain information concerning the assassination of Babacar Sèye. Various journalist associations condemned the decision as a violation of freedom of the press and a restraint on the free flow of information.

The quality of journalism has improved considerably in recent years. Independent newspapers have become less strident and more probing in their analyses. *Sopi*, the PDS organ, and other opposition papers adopted a more civil tone when PDS and PIT entered the government in 1991 but again became strident during and after the 1993 national election campaigns. For its part, the progovernment *Le Soleil* now includes a page or so on opposition party activities and prints interviews with opposition leaders.

In April 1991, the government created a mass media advisory commission to give opposition parties regular access to state-run radio and television. This was a major breakthrough since opposition parties had been granted radio and TV access only during the 1983 and 1988 election campaigns. The new policy has led to regular coverage of party activities and vigorous debates of various public issues by government, PS, and opposition leaders.

The mass media in Senegal is changing rapidly and becoming more sophisticated and cosmopolitan. During the early 1990s, Radio Sénégal gave Radio France International an FM band and eighteen hours of tranmission time. At the same time, Canal Horizons, a French pay TV entertainment channel, began operating in Senegal.[25] Senegalese radio and television broadcasting has become more varied with a larger Senegalese content. One can now see and hear more programming in Wolof and other local languages. Television now offers political debates, coverage of political party activities, variety shows, sermons by religious personalities, talk shows, and locally produced musical videos by Senegal's leading musical artists. Despite the freer climate in the mass media, however, radio and TV programming still tend to reflect a progovernment bias. Until recently, the government was reluctant to permit private, independent Senegalese radio stations from operating. In July 1994, SUD FM became the first private Senegalese radio station to go on the air.

Senegalese in the peripheral areas distant from the capital have complained about poor radio and TV reception and are asking the government for stronger broadcasting facilities. While the radio continues to be the most important modern medium for transmitting popular culture in the rural areas, television has become increasingly more important in creating a modern Dakar-Wolof urban culture.

Notes

1. For an analysis of demographic trends in Senegal, see Mohamed Mbodj, Babacar Mane, and Waly Badiane, "Population et développement: Quelle politique" [Population and Development: Which Policy?], in Momar Coumba Diop, ed., *Sénégal: Trajectoires d'un état* [Senegal: Trajectories of a State] (Paris: Editions Karthala, 1992), pp. 177–204.

2. The 1988 provisional census figures showed the following membership figures for Senegal's three main brotherhoods: Tijanis, 50.4 percent; Mourides, 34.2 percent; and Qadiri, 6.7 percent. These figures reflected an increase in Mouride membership at the expense of the two other brotherhoods. See François Zuccarelli, "Les Catholiques du Sénégal" [The Catholics of Senegal], *L'Afrique et l'Asie Modernes*, No. 165 (Summer 1990): 79.

3. The Mourides are the most written about Islamic brotherhood in Senegal. Because of the attention they receive, their influence in the country is perhaps somewhat overstated in the literature.

4. See, for example, "Les explications de Thierno Mountaga Tall" [Thierno Mountaga Tall's Explanations], *Muntu*, No. 44 (June 1989) for Tall's explanation of the cause of the interethnic conflict in Mauritania and the events leading to the 1989 Senegal-Mauritanian crisis.

5. For accounts of Ahmed Niasse's efforts to launch a radical Islamic party, see Moriba Magassouba, *L'Islam au Sénégal: Demain les mollahs?* [Islam in Senegal: Tomorrow the Mullahs?] (Paris: Editions Karthala, 1985), pp. 130–137; and François Zuccarelli, "A propos de l'intégrisme sénégalais" [Concerning Senegalese Fundamentalism], *L'Afrique et l'Asie Modernes*, No. 154 (Autumn 1987): 17–18.

6. For an interesting discussion of the stance of Senegalese political parties toward preserving a secular state and the prospects for an Islamic republic in Senegal, see Magassouba, *L'Islam au Sénégal*, pp. 138–212.

7. For a detailed analysis of the current status of the Catholic community in Senegal, see Zuccarelli, "Les Catholiques du Sénégal," pp. 78–96.

8. For the best discussion of the dynamics of Wolof society, see Abdoulaye-Bara Diop, *La société Wolof, tradition et changement: Les systèmes d'inégalité et de domination* [Wolof Society, Tradition and Change: Systems of Inequality and Domination] (Paris: Editions Karthala, 1981); and *La famille Wolof* [The Wolof Family] (Paris: Editions Karthala, 1985).

9. For some of the historical background to the separatist uprising in the Casamance, see Dominique Darbon, *L'Administration et le paysan en Casamance: Essai d'anthropologie administrative* [The Administration and the Peasant in Casamance: An Essay in Administrative Anthropology] (Paris: Pedone, 1988); and Dominique Darbon, "Le culturalisme Bas-Casmançais" [Lower Casamance Culture], *Politique Africaine*, No. 14 (1984): 125–128.

10. For a concise analysis of the background to the conflict, see Michael Horowitz, "Victims of Development" *Development Anthropology Network* 7, No. 2 (Fall 1989): 1–8.

11. For a recent account of the current status of the Lebanese community, see Said Boumedouha, "Adjustment to West African Realities: The Lebanese in Senegal," *Africa* 60, No. 4 (1990): 538–549.

12. ENDA, a Dakar-based NGO that has supported the activities of community organizations in urban and rural settings, has produced numerous monographs describing the relationships between solidarity networks, community values, and community action projects. See, for example, Emmanuel Seyni Ndione, *Dynamique urbaine d'une société en grappe: Un cas, Dakar* [Urban Dynamics of a Society in Change: The Dakar Case] (Dakar: ENDA, 1987).

13. For the role of Senegalese Islam in providing help to the needy, see Robert Vuarin, "L'Enjeu de la misère pour L'Islam sénégalais" [The Stakes of Misery for Senegalese Islam], *Revue Tiers Monde* 31, No. 123 (July–September 1990): 601–621.

14. For a study of the richness of urban associational life, see Michèle O'Dèye, *Les associations en villes africaines: Dakar-Brazzaville* [Associations in African Cities: Dakar and Brazzaville] (Paris: Editions L'Harmattan, 1985).

15. For more details on this association, see Daniel Descendre, *L'autodétermination paysanne en Afrique: Solidarité ou tutelle des ONG partenaires* [Peasant Self-Determination in Africa: Solidarity or External NGO Tutelage] (Paris: Editions l'Harmattan, 1991).

16. For a detailed analysis of the status of Senegalese women, see Lucy E. Creevey, "The Impact of Islam on Women in Senegal," *The Journal of Developing Areas* 25 (April 1991): 347–368. For a Senegalese perspective on the UN Decade for Women and its impact on Senegalese women, see Fatou Sow, "Senegal: The Decade and Its Consequences," *Issue* 17, No. 2 (1989): 32–36.

17. For example, see Mariama Ba, *Une si longue lettre* [A Very Long Letter] (Dakar: Nouvelles Editions Africaines, 1980) and Aminata Sow Fall, *La grève des battù* [The Beggars' Strike] (Dakar: Nouvelles Editions Africaines, 1980).

18. For a discussion of Senegal's working women, see Francine Kane, "Femmes prolétaires du Sénégal, à la ville et aux champs" [Proletarian Women of Senegal, in the city and the countryside], *Cahiers d'Etudes Africaines* 17, No. 65 (1976): 77–94.

19. On the *Set-Sétal* phenomenon, see Jacques Bugnicourt, "Soudain, les murs de Dakar fleurient sous les fresques" [Suddenly, Dakar's Wall Flower Under the Murals] *Le Monde Diplomatique* (April 1991): 28; and the exceptionally revealing and perceptive article by Mamadou Diouf, "Fresques murales et écriture de l'histoire: Le Set/Sétal à Dakar" [Mural and Written Frescoes of History: The Set/Setal phenomenon in Dakar] *Politique Africaine*, No. 46 (June 1992): 41–54.

20. For a fascinating discussion of the *griot*'s training, see Assane Sylla, *La philosophie morale des Wolof* [The Moral Philosophy of the Wolof] (Dakar: Sankoré, 1978), pp. 121–123. For a fascinating analysis of the cultural influence of griots in Senegal today, see Cornelia Panzacchi, "The Livelihoods of Traditional Griots in Modern Senegal," *Africa* 64, No. 2 (1994): 190–210.

21. For excellent examples of Senegalese folktales, see Birago Diop, *Les contes d'Amadou Koumba* [The Tales of Amadou-Koumba] (Paris: Présence Africaine, 1961).

22. For an analysis of Senegalese soccer and other sports associations, see Jean-Marie Mignon, *Les associations sportives au Sénégal* [Sports Associations in Senegal] (Bordeaux: Centre d'Etude d'Afrique Noire, 1987).

23. See "Coupe d'Afrique des nations: Un ballon trés politique" [The African Cup Games: A Very Political Event], *Jeune Afrique*, No. 1620 (January 24–January 31, 1992): 5–6.

24. Although expanding, adult functional literacy programs have not received much support by the government, have been heavily dependent upon NGO and donor financing, and have not generated sufficient reading materials to promote the development of local libraries in indigenous languages.

25. Prominent Senegalese associated with this new venture include Habib Thiam, Moustapha Niasse, Fara N'Diaye, a former lieutenant of Abdoulaye Wade's, a prominent marabout, and several Senegalese business leaders. See Ariane Poissonnier, "Sénégal: Images trés privées" [Senegal: Very Private Images], *Jeune Afrique*, No. 1543 (July 25–August 1, 1990): 27.

6

TOWARD
THE YEAR 2000:
WHITHER SENEGAL?

I N THE MID-1990S, Senegal was going through its most difficult economic and social crises since independence. The *grands projéts* of the 1970s and 1980s had not achieved their goals in leading Senegal to economic prosperity. Donor patience was wearing thin, and it was unlikely that Senegal would be able to obtain the same levels of economic aid that it had enjoyed during the 1980s and early 1990s. In the mid-1990s, the government also had to deal with the inflationary effects of the January 11, 1994, devaluation of the CFA franc, which threatened to further erode Senegalese living standards. Moreover, the Diouf regime seemed to have no clearcut strategy to overcome the economic crisis. To many observers, the prospects of Senegal's climbing out of the economic morass by the year 2000 seemed bleak.[1]

The deterioration of the political climate following the Sèye assassination in May 1993 and the rioting of February 16, 1994, which led to the death of five Senegalese policemen, heightened the sense of crisis. Senegalese democratic institutions and political stability were further threatened when the government reacted to the riots by banning political opposition demonstrations and arresting opposition leaders such as Abdoulaye Wade and Landing Savané. The image of a democratic, financially sound, and prosperous Senegal by the year 2000 that Diouf has presented in his 1993 presidential campaign did not seem to be just around the corner.

The Mystique of the Year 2000

Both Senghor and Diouf offered a hopeful vision of the future incarnated in the Mystique of the Year 2000. Senghor first launched the Mystique of the Year 2000 campaign in December 1969 in his report to the Seventh UPS National Party Congress,[2] projecting an image of a modern and prosperous Senegal that would have tripled real per capita income and entered the ranks of the world's industrialized nations by the turn of the millennium. During the early 1990s, it became clear that Senghor's vision would not be realized. Instead of tripling real per capita income, Senegal would be doing well to reverse the steady decline that had taken place since independence. Rather than entering the ranks of the world's industrialized nations, Senegal was going through a phase of deindustrialization as inefficient industries went out of business and others streamlined their personnel. During the the late 1980s and early 1990s, Senegal's industrial sector had lost 20,000 jobs.

Despite the gloomy economic realities and the failure of most of the *grands projéts* launched while he was prime minister, Abdou Diouf maintained his predecessor's optimism about the future and the Mystique of the Year 2000. The constitutional revisions accompanying the electoral reform of 1991 extended the president's mandate from five to seven years, which meant that Diouf could serve until the very end of the century.

In the 1993 election campaign, Diouf formulated a *contrat programme* for the year 2000 to revitalize the Senegalese economy and propel it to better days.[3] Diouf's program had three major planks: (1) the revitalization of Senegal's productive capacity, especially in agriculture; (2) improvement in the quality of life—including more and higher-quality education, the allocation of a larger percentage of the national budget to the health sector, decent and less expensive housing for Senegal's urban populations, greater support of the arts and cultural activities, and the like; and (3) the development of an integrated West African economic community with Senegal taking a leading role in promoting greater interregional trade and a unified and stable monetary system. Diouf's program also called for the creation of 20,000 new jobs a year in the private sector and massive state financing to stimulate the launching of new private-sector enterprises. While Diouf's *contrat programme* clearly reflected the aspirations of Senegalese for a better life, it was less clear whether the platform embodied a real economic strategy for getting Senegal out of the economic doldrums or simply an appealing election year wish list to convince the Senegalese people that the Diouf regime was acting on behalf of their interests.

Diouf's optimistic projections contrasted with the more somber perspective appearing in a study commissioned in the late 1980s by the Senegalese government as part of the preparation for the Eighth Social and Economic Development Plan (1989–1995). Instead of looking toward the year 2000, the study projected different scenarios for the year 2015.[4] By then, the Senegalese population would grow to 16 million and Senegal would be a predominantly urban society with 56 percent of its citizens living in towns and cities. The study listed several factors holding the economy back and making Senegal increasingly dependent upon external resources to finance development investments: (1) Senegal was a consumer society with consumption outstripping its productive capacity; (2) the educational system was becoming less and less able to meet the country's real needs; (3) the degradation of the environment fueled by growing demographic pressure on Senegal's fishing, forest, land, and water resources was undermining Senegal's natural resource base; (4) the country suffered from the low productivity of state investments, especially in the area of high-cost irrigated agriculture; (5) the state was still intervening too much in the Senegalese economy and Senegalese depended too much upon the state to provide for their needs; (6) the urban environment was deteriorating because of air pollution, inadequate garbage collection and sanitation facilities, and the chaotic development of new neighborhoods lacking basic urban infrastructure; (7) the economy was unable to generate enough jobs to absorb the massive flow of young Senegalese entering the labor market each year; and (8) because of inadequate employment opportunities, the country was in danger of losing its best-trained and most dynamic elements to the industrialized world.

One of the few bright spots of the study was its finding that the various associations, self-help groups, and economic organizations that had emerged in recent years showed high levels of organizational capacity and initiative in developing solutions to difficult problems. The study also noted that Senegal's favorable geographic location provided it with many opportunities for improving its ability to compete in such areas as tourism, international transport and communications, research, and other service-oriented activities.

Diouf's *contrat programme* for 2000 reflected some of the suggestions made in the study by placing priority on making improvements in the educational system, decentralizing government and transferring more authority to local bodies, pursuing West African regional economic integration, promoting integrated agropastoral agricultural production systems, and protecting and developing Senegal's natural resource base.

Unlike Diouf, opposition leaders offered no alternative plan for the year 2000. Instead, they campaigned largely on the theme of "Throw the rascals out who have ruined Senegal's economy and transformed Senegal into a beggar nation heavily dependent upon foreign aid to keep the country afloat." In the mid-1990s, however, the Mystique of the Year 2000 meant little to most Senegalese who were struggling to survive and adapt to the changing economic conditions.

Senegal's Political Future: Democracy or Disintegration?

The contours and quality of Senegal as an African democracy in the year 2000 will be affected by the outcome of two apparently contradictory trends. During the early 1990s, Senegal experienced both the strengthening of its democratic institutions and the growing alienation of the public, in general, and youth, in particular, from politics.

The democratic institutions were strengthened by an impressive list of changes in the political system, including: (1) the reduction of central government control over local government institutions and the transfer of more powers to locally elected officials in 1990; (2) the 1991 reform of the electoral code, which expanded the electorate to give youth a greater voice in politics, provided for mechanisms and procedures approved by most of Senegal's opposition parties to insure fair and open elections, and revised the electoral regime to insure broader representation in the National Assembly; (3) the measures taken to insure opposition parties regular and greater access to state-run media; (4) the openness of the 1993 presidential and legislative elections; (5) the strengthening of civil society as reflected in the emergence of relatively autonomous interest groups, such as peasant and consumer associations, new business organizations and trade unions, and women's groups, as well as independent newspapers not dominated by the ruling party or subordinated to the state; and (6) the declining role of maraboutic intervention in Senegalese elections.[5]

Faced with a grave social and economic crisis, Diouf also reached out to the opposition to broaden his government after the 1993 national elections. At the same time, opposition political leaders like Landing Savané and Iba Der Thiam, though critical of government policy, seemed willing to engage in dialogue with the government rather than resort to demagogic tactics. The seriousness of the opposition and its apparent desire to avoid heightening social tensions and the disintegration of the country offered some hope for the future of Senegalese democracy.

The gains made in strengthening democratic institutions were undermined, however, by the drawn-out process of validating the results of the 1993 presidential elections; the Babacar Sèye affair, the most serious case of political assassination since independence; the February 16, 1994, riots; the government's jailing of Wade, Savané, and other opposition leaders; and accusations by Amnesty International that the regime had tortured political prisoners. The riots placed a heavy strain on Senegal's fragile democratic institutions and pointed to Diouf's apparent inability to maintain control over a worsening situation.

The rioting was, in part, a result of the growing frustration of large segments of urban Senegal with traditional politics. This trend was reflected by the record low voter turnouts in the national elections;[6] the even smaller turnout of young people voting in the 1993 elections despite the appeals made to them by all political parties; a decline in Wade's credibility as an alternative to Diouf and the PS; the widespread belief that Senegal's political leaders did not share the sacrifices they were asking the people to accept to overcome the country's economic crisis; and the rising number of strikes, protests, and other forms of social agitation by urban youth, students, business associations, and trade unions.

The future of the PS as Senegal's ruling party may also be threatened by the current crisis. Prime Minister Habib Thiam has become a political liability to the party. The Dakar-Thiès metropolitan area, which contains nearly a third of Senegal's population, no longer supports the PS. The July 1994 PS Party Congress called for a reorganization of party structures in the Cap Vert region in an effort to make a comeback in the capital in the municipal elections originally scheduled for 1995. The sharp decline in urban purchasing power following the 1994 devaluation will make it very difficult, however, for the PS to make significant gains in popularity.

The main bastions of the party remain in the hinterland. The overwhelming support that voters in the Senegal River region gave to Diouf and the PS in 1993 may not be forthcoming in the future, however, especially if the government decides to allocate large tracts of potentially rich irrigable land to expatriate agrobusinesses or to Senegalese businessmen, politicians, and religious leaders from outside the region. The solid support the PS has enjoyed in the peanut basin is also likely to dwindle in the 1998 legislative elections because of declining maraboutic authority, the disappearance of the older generation of religious leaders who loyally backed Senghor and Diouf, dwindling patronage, and the emergence of well-organized and politically sophisticated peasant associations not affiliated with the PS. The PS will also have to run in a nonpresidential election year and the party candidates will have to run on their own merits. By then, Diouf, if he is still in office, will be close to lame duck status.

The municipal and rural council elections originally scheduled for November 1995 are likely to be delayed until 1996 to coincide with regional council elections and hold down costs. These elections should provide some clues as to the PS's current strength. In the past, opposition parties have tended to boycott local elections. However, in 1995, they were determined to present candidates for local elections, especially in the towns. If they wish to oust the PS, they will need to organize at the grassroots level and seriously contest elections such as these. Obtaining a foothold in the hinterland will be crucial if they are to successfully challenge the PS in the 1998 legislative elections.

Senegal's Economic Future: Prosperity or Decline?

In the mid-1990s, donor pressure finally forced the Senegalese government to take more drastic measures to check government spending and restructure the Senegalese economy. These steps included reducing state personnel costs from 60 percent to only 40 percent of the total national budget and accepting the 50 percent devaluation of the CFA franc. Both measures were sure to reduce living standards in the short-run and be bitterly opposed by Senegal's urban populations.

In January 1994, the National Assembly gave Diouf extensive emergency powers to control wages and prices for a limited period. Failure to prevent hyperinflation would wipe out the competitive advantages to be gained by a devalued currency and further destabilize the economy.

In return for biting the bullet, Senegal expected the donor community to provide sufficient aid during the difficult adjustment period to keep the government solvent and minimize the social costs of the adjustment, which, if unchecked, could destabilize the regime. In the next two or three years, foreign aid will be used primarily to eliminate Senegal's foreign debt, restore the state's solvency, and cushion the negative effects of devaluation on living standards by financing state subsidies for basic commodities, modest wage increases, and employment-generating projects. After a successful adjustment period, public investments theoretically could again be directed toward more directly productive activities.

Assuming that inflationary pressures can be held down to reasonable levels, what will the revamped Senegalese economy look like as the country moves toward the year 2000? One scenario pictures a revitalization of Senegal's traditional rural economy. The higher prices for agricultural commodities like peanuts, cotton, rice, and millet may very well stimulate Senegalese farmers to produce more. Peanut production, which averaged around 700,000 tons in the early 1990s, might increase somewhat but it is unlikely that the peanut will regain its former prominence. Population pressure and declining soil fertility in the peanut basin preclude any big leap forward in peanut or millet production. Cotton production is also unlikely to experience dramatic jumps. In early 1994, producers were smuggling cotton into Gambia, where prices were higher than in Senegal. The peanut basin, which still contains more than half of Senegal's rural population, has little potential for agricultural development. The Casamance, Eastern Senegal, and the Senegal River Valley are more likely candidates for agricultural expansion.

The greatest potential for major gains in agricultural production lies in the underutilized Senegal River region, which has seen steady increases in rice production since the completion of the anti-salt Diama dam in Senegal and the Manantali dam in Mali in the mid and late 1980s. However, these increases have barely compensated for the drop in millet and sorghum production. The Senegalese government and donors have encouraged rice production in the region in order to eliminate the need to import 300,000 to 450,000 tons of rice a year. In the early 1990s, unsubsidized Senegalese rice cost nearly double the price of imported broken rice from Asia. On the surface, the devaluation made Senegalese rice more competitive with imported rice; however, devaluation also meant higher prices for imported inputs, such as machinery and spare parts for maintaining the large dams, motor pumps, and fuel to run the motor pumps. These increases will lead to a sharp rise in production costs. An alternative to making rice the focus of production is to develop a more diversified agricultural economy in the region by promoting livestock, fishing, and horticulture in addition to rice. In the mid-1990s, only 5 percent of the region's potential irrigable land was being exploited. This percentage will have to increase dramatically for Senegal to make greater inroads toward its goal of obtaining food self-sufficiency.

In the modern industrial and commercial sectors, which have been traditionally heavily regulated and protected by the state, the moment of truth is coming. Donor pressure and economic conditions are moving Senegal further and further on the path of economic liberalization. With its back against the wall, the government seems to be endorsing policies to accelerate privatization of state enterprises, end state monopolies, reduce subsidies, and revamp the Labor Code to make it easier to fire workers. By the beginning of 1995, the government had ended import monopolies on rice, sugar, and oilseed products and was preparing to privatize SONOCOS, despite fierce opposition by SONOCOS's management, trade unions, and the political opposition. In 1994, the government, with the support of the World Bank, was making plans to create a Private Sector Foundation to promote private enterprise and activating commissions to explore ways of making the economy more competitive. The government-sponsored July 1994 conference on the national economy, which included representatives from civil society, trade unions, and the private sector, called for a greater role for the private sector and stressed the need for Senegal to develop a dynamic export sector to lead economic growth.[7]

Since the beginning of the 1980s, Senegal has cleverly managed to drag its feet in implementing many donor conditions for offering structural adjustment loans. This strategy will be more difficult to maintain in the future as donors become more insistent and the government's bargaining power declines.

The devaluation has given Senegal's import substitution and export industries a competitive edge in pricing. It remains to be seen whether the industrial sector—which, for the most part, has antiquated production facilities—will be able to take advantage of the new situation. For the first time in years, Senegalese banks in 1995 were awash in liquidity thanks to the repatriation of capital from abroad following devaluation. These same banks, however, remained reluctant to provide credit for Senegalese enterprises.

During the remainder of the 1990s, Senegal's prospects for economic recovery will be influenced by more than the soundness of its economic policies. External factors like world market commodity prices, stable oil prices, aid levels, and access to African and European markets will greatly affect Senegal's prospects for economic recovery.

Even if Senegal manages to sharply increase its agricultural and industrial exports, gains at the macroeconomic level will not necessarily lead to improvements in living standards for Senegalese. On the contrary, current austerity programs and the need to make Senegalese agriculture and industry more competitive will probably require restrictions on wage increases in the private sector and only modest increases in producer prices for agricultural exports. Living standards are

Figure 6.1 Harvesting fish along the Senegal River. Much of Senegal's economic future depends upon full utilization of the river's resources. (Photo by Julie Stedman)

thus likely to go down before they go up. Moreover, privatization could mean that foreign companies may take over many of Senegal's large-scale industries and reap most of the advantages of economic recovery.

Senegal needs political and social stability in the cities and peace in the Casamance and the Senegal River Valley to take full advantage of its economic potential and to revitalize the tourist industry, one of the country's major sources of foreign currency. Senegal's future, to a large extent, depends on developing its rich human resources. Given the current economic situation, it is difficult to see how Senegal can meet the demand for more schools and better-quality education to keep up with its rapidly growing populations without extensive external support. The devaluation has also dealt a crippling blow to Senegal's university system by sharply increasing the cost of higher education while making it more difficult for professors and students to obtain essential equipment, books, and other materials needed for research and learning.

Toward the Year 2000:
Prospects for the Future

Despite the grimness of the present political, economic, and social situation, there are still grounds for hope that the Senegalese will be able to overcome the crises of the mid-1990s. Notwithstanding the escalation in political violence, the Senegalese are likely to seek some sort of compromise to break the recent cycle. Although Abdoulaye Wade has often gone to the brink in appealing to the street to bring down Diouf, he has also backed off when the situation began to get out of hand. And, though not above taking repressive measures to clamp down on his political opponents, Diouf has almost always kept the door open for reconciliation with the opposition.

In March 1995, the negotiations between Diouf and Wade that had begun at the beginning of the year ended with the return of the PDS to the ruling government coalition.[8] Wade once again became minister of state, and his party received four minor cabinet posts. In order to accommodate the PDS without antagonizing his own party, Diouf simply added four more ministerial-level positions to the cabinet. Djibo Ka, the interior minister and a close associate of the president, was the only major PS figure to leave the government, while Habib Thiam stayed on as prime minister.

The rallying of Wade and the PDS to the "enlarged government majority" pointed to a new period of political stability and continuity in Senegal. As minister of state directly attached to the presidency, Wade asserted that he would make major changes in government practices to reduce corruption and would invite in-

Figure 6.2 President Diouf flanked by Prime Minister Habib Thiam and State Minister Abdoulaye Wade. (Photo courtesy of Le Soleil*)*

ternational experts to audit government expenditures. While Wade emphasized that the PDS's participation in the government meant change, the PS insisted that the government would continue its current economic policies. Prime Minister Thiam predicted that the economy would be viable in two years, thanks to his government's reform policies.

The new government reflected a marriage of convenience. For Diouf, Wade's entry meant co-opting the most important political opposition party and having it share the responsibility for making the difficult and politically unpopular economic decisions needed to satisfy the donors. For Wade and the PDS, the return to government brought an end to harassment by the state and access to power and government resources.

Wade's rallying did not surprise the other parties in the opposition. Nevertheless, it meant the end of the political alliance that had brought together Wade, Landing Savané, and Mamadou Dia in the Bokk Sopi Senegaal movement, created in September 1994 and presided over by Wade to pressure the government to accept major reforms. It was inconceivable that Wade could remain president now that he was in the government. Madior Diouf of the RND, which had remained outside the Bokk Sopi Senegaal, called for reviving the old CFD coalition. Other opposition leaders such as Iba Der Thiam and Landing Savané saw Wade's rallying as signifying business as usual and vowed to continue their struggle for reform. All opposition political leaders agreed that there were too many ministers in the government. The relatively moderate language used by Senegalese opposition leaders suggested that they intended to play the role of a loyal and constructive opposition that would work through the system and not appeal to the street to bring the government down.

Wade expressed the hope that he could continue to maintain good personal relationships with his former allies in Bokk Sopi Senegaal, and Diouf implied that he would be open to bringing more opposition parties into the government if they would accept his terms and work together with him to solve the current crisis. The willingness of the government to reach out to its opponents and the willingness of the opposition to retreat from inciting the street to violence once again revealed the proclivity of Senegal's elites to seek a peaceful resolution to political conflict through negotiation and compromise.

Senegal's Western-educated elites take pride in Senegal's status as a democratic model for Black Africa. Most have a strong attachment to democratic values and are thus likely to seek compromise to preserve Senegal's fragile democracy. Most also fear the "Algerianization" of the country and will reject efforts by radical Islamic extremist groups like the Moustarchidines to transform Senegal into an Islamic Republic. In February 1995, the government banned a meeting that was to be held by Cheikh Tidjiane Sy, the father of the leader of the Moustarchidines, because it feared that the meeting might be used to stir up antigovernment sentiments and provide a platform for radical Islamic fundamentalism that could again lead to violence.

While it is probable that Senegalese democracy will survive into the next century, the political landscape in the year 2000 may be very different from what it is today. It is by no means apparent that the PS will maintain its position as the ruling party. Moreover, a new generation of political leaders may be waiting in the wings to replace the Dioufs and Wades who represent that generation of political leaders formed before independence. By the year 2000, 80 percent of Senegal's population will have been born after independence and only a tiny fraction of the national leadership will have experienced growing up under colonial rule. The new leadership will likely be more pragmatic, more Islamic, and less attached to France than the political generation that came to power at independence. Women, youth, and representatives of peasant associations will have a greater voice in Senegalese politics, and Senegalese politicians will be paying more attention to these groups and making greater use of radio and television in campaigning. At the same time, the political influence of the Muslim brotherhoods as a coherent power block will probably decline as the urban sector becomes an increasingly larger part of the electorate. Radical Islamic elements may also gain some ground, especially if the social and economic situation continues to deteriorate, but it is unlikely that they will become strong enough to challenge Senegal's status as a secular state.

The road toward the year 2000 will be a bumpy one. The Senegalese state will have to learn to live with less, and many Senegalese may be forced to tighten

Figure 6.3 Going to the polls. Senegal has one of Black Africa's rare multiparty democracies. (Photo by Michel Renaudeau)

their belts still further, if economic recovery is to take place. Senegalese society will have to rely even more on its traditional local, national, and international solidarity networks to sustain the country's poor during a difficult transition period. Perhaps the greatest challenge Senegal faces during the rest of the century is how to retain the support of Senegalese youth for democratic processes while meeting their rapidly growing needs for education and jobs. Failure to meet this challenge could foster endless social agitation, undermine political stability, and set back recent efforts to strengthen democratic institutions. Despite the many obstacles in their path, the Senegalese have the capacity to develop their own unique synthesis of African, Islamic, and Western values and to overcome the crises which they are now confronting as they move toward the year 2000.

Notes

1. For a pessimistic view of Senegal's economic future and biting critique of Senegalese economic policy, see Jean-François Bayart, "L'Afrique de papa: ça suffit!" [The Old Africa: That's Enough], *Jeune Afrique*, No. 1684 (April 14–21, 1993): 50–53.

2. Senghor's report was published as *Le plan du decollage économique ou la participation responsable comme moteur du développement* [The Economic Take-off Plan or Responsible Participation as the Motor for Development] (Dakar: Grande Imprimerie Africaine, n.d.).

3. For a presentation of Diouf's program for the year 2000, see *Le Soleil*, December 19–20, 1992.

4. See Souleymane Bachir Diagne, Guy Le Moine, and Paul Ndiaye, *Etude Prospective: Sénégal 2015* [Study of the Future: Senegal in the Year 2015] (Dakar: Ministère du Plan et de la Coopération, July 1989). This impressive study was largely the result of a broad collaboration among numerous Senegalese government officials, social scientists, and scholars.

5. For an analysis of the decline of maraboutic authority, particularly in the political domain, see Donal B. Cruise O'Brien, "Le contrat social sénégalais à l'eprueve" [The Testing of the Senegalese Social Contract], *Politique Africaine*, No. 45 (March 1992): 9–20; and Donal B. Cruise O'Brien, "Charisma Comes to Town: Mouride Urbanization 1945–46," in Donal B. Cruise O'Brien and Christian Coulon, eds., *Charisma and Brotherhood in African Islam* (Oxford: Clarendon Press, 1988), pp. 137–155.

6. It is, of course, possible that the higher voter turnouts in the 1960s and 1970s were more the result of government inflation of the figures than a reflection of the real turnout. During the early 1990s, abstention rates in countries such as Mali and Benin that had recently established multiparty systems were also higher than in previous elections under one-party regimes.

7. For a summary of the conclusions of this conference, see *Marchés Tropicaux*, August 5, 1994, pp. 1648–1651; and *Le Soleil*, July 23–24 and July 25, 1994.

8. For details on the composition of the new government and the initial reaction of the political opposition, see *Le Soleil*, March 15, 16, 17, and 18–19, 1995.

Selected Bibliography

General Works

Colvin, Lucie Gallistel. *Historical Dictionary of Senegal*. Metuchen, N.J.: Scarecrow Press, 1981.

Decraene, Philippe. *Le Sénégal* [Senegal]. Paris: Presses Universitaires de France, 1985.

Makedonsky, E. *Le Sénégal, la Sénégambie* [Senegal, Senegambia]. Vols. 1 and 2. Paris: Editions L'Harmattan, 1987.

Nelson, Harold D., et al. *U.S. Army Handbook for Senegal*, 2nd ed. Washington, D.C.: U.S. Government Printing Office, 1974.

Senegal, Republic of. *Atlas national du Sénégal* [National Atlas of Senegal]. Paris: Institut de Géographie National, 1977.

History

Barry, Boubacar. *Le Royaume du Waalo: Le Sénégal avant la conquête* [The Kingdom of Waalo: Senegal Before the Conquest]. Paris: François Maspero, 1972.

―――. *La Sénégambie du XVè au XIXè siècle: Traite négrière, Islam, et conquête coloniale* [The Senegambia from the Fifteenth to the Nineteenth Century: The African Slave Trade, Islam, and the Colonial Conquest] Paris: Editions L'Harmattan, 1988.

Cohen, William B. *Rulers of Empire: The French Colonial Service in Africa*. Stanford: Stanford University Press, 1971.

Crowder, Michael. *Senegal: A Study of French Assimilation Policy*. London: Oxford University Press, 1962.

Curtin, Philip D. *Economic Change in Precolonial Africa: Senegambia in the Era of the Slave Trade*. Madison: University of Wisconsin Press, 1975.

Delavignette, Robert. *Freedom and Authority in French West Africa*. London: Oxford University Press, 1950.

Diagne, Pathé. *Pouvoir traditionnelle en Afrique Occidentale* [Traditional Political Power in West Africa]. Paris: Présence Africaine, 1967.

Diop, Cheikh Anta. *L'Afrique noire pré-coloniale* [Precolonial Black Africa]. Paris: Présence Africaine, 1960.

Duquenot, Nicole Bernard. *Le Sénégal et le Front Populaire* [Senegal and the Popular Front]. Paris: Editions L'Harmattan, 1986.

Gellar, Sheldon. *Structural Changes and Colonial Dependency: Senegal, 1885–1945*. Beverly Hills, Calif.: Sage Publications, 1976.

Johnson, G. Wesley, Jr. *The Emergence of Black Politics in Senegal: The Struggle for Power in the Four Communes, 1900–1920*. Stanford: Stanford University Press, 1971.

Klein, Martin A. *Islam and Imperialism in Senegal: Sine-Saloum, 1847–1914*. Stanford: Stanford University Press, 1968.

Robinson, David W. *Clerics and Chiefs: The History of Abdul Bokar Kane and the Futa Toro.* New York: Oxford University Press, 1976.

————. *The Holy War of Umar Tal: The Western Sudan in the Mid-nineteenth Century.* Oxford: Clarendon Press, 1985.

Schachter-Morgenthau, Ruth. *Political Parties in French-Speaking West Africa.* London: Oxford University Press, 1964.

Suret-Canale, Jean. *French Colonialism in Tropical Africa, 1900–1945.* London: C. Hurst & Company, 1971.

Trimingham, J. Spencer. *A History of Islam in West Africa.* London: Oxford University Press, 1962.

Zuccarelli, François. *La vie politique sénégalaise (1789–1940)* [Senegalese Political Life (1789–1940)]. Paris: CHEAM, 1988.

Politics and Government

Barker, Jonathan S. "The Paradox of Development: Reflections on a Study of Local-Central Relations in Senegal." In *The State of the Nations,* edited by Michael Lofchie, 47–63. Berkeley: University of California Press, 1971.

————. "Political Space and the Quality of Participation in Rural Africa: A Case from Senegal." *Canadian Journal of African Studies* 21, No. 1 (1987): 1–16.

Coulon, Christian. *Le marabout et le prince: Islam et pouvoir au Sénégal* [The Marabout and the Prince: Islam and Power in Senegal]. Paris: Pedone, 1981.

————. "Senegal: The Development and Fragility of Semidemocracy." In *Democracy in Developing Countries,* edited by Larry Diamond, Juan J. Linz, and Seymour Martin Lipset, Vol. 2, 141–177. Boulder: Lynne Rienner, 1988.

Coulon, Christian, and Donal B. Cruise O'Brien. "Senegal." In *Contemporary West African States,* edited by Donal B. Cruise O'Brien, John Dunn, and Richard Rathbone, 145–164. Cambridge: Cambridge University Press, 1989.

Desouches, Christine. *Le Parti Démocratique Sénégalais: Une opposition légale en Afrique* [The Senegalese Democratic Party: A Legal Opposition in Africa]. Paris: Berger-Levrault, 1983.

Dia, Mamadou. *Vicissitudes de la vie d'un militant du Tiers-Monde* [Vicissitudes of the Life of a Third World Militant]. Paris: Publisud, 1985.

Diagne, Pathé. *Crise économique et devenir de la démocratie* [Economic Crisis and the Future of Democracy]. Dakar: Sankoré, 1984.

Diop, Momar Coumba, and Mamadou Diouf. *Le Sénégal sous Abdou Diouf: Etat et société* [Senegal Under Abdou Diouf: State and Society]. Paris: Editions Karthala, 1990.

Fall, Mar. *L'Etat Abdou Diouf ou le temps des incertitudes* [The Abdou Diouf Regime or Times of Uncertainty]. Paris: Editions L'Harmattan, 1986.

Fatton, Robert, Jr. "Clientelism and Patronage in Senegal." *African Studies Review* 29, No. 4 (December 1986): 61–78.

————. *The Making of a Liberal Democracy: Senegal's Passive Revolution: 1975–1985.* Boulder: Lynne Rienner, 1987.

Foltz, William J. *From French West Africa to the Mali Federation.* New Haven, Conn.: Yale University Press, 1965.

Gautron, Jean-Claude, and Michel Rougevin-Baville. *Droit public du Sénégal* [Senegalese Public Law]. Paris: A. Pedone, 1970.

Gellar, Sheldon. "State Tutelage vs. Self-Governance: The Rhetoric and Reality of Decentralization in Senegal." In *The Failure of the Centralized State in Africa: Institutions and Self-Governance*, edited by James S. Wunsch and Dele Olowu, 130–147. Boulder: Westview Press, 1990.

Hayward, Fred M., and Siba Grovogui. "Persistence and Change in Senegalese Electoral Processes." In *Independent Elections in Africa*, edited by Fred Hayward, 239–270. Boulder: Westview Press, 1987.

Hesseling, Gerti. *Histoire politique du Sénégal: Institutions, droit et société* [Political History of Senegal: Institutions, Law, and Society]. Paris: Editions Karthala, 1985.

Lo, Magatte. *Syndicalisme et participation responsable.* [Trade Unionism and Responsible Participation]. Paris: Editions L'Harmattan, 1987.

Markovitz, Irving. *Leopold Sedar Senghor and the Politics of Negritude.* New York: Atheneum, 1969.

Ngom, Benoit. *L'Arbitrage d'une démocratie en Afrique: Le Cour Suprême du Sénégal* [Arbiter of an African Democracy: The Supreme Court in Senegal]. Paris: Présence Africaine, 1989.

Nzouankeu, Jacques Mariel. *Les partis politiques sénégalais* [Senegalese Political Parties]. Dakar: Clairafrique, 1984.

O'Brien, Donal B. Cruise. "Le contrat social sénégalais à l'epreuve" [The Testing of the Senegalese Social Contract]. *Politique Africaine*, No. 45 (March 1992): 9–20.

———. *Saints and Politicians: Essays in the Organization of a Senegalese Peasant Society.* Cambridge: Cambridge University Press, 1975.

O'Brien, Rita, ed. *The Political Economy of Underdevelopment: Dependence in Senegal.* Beverly Hills, Calif.: Sage Publications, 1979.

Schumacher, Edward J. *Politics, Bureaucracy, and Rural Development in Senegal.* Berkeley: University of California Press, 1975.

Young, Crawford, and Babacar Kanté. "Governance, Democracy and the 1988 Senegalese Elections." In *Governance and Politics in Africa*, edited by Goren Hyden and Michael Bratton, 57–74. Boulder: Lynne Rienner, 1992.

Zuccarelli, François. *Un parti politique africain: L'Union Progressiste Sénégalaise* [An African Political Party: The Senegalese Progressive Union]. Paris: R. Pichon and R. Durand-Auzias, 1970.

———. *La vie politique sénégalaise (1940–1988)* [Senegalese Political Life (1940–1988)]. Paris: CHEAM, 1988.

The Economy

Amin, Samir. *Le monde des affaires sénégalais.* [The Senegalese Business World]. Paris: Editions de Minuit, 1969.

Berg, Elliot. *Adjustment Postponed: Economic Policy Reform in Senegal in the 1980s.* Bethesda, Md.: Development Alternatives, Inc., 1990.

Boone, Catherine. "The Making of a Rentier Class: Wealth Accumulation and Political Control in Senegal," *Journal of Development Studies* 26, No. 3 (1990): 425–449.

————. *Merchant Capital and the Roots of State Power in Senegal, 1930–1985.* New York: Cambridge University Press, 1992.

Casswell, Nim. "Autopsie de l'ONCAD: La politique arachidière du Sénégal, 1966–1980" [Autopsy of ONCAD: Senegalese Peanut Policy, 1966–1980]. *Politique Africaine,* No. 14 (1984): 38–73.

Copans, Jean. *Les marabouts de l'arachide* [The Peanut Marabouts]. Paris: Le Sycomore, 1980.

Dia, Mamadou. *Le Sénégal trahi: Un marché d'esclaves* [Senegal Betrayed: A Market of Slaves]. Paris: Selio, 1988.

Diagne, Souleymane Bachir, Guy Le Moine, and Paul Ndiaye. *Etude prospective: "Sénégal 2015"* [Study of the Future: "Senegal 2015"]. Dakar: Ministère du Plan et de la Coopération, July 1989.

Dijk, Meine Pieter van. *Sénégal: Le secteur informel de Dakar* [Senegal: The Informal Sector of Dakar]. Paris: Editions L'Harmattan, 1986.

Diop, Abdoulaye-Bara. "Les paysans du bassin arachidier: Conditions de vie et comportements de survie" [The Peasants of the Peanut Basin: Living Conditions and Survival Behaviors]. *Politque Africaine,* No. 45 (March 1992): 39–61.

Diouf, Mahktar. "La crise de l'ajustement" [The Adjustment Crisis]. *Politique Africaine,* No. 45 (March 1992): 62–85.

Duruflé, Gilles. *L'ajustement structurel en Afrique: Sénégal, Côte d'Ivoire, Madagascar* [Structural Adjustment in Africa: Senegal, the Ivory Coast, Madagascar]. Paris: Editions Karthala, 1988.

————. *Le Sénégal peut-il sortir de la crise? Douze ans d'ajustement structurel au Sénégal* [Can Senegal Break Out of the Crisis? Twelve Years of Structural Adjustment in Senegal]. Paris: Editions Karthala, 1994.

Engelhard, Philippe. *Enjeux de l'aprés-barrage: Vallée du Sénégal* [Post-Dam Stakes: Senegal River Valley]. Paris: Enda, 1986.

Gellar, Sheldon. "Circulaire 32 Revisited: Prospects for Revitalizing the Senegalese Cooperative Movement in the 1980s." In *The Political Economy of Risk and Choice in Senegal,* edited by John Waterbury and Mark Gersovitz, 123–159. London: Frank Cass, 1987.

Gellar, Sheldon, Robert B. Charlick, and Yvonne Jones. *Animation Rurale and Rural Development: The Experience of Senegal.* Ithaca, N.Y.: Cornell University Rural Development Committee, 1980.

Giri, Jacques. *Le Sahel au XXIè siècle* [The Sahel in the 21st Century]. Paris: Editions Karthala, 1989.

Mackintosh, Maureen. *Gender, Class and Rural Transition: Agribusiness and the Food Crisis in Senegal.* London: Zed Press, 1989.

Rocheteau, Guy. *Pouvoir financier et indépendance économique: Le cas du Sénégal* [Financial Power and Economic Independence: The Senegalese Case]. Paris: Editions Karthala, 1982.

Senghor, Léopold Sédar. *On African Socialism.* New York: Frederick A. Praeger, 1964.

Sy, Cheikh Tidiane, ed. *Crise du développement rural et desengagement de l'etat au Sénégal* [The Crisis of Rural Development and the Disengagement of the State in Senegal]. Dakar: Nouvelles Editions Africaines, 1988.

Terrell, Katherine, and Jan Svejnar. *The Industrial Labor Market and Economic Performance in Senegal.* Boulder: Westview Press, 1989.

Van Chi Bonnardel, Regine Nguyen. *La vie des relations au Sénégal: La circulation des biéns* [Relational Life in Senegal: The Circulation of Goods]. Dakar: IFAN, 1978.

Vanhaeverbeke, André. *Rémuneration du travail et commerce extérieur: Essor d'une économie exportatrice et termes de l'échange des producteurs d'arachides au Sénégal* [Remuneration of Labor and Foreign Trade: Progress of an Export Economy and the Terms of Trade of Peanut Producers in Senegal]. Louvain: Centre de Recherches des Pays en Développement, 1970.

Waterbury, John, and Mark Gersovitz, eds. *The Political Economy of Risk and Choice in Senegal.* London: Frank Cass, 1987.

World Bank. *Senegal: Tradition, Diversification, and Economic Development.* Washington, D.C.: World Bank, 1974.

————. *The World Bank and Senegal, 1960–1987.* Washington, D.C.: World Bank, 1989.

Senegal and the World

Bayart, Jean-François. *La politique africaine de François Mitterrand* [The African Policy of François Mitterrand]. Paris: Editions Karthala, 1984.

Biarnés, Pierre. "La diplomatie sénégalaise" [Senegalese Diplomacy]. *Revue Française d'Etudes Politiques Africaines,* No. 149 (May 1978): 62–78.

Bourgi, Albert. *La politique française de coopération en Afrique: Le cas du Sénégal.* [French Aid Policy in Africa: The Senegal Case]. Paris: R. Pichon et R. Durand-Auzias, 1979.

Club du Sahel/CILSS. *From Aid to Investment . . . to Financial Support.* Paris: Club du Sahel/CILSS, January 1990.

Colvin, Lucie Gallistel. "International Relations in Precolonial Senegal." *Presence Africaine,* No. 93 (1975): 215–230.

Dia, Mamadou. *The African Nations and World Solidarity.* New York: Frederick A. Praeger, 1961.

Diop, Momar-Coumba, ed. *Le Sénégal et ses voisins* [Senegal and Its Neighbors]. Dakar: Sociétées-Espaces-Temps, 1994.

Ethiopiques. "Francophonie et développement." *Ethiopiques* (May 1985). Special Issue.

Parker, Ron. "The Senegal-Mauritania Conflict of 1989: A Fragile Equilibrium." *The Journal of Modern African Studies* 29, No. 1 (1991): 155–171.

Skurnik, W.A.E. *The Foreign Policy of Senegal.* Evanston, Ill.: Northwestern University Press, 1972.

Zarour, Charbel. "La coopération arabo-sénégalaise" [Arab-Senegalese Cooperation]. *Afrique et Développement* 11, Nos. 2–3 (1986): 261–287.

Social Structures

Adams, Adrian. *Le long voyage des gens du fleuve Sénégal* [The Long Journey of the Senegal River People]. Paris: François Maspero, 1977.

Behrman, Lucy C. *Muslim Brotherhoods and Politics in Senegal.* Cambridge: Harvard University Press, 1970.

Bugnicourt, Jacques, Seyni Emmanuel Ndione, and Maximillien Sagna. *Pauvreté ambigüe: Enfants et jeunes au Sénégal* [Ambiguous Poverty: Children and Youth in Senegal]. Dakar: ENDA, 1987.

Caverivière, Monique, and Marc Debene. *Le droit foncier sénégalais* [Senegal Land Tenure Law]. Paris: Berger-Levrault, 1988.

Colvin, Lucie Gallistel, ed. *The Uprooted of the Western Sahel: Migrants' Quest for Cash in the Senegambia.* New York: Praeger Publishers, 1981.

Creevey, Lucy E. "The Impact of Islam on Women in Senegal." *The Journal of Developing Areas* 25 (April 1991): 347–368.

Darbon, Dominique. *L'Administration et le paysan en Casamance: Essai d'anthropologie administrative* [The Administration and the Peasant in the Casamance: An Essay in Administrative Anthropology]. Paris: Pedone, 1988.

Diop, Abdoulaye-Bara. *La famille Wolof* [The Wolof Family]. Paris: Editions Karthala, 1985.

———. *La société Wolof tradition et changement: Les systèmes d'inégalité et de domination* [Wolof Society: Systems of Domination and Inequality]. Paris: Editions Karthala, 1981.

Diop, Majhemout. *Histoire des classes sociales dans l'Afrique de L'Ouest: Le Sénégal* [History of Social Classes in West Africa: Senegal]. Paris: François Maspero, 1972.

Magassouba, Moriba. *L'Islam au Sénégal: Demain les mollahs?* [Islam in Senegal: Tomorrow the Mullahs?] Paris: Editions Karthala, 1985.

Ndione, Emmanuel Seyni. *Dynamique urbaine d'une société en grappe: Un cas, Dakar* [Urban Dynamics of a Society in Change: The Dakar Case]. Dakar: ENDA, 1987.

O'Brien, Donal B. Cruise. "Charisma Comes to Town: Mouride Urbanization, 1945–1986." In *Charisma and Brotherhood in African Islam,* edited by Donal B. Cruise O'Brien and Christian Coulon, 135–155. Oxford: Clarendon Press, 1988.

———. *The Mourides of Senegal: The Political and Economic Organization of an Islamic Brotherhood.* London: Oxford University Press, 1971.

O'Brien, Rita Cruise. *White Society in Black Africa: The French of Senegal.* Evanston, Ill.: Northwestern University Press, 1972.

O'Dèye, Michele. *Les associations en villes africaines: Dakar-Brazzaville* [Associations in African Cities: Dakar-Brazzaville]. Paris: Editions L'Harmattan, 1985.

Pélissier, Paul. *Les paysans du Sénégal: Les civilisations agraires du Cayor à la Casamance* [Peasants of Senegal: Agrarian Civilizations from Cayor to the Casamance]. Saint-Yrieix: Imprimerie Fabregue, 1966.

Zuccarelli, François. "Les Catholiques du Sénégal" [The Catholics of Senegal]. *L'Afrique et l'Asie Modernes,* No. 165 (Summer 1990): 78–96.

Culture

Ba, Mariama. *Une si longue lettre* [A Very Long Letter]. Dakar: Nouvelles Editions Africaines, 1980.

Blondé, Jacques, Pierre Dumont, and Dominique Gontier. *Lexique du français du Sénégal* [Lexicon of Senegalese French]. Dakar: Nouvelles Editions Africaines, 1979.

Diop, Birago. *Les contes d'Amadou-Koumba* [The Tales of Amadou-Koumba]. Paris: Présence Africaine, 1961.

Diop, Cheikh Anta. *Egypte ancienne et Afrique noire* [Ancient Egypt and Black Africa]. Dakar: IFAN, 1989.

Dumont, Pierre. *Le français et les langues africaines au Sénégal* [French and African Languages in Senegal]. Paris: Editions Karthala, 1983.

Fall, Aminata Sow. *La Grève des battû* [The Beggars' Strike]. Dakar: Nouvelles Editions Africaines, 1980.

Fougeyrollas, Pierre. *Modernisation des hommes: L'exemple du Sénégal* [Modernization of Man: The Example of Senegal]. Paris: Flammarion, 1967.

Hymans, Jacques Louis. *Léopold Sédar Senghor: An Intellectual Biography.* Edinburgh: Edinburgh University Press, 1971.

Kane, Cheikh Amadou. *Ambiguous Adventure.* New York: Collier Books, 1969.

Mignon, Jean-Marie. *Les associations sportives au Sénégal* [Sports Associations in Senegal]. Bordeaux: Centre d'Etude d'Afrique Noire, 1987.

Sembène, Ousmane. *God's Bits of Wood.* Garden City, N.Y.: Anchor Books, 1970.

Sylla, Assane. *La philosophie morale des Wolof* [The Moral Philosophy of the Wolof]. Dakar: Sankoré, 1978.

About the Book and Author

A West African nation with an extremely rich political and cultural heritage, Senegal continues to serve as a role model for Francophone Africa despite its weak economic base and small population. Senegal's status as both a Sahelian and a maritime country brought its people into early contact with Islam and the West, making the country a crossroads where traditional African, Islamic, and European cultures met and blended.

Sheldon Gellar begins his exploration of Senegal by examining the influence of Islam, Western imperialism, and French colonial rule and by tracing the country's political, economic, and social evolution since independence. This expanded second edition also analyzes developments since 1983, looking in particular at the state of multiparty democracy, the 1993 national elections, the deterioration of the political climate following the assassination of the vice president of the Constitutional Council, the 1994 devaluation of the CFA franc, and the return of Abdoulaye Wade to the government coalition in 1995.

Despite its inability to break out of severe and chronic economic crises, Senegal has managed to solicit high levels of foreign aid and has gained a significant profile on the international scene. Gellar closes with an evaluation of the social and cultural trends that have contributed to Senegal's emergence as one of Africa's most important cultural centers.

Sheldon Gellar is senior research associate at the Harry S. Truman Institute, The Hebrew University of Jerusalem.

Index